FELLATIO
MASOCHISM
POLITICS
AND LOVE

FELLATIO
MASOCHISM
POLITICS
AND LOVE

LEO ABSE

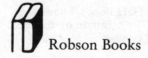

Robson Books

First published in Great Britain in 2000 by Robson Books,
10 Blenheim Court, Brewery Road, London N7 9NT

A member of the Chrysalis Group plc

British Library Cataloguing in Publication Data
A catalogue record for this title is available from the British
Library

The author is grateful to Marlene Dietrich for supplying the
photographs reproduced in this book, which are included at
her express request.

ISBN 186105 351 7

Typeset by FiSH Books, London
Printed in Great Britain by Butler & Tanner Ltd,
Frome and London

Contents

Acknowledgements

Without the assistance of Frances Hawkins, my indefatigable amanuensis, this work would not have been produced; only her constant invigilation, critical appraisements and preliminary editing ensured it was brought to a conclusion.

I am indebted to my psychoanalyst brother, Dr Wilfred Abse, Emeritus Professor of Psychiatry at the University of Virginia, whose critique of the draft of an early section of the book led me into much deeper waters. I owe, too, a further debt to Geoffrey Goodman, editor and biographer, who, in so many dialogues, helped me to shape the political dimensions of this book.

At my late age, friends are much needed to incite and encourage me to persist in writing. At least some of the responsibility for this essay must therefore fall upon: Gillon Aitken, literary agent; Reva Berstock, psychoanalyst; Michael Bloch, biographer; Rabbi Sidney Brichto; Stuart Cameron, administrator; Paul Cavadino, penologist; Stephen Cretney of All Souls; Jürgen-Michael Gottinger, management consultant; Gerald Abrahams, geriatrician; David Hughes, political editor; Brett Kahr, psychotherapist and composer; Fred Kendall, publisher; Charles Leeming, solicitor; Graham Little, political scientist; Richard Martin, economist; David Parfitt, painter; Dacre Punt, designer; Jeremy Robson, publisher; Andrew Ross, botanist; Ivan Sadka, solicitor; Peter Soar, solicitor; Mike Steele, lobby correspondent; Richard Tilleard-Cole, psychiatrist; Ernest Woolf, psychoanalyst; and my class-mate, Bert Greatrex. My historian son, Tobias, has as ever, vainly tried to protect me from extravagances and for this, and much else, I continue to be grateful.

I owe, too, special thanks to my physician Stephen Hirst who, to the dismay of my enemies, has kept me alive.

To
Ania Czeputkowska

Give up philosophy because I'm an old man?
It's at the end of a race that you break into a burst of speed

Diogenes

Introduction

Sixty-five years ago, as a callow provincial youth of 17, I was for the first time proffered a blow job. Although, like most old people, I suffer severely from nominal amnesia I have no difficulty in recalling the exact address where the event occurred. I was, as part of my rites of passage, in an up-market bordello standing behind the Montparnasse Station in Paris at 31 Boulevard Edgar-Quinet – 'Le Sphinx' which, with much celebration, had been formally opened by the Mayor of Paris. Today I would find the setting – a pot pourri of Karnac and Pompeii, red plush and overblown chandeliers – burlesque; then, on entering, I was dazzled, frightened and forlorn.

As I stood near the door, immobile, wanting to run back out but rooted, not by desire but by my self-imposed task of initiation, the middle-aged madam, at one glance, took in the situation. She looked round, beckoned to one of the scantily dressed young women draped around a glittering bar, and then spoke to her in a French patois well beyond the boundaries of my schoolboy French. In seconds, a glass of champagne was placed in one of my hands and the other was grasped by the girl, who immediately led me upstairs to the statutory brothel bedroom with pink sheets and mirrored walls and ceiling.

This was my first visit abroad, and anticipating a practice that more than half a century later seems to have become fashionable, I was mixing sex with politics. As the chairman of the Young

Socialists in Cardiff, I was their delegate to an international young people's conference for peace in Paris, one, of course, organised by communist parties and their fellow travellers of whom, like so many bright youngsters of those days, I was one. I had been told as a preliminary to participating in the conference to visit a young Englishman living in Paris for a briefing; he proved to be the son of Edgar Wallace, the best-selling crime writer of the 1930s, and it was he, while I was receiving his political catechism, who, at my prompting, directed me to Le Sphinx. He thoroughly recommended it.

His recommendation gave me little help when the young woman lay beside me. Frightened, I did not respond to her advances, and no doubt as part of her routine she sought to encourage me by moving on to fellatio, a name and practice unknown to me, as it would have been, I am certain, to almost all pre-war young men and women of the middle and working classes in South Wales. I recoiled with amazement and horror, all my castration anxieties aroused, and in the subsequent mêlée the girl fled the room. The sage madam quickly re-emerged with an older woman – all of 30 years, no doubt – who settled me down, soothed me and more gently gave me my initiation. I left Le Sphinx, with a manly step, able to proceed to the conference and make my now absurdly confident and optimistic contribution.

The sceptics who may regard my behaviour as a teenager as idiosyncratic fail to understand the gulf between today's sexual mores and that genuinely in place in Britain in the 1920s and 1930s. Sex certainly did not begin, as Larkin tells us, in the sixties, but fellatio probably did. Rules and conventions, only rarely broken, governed the play between pre-war young unmarried people; 'necking' was acceptable and expected but foreplay, within strict boundaries, remained foreplay. 'French' kissing, the insertion of a tongue into your mouth, was regarded as 'hot stuff'. It has been pleaded in mitigation of Clinton's behaviour that he was brought up in Arkansas, a good Baptist region where: 'It ain't a sin if you don't stick it in'; such extensive permissiveness certainly did not prevail in Methodist South Wales. In innocence we sang to the accompaniment of records by the great saxophonist Charlie Parker, not knowing that the line 'You go to my head... Like the bubbles in a glass of champagne' were from the theme song of New York's oral eroticists, a vehicle for coded messages in East Coast jazz clubs. We did not know that in the vocabulary of those clubs having head meant fellatio. It may be that there is some truth in the suggestion that boy babies of the rich were initiated into fellatio by their nurses who used it to quiet and comfort their crying charges and that, as a result, some upper-class adults, out of nostalgia, enjoyed the practice; but in the pre-war world of the overwhelming majority, mothers, not nurse-maids, brought up their children, and there was certainly no such impress left upon their sons, my contemporaries.

Most of us were brought up in a much more restricted world. Among the middle classes sexual intercourse commenced on the wedding night and virginity was ended by the husband; more usually among the working classes, a formal engagement meant intercourse began. Indeed, such were the constraints that only after the engagement had been announced would a young woman dare to put her arm into that of her fiancé and give a clear signal that they were a courting couple.

And the State colluded in the imposition upon the unmarried of these regulatory modes. If discovered to be broken, the punishment accorded the girl and her bastard child was reflected in a derisory financial award, a pittance that could be awarded for the child under affiliation proceedings. It was a ceiling I was only able to break through in one of my Private Members' Acts in the 1960s; and it was even later before my agitation for the ending of breach of promise actions was successfully concluded.

More, the censorship laws and societal conventions ensured that access to sexual instruction was severely restricted. The only sexual manual likely to have been read by my peers – and that only by a handful of the more literate of us – was Norman Haire's *Encyclopaedia of Sexual Knowledge*, which ran into ten editions between 1934 and 1944. With the aid of some fellow physicians, he made a bid to explain to us the anatomy of our sexual organs and the mechanics and aberrations of sexual behaviour free, they declared, from the 'sloppy sentimentalism and religious mush which disfigured previously published books on sexual enlightenment'. But nowhere within the tome was there any mention of the practice of fellatio within a heterosexual relationship, and such was the environment in which they were writing that when they described, briefly, cunnilingus as the 'genital kiss', they resorted to teleology. In stern medical tones they commended its usefulness in lubricating the female genital organs in order to assist penetration; pleasure was evidently not the purpose. But the encyclopaedia, although so tentative and mortified, was not available in either the public or miners' libraries of my youth. As for Krafft-Ebing and *The Kama Sutra*, they were confined to collections of the wealthy; for hoi polloi, they were unknown works.

Even after World War II, as the massive survey conducted in the 1950s with the aid of the Hulton Press by anthropologist Geoffrey Gorer revealed, sexual behaviour in England remained remarkably rigid and constrained. As a young solicitor when, almost daily, I was appearing in cases involving allegations of persistent cruelty against husbands, I never encountered any suggestion that a demand for fellatio had been made. Insistence on anal sex was often a matter of complaint although, often, I suspect, it was a belated objection. There is, however, but one case within my recall when a man was charged with causing grievous bodily harm which included forcing a woman to give him fellatio; it is claimed that the disbelieving judge asked the pert question, 'Didn't she have any teeth?'

It has been suggested that the widely relished and widely distributed sleazy 1970s film *Deep Throat* brought fellatio into the mainstream in Britain; doubtless the film did incite mimetic responses but its influence can be overestimated. As the film's euphemistic title reveals, some inhibitions were holding firm and circumlocution was still required to speak of oral sex. *Patridge's Dictionary of Slang and Unconventional English* tells us that even the use of 'blow job' to describe fellatio only became current after 1970, and even Mills & Boon did not feature oral sex in any of its books until well into the 1980s. Nowadays, of course, all former reticences have been abandoned; any visit to a London West End public telephone booth tells us that, among all the fetishes bluntly advertised, the blow job is the main lure. And the advertising industry itself, divining the desires of the consumer, has long since discovered its seductiveness: in less than subtle innuendo, the pleasures of a perfume, a car, an ice cream, are equated with those of oral sex, ensuring that that excitation is never far removed from the soft-porn advertising enveloping our TV screens.

More overtly, it is a prominent feature of the hard VCD pornography sold by the millions, and almost invariably speedily enters into the 'dirty talk' which can be obtained by picking up the telephone. And the new communication technologies, all sharing the ability to create, receive or send pornographic material in privacy, with minimum effort, and bringing a sense of safety from the oversight and opprobrium of others, have created new opportunities which have been fully exploited to pedal the claims of fellatio. Predictably, when the Clinton-Lewinsky story emerged, the e-mail routes buzzed with jokes, almost all concerned with the mechanics of the scandal and frequently revealing admiration for and envy of the president's sexual play.

No-one can grow up today, as my generation did, in ignorance of the practice. Sex manuals now are widely circulated, giving women full instruction and telling how the mouth can be made 'a snug fit', how to take total control by using two hands, 'one to stimulate him elsewhere (nipples, testicles, anus), the other as a guide', always remembering that 'most feeling is at the head of his penis not the bottom'. One of the most successful manuals (circulation-wise) provides women with a 'ten-step guide to the best fellatio he's ever had'. And nowadays populist orthodox rabbis, yielding to the mood of their congregants, still insist upon medieval rules which condemn coitus interruptus and any sexual intercourse during menstruation and a week thereafter, but reassure their flock that oral sex can be kosher.

In response to this and similar types of advocacy and conduct, there has arisen a popular notion, steadfastly held by the prim and would-be censors, that we now have a society without sexual restraints, and the responsibility for what they regard as present-day licentiousness rests on those like myself who, by our legislation, undermined the old legal and societal taboos. They cannot acknowledge the consequences of the 'mass of misery, enormous and appalling' which Haire declared ignorance of sexual matters created in pre-war Britain and they will not acknowledge the extent of the relief brought to those enduring appalling distortions of the human spirit as a consequence of the punitive laws impinging upon human relationships. Until our intervention, our laws relating to divorce, suicide, illegitimacy, adoption and homosexuality were unbecoming to any society claiming to be civilised.

But the most grave error of the puritans is their charge that our advocacy of reforms has led to sexual freedom which they claim is the cause of so many of the ills of present-day society. Indeed, such intimacies as fellatio, if uninformed by tenderness and bereft of whole relationships between the protagonists, tell us how unemancipated, not how liberated, our society has become. It is a poor defence by those of us responsible for reforming legislation and now standing accused of heralding in an ugly salacious era, merely to plead 'it was ever so'; and that the widespread underground Victorian and Edwardian pornography and prostitution, male and female, are only being pulled out of their netherworld by hard-porn video, seedy television, scavenging tabloids and the network; and that now, what always was, has simply been made visible; that hypocrisy has diminished, and that it is not perversion, promiscuity and lasciviousness which have increased.

Such apologias are flawed. They rest upon the false assumption which too many reformers share with their censorious critics – the belief that our society has attained an immeasurably greater freedom than that of our grandparents. Gains there have been but the losses are heavy, for, despite presidential approval, widespread and compulsive fellatio and even more way-out practices all advertise our society's hang-ups, not its freedoms. When, in 1998, a Cabinet Minister's visit to Clapham Common brings about his resignation, we witness the paradox of our times – that the claimed increasingly liberal attitude to sexuality is coupled with increasing intolerance by so many for politicians who transgress yesterday's guidelines. Today the media of our so-called permissive society, reflecting so many of their readers' compulsive and desperate need for constant titillation, plays the part of Mrs Grundy. With pursed lips and with relish, they recite as rarely before, and at inordinate length, accounts of the sexual behaviour and orientation of the well-known. Before 1998 was out, when another Cabinet Minister, the Minister of Agriculture, was 'outed' by the tabloids, the voyeurism within our society reached its apogee, emphasising yet again how unrelaxed, not how emancipated, we are when confronted with issues of sexual deviation. And our uneasy laughter at Clinton's antics, which we either share in fact or vicariously covet, will again confirm the poet's insight: 'Not all are free who mock their chains.'

In politics one can choose one's enemies but not one's allies, and not a few of those assisting me in my campaigns for social reforms unwittingly taught me that conscious investment in the ideals of sexual freedom can be accompanied by a savagely puritanical but unconscious conscience that operates unceasingly and relentlessly beneath the veneer. The conscious and oft times defiant attitudes of the seemingly emancipated are so often mere masks concealing continuing subjugation to persistent and contrary childhood attitudes. I do not wholly exempt myself from the syndrome; not for nothing did my wife, in the midst of the clamour that so often accompanied my divorce reform efforts when I was stereotyped as a champion of the libertines, tease me about my own essential puritanism.

Clinton's behaviour pattern, so especially determined by his tragic childhood, is in many respects a paradigm of the psychic enslavement which oppresses so many in our contemporary society. Side by side with his liberal pretensions, his pro-abortion and anti-homophobic stances, is his compulsive unzipping, the tic from which he could not free himself, although it was leading him to political destruction. In his bondage to joyless, impersonal oral sex which Monica Lewinsky says he prefers to sexual intercourse, he remains, as an adult, ensnared in the coils of the sado-masochistic childhood with which he was cursed. Fellatio can be foreplay, giving an intimation of a love that can only be inadequately told in words, but it is a dangerous messenger and, for Clinton, it is a carrier not of love but of all the sado-masochism which enveloped his first household. It is this dimension which distinguishes the Clinton affair, and which has so excited the voyeurism of so many. It cannot be simply slotted into the category of those politicians I have known, clever and fluent, who are perpetually adolescent, and who, lacking a sense of self-worth, relieve their depression with recurrent affairs of little importance which offer an escape into guilt-free, disposable relationships. Unlike these politicians, Clinton, certainly in recent years, does not sleep around; indeed, in singular fashion, what has demonstrably excited so much attention and so much rapport is his penchant for *not* bedding his women. Unlike the priapic Jack Kennedy, he prefers his extra-marital activities to be kept well outside the sheets and the duvet.

Clinton's biological father, William Blyth, who had five wives and several illegitimate children, died before Bill Clinton was born. The third man his compulsive-gambler mother married was a violent alcoholic, ready to display and use force in the domestic brawls which were part of the background to Bill Clinton's childhood. In his earliest years Clinton had to endure a temporary abandonment by his mother and the searing experience of being a disputed trophy as his mother and grandmother savagely fought each other. By the time Clinton was 14 years old, the growing son, to protect his mother, was breaking down locked doors to gain entry into rooms where the step-father was beating up his wife. At 15, Bill Clinton was swearing a deposition against his step-father after calling the police to the home to arrest the violent man, but the mother, within three months of divorcing him, and evidently nostalgic for the masochistic needs her third husband had supplied, remarried him. For Clinton, fellatio is a re-enactment: there he finds the pleasures of the earliest pains of his childhood for, such is our biological endowment, pain and pleasure are never far apart. And perhaps no physical act can more nicely bring together, for both parties, a greater simultaneous release of sadism and masochism.

It is true that Clinton has a family background that provides us with a singularly florid example of those who opt for oral rather than vaginal intercourse. However, at a time when the condom can provide safe sex and when the pill can ensure no unplanned consequences, it would surely be too reductive to suggest that the ubiquity and popularity of fellatio can be wholly and simply explained as a regressive phenomenon emerging from the appalling increase in dysfunctional and fatherless families. That is only part of the dreary story, probably a considerable part, but the resonances and dissonances provoked by the Clinton scandals warn us that such an explanation is incomplete. It certainly does not tell us why in February 1998, when the world teetered on the edge of a war that had the potential to destabilise the Middle East and cost the lives of millions, the attention of the British public and media, following the USA example, until the very last days of the fateful military decision, was focused not on the Iraqi crisis, but on Clinton's ejaculations. Such Anglo-Saxon salaciousness was sustained throughout 1998 as Clinton inflamed Islamic countries with his absurd retaliatory and fruitless bombings of Afghanistan and Sudan, a prurience ever contributing to the danger that a harassed President can be tempted to try and escape from a threatening domestic scene by diverting attention to untimely populist military adventures. And still the public and media remained riveted by the tactile details of the President's escapades: when, in September 1998 the American Treasury told the President to warn America the world was teetering on the edge of a grim recession, his declaration that 'the global economy' was 'confronted with the biggest financial challenge facing the world in half a century' was barely heard amidst the clamour surrounding the publication of the Starr report, and then the release of 243 minutes of video tapes, replete with excruciatingly intrusive questioning, ensured that the most powerful and sophisticated Government on earth was transfixed and mesmerised.

That there can remain in place, at such hazardous moments, an overwhelming prurient interest in Clinton's method of attaining tumescence surely tells us that fellatio cannot always be treated as a political irrelevance, a mere frolic. Rather, is its present ubiquity, and the excitations and voyeurism its practice provokes, a symptom of a grave and pathological societal condition?

Fellatio – The 'Innocent' Origin

When the Clinton-Lewinsky affair became public, there were immediately many refinements of the criticism Clinton's behaviour attracted; the dominant criticism, the one which was ultimately to find expression in the impeachment indictment brought before the Senate, was the most hypocritical. The accusers declared themselves non-judgemental in their attitude to his sexual behaviour but affected to find his lying about his sexual antics intolerable. This was the most transparent of the hypocrisies which were donned by his critics; without exception, everyone lies about, or conceals, his or her sexual fantasies and behaviour. And forcing someone to lie so that one can condemn the offender rather than acknowledge one's own attraction to the 'offence' is sickeningly devious and, in the end, the American public so appeared to have perceived it. One of the most obscene occasions I ever witnessed in the Commons was the condemnation of the hapless John Profumo for lying to the House. I was surrounded by men, the majority of whom would have given their right arm to have secretly spent the night in bed with Christine Keeler.

This form of hypocrisy, so evident in many of the comments on the Clinton scandal, provides a little corroboration of the spuriousness of the assertion that we live in a permissive society. Indeed, the search for 'non-sexual' justifications enabling condemnations of conduct we desire and often act out ourselves

1

tells of the often unconscious guilt pervading our 'liberated' society. In the Wales of my youth, the antics of Lloyd George, the most notorious of our libidinous politicians in the twentieth century, sardonically and with delicious irony were described as a scattering around of his Maker's image, surely a more sophisticated and far less morbid response to a public man's misbehaviour than prevails today. Now, in the Starr report and in the notorious video interrogation of the President, under the cover of condemnation of Clinton's lies, the scavenging prosecutor and his minions revelled in detailing Clinton's fumblings, once again showing to the world the radical ambivalence of the puritanic and the prurient, of the Edenic and the Fallen, that is at the very heart of North American culture.

But from the beginning, uneasy about condemnation based solely upon the shaky foundation of Clinton's perjury, more subtle efforts were made by some of his American women critics, and not a few militant feminists here, to condemn Clinton without disclosing their true ambivalences about fellatio; sometimes, almost desperately, they strove to distance themselves from the seductions and the repellences which the idea of the practice of fellatio aroused in them. Their denunciations of the President were prefaced by a declaration of neutrality. It was not oral sex they condemned but Clinton's abuse of power: that, they insisted, was the gravamen of the charge.

Even initially, such an indictment by 'neutrals' seemed fevered. Although a man in authority can, by pelf or place, offer a young employee inducements to which she succumbs, short of the threat of torture or death there are limits to the power of any man, even a president, to command an unwilling woman to pleasure him by way of oral sex. As Paula Jones's response to Clinton's alleged overtures make only too clear, it takes two to tango. Those who conjured up the picture of a powerful, magnetic president humiliating a woman, ordering her, despite her protests, to go literally on her knees, unzip him and bring him to tumescence, were writing pornography, not a critique on the exercise of presidential power. What is noteworthy, however, is that despite the evidence that later emerged that Monica Lewinsky was flaunting her knickers within minutes of their first meeting and was on her knees giving him oral sex a few hours after, and despite her emphatic television assertion that her behaviour was her own choice, still the charge lingers on that Clinton abused his power over the intern. It is difficult to interpret such a formulation other than as an avoidance stratagem designed to deny women's complicity in fellatio.

It was an approach which Starr followed. Too excited by his own pornography to affect the 'neutrality' of such critics, he nevertheless, quite contrary to the evidence he could not resist presenting, overtly sought to exculpate Lewinsky. In the Starr report we are told that 'in the evaluation of prosecutor and investigators Ms Lewinsky had provided truthful information. She had not falsely inculpated the President. Harming him, she had testified, was "the last thing in the world I would do".'

Such a winsome presentation of Lewinsky is, to say the least, unconvincing. It is abundantly clear that she stalked the vulnerable President with extraordinary persistence, using every possible occasion to get near Clinton's crotch, and it is no less clear that the sinning Clinton was literally holding back, his glands expressing his reluctance as, to her fury, again and again Lewinsky could not bring him to a climax. Guilt inhibited the half-hearted would-be adulterer; he could toy with the menu but never yield to the main course. When at last she finally brought him to ejaculation, triumphantly she retained the stains on her dress until handing it over to the prosecutor and ensuring Clinton's nemesis as a credible political leader.

To generalise from the particular behaviour of a hysterical personality could be misleading; but caricature though it may be, it does illustrate that no valid scrutiny of the phenomenon of fellation can be made if it is viewed simply as a selfish expression of the male within an alleged tradition that pleasurable sex is something that women give and only men get.

Indeed, Freud's clinical investigations brought him to a quite contrary conclusion. Writing almost 90 years ago, he affirmed:

The inclination to take a man's sexual organ into the mouth and suck at it, which in respectable society is considered a loathsome sexual perversion, is nevertheless found with great frequency among women of today – and of earlier times as well, as ancient sculptures show – and in the state of being in love it appears completely to lose its repulsive character. Fantasies derived from this inclination are found by doctors even in women who have not become aware of the possibilities of obtaining sexual satisfaction in this way by reading Krafft-Ebing's *Psychopathia Sexualis* or from other sources of information. Women, it seems, find no difficulty in producing this kind of wishful fantasy spontaneously.

Freud's finding that fellatio for many women is no mimetic exercise but is a 'spontaneous' acting out of a wishful fantasy finds some corroboration in its almost complete absence from the popular erotica circulating in Vienna at the beginning of the century. In the unlikely event that Freud's upper-middle-class women patients gained access to the libraries of their husbands or lovers, they would have found little in those contemporary erotica productions to instruct them in the joys of oral sex.

At the very time when Freud was composing the handful of essays which contain an exploration into the oetiology of fellatio, there was circulating in Austria Eduard Fuchs' recently published *Geschichte der Erotischen Kunst*. It is an extraordinary and lavishly illustrated history of erotic art. Six volumes of this work are within my possession and I fear I acquired them in less than creditable circumstances. Perhaps today they would be described as loot, but in war-time we servicemen had a different description of our usually petty pillaging: goods were 'liberated', and this was my one act of liberation. As the war came to its conclusion I moved up with my small RAF unit from Italy into Austria. With the Russians still reluctant to permit us entry into Vienna, which they had already occupied, I was forced to halt awhile at Styria's capital, Graz, then rotten with Nazis even as it is with neo-Nazis today. It was the little town which had another notoriety for, by a curious coincidence, it was here that, simultaneously, there had lived the psychiatrist Krafft-Ebing and the novelist Leopold von Sacher-Masoch, the aristocratic intellectuals whose names have been enshrined in every review of pornography. As my billet for the few days I was to remain in Graz, I chose the home of a repellent elderly man whose study contained a collection in equal portions of pornography and no less obscene Nazi propaganda. Fuchs' work, published in 1909, lay on his shelves, and I found the opportunity irresistible. I told my Nazi 'host', whose hatred and fear oozed out of every one of his pores, that I was purchasing them, gave him a derisory sum and somehow, when demobilisation eventually came, lugged them back to Wales.

Now, as I peruse them more than half a century later, I find among them thousands of reproductions of paintings, drawings and caricatures depicting flagellation, narcissism, lesbianism and voyeurism, breast fondling, straight and anal sex all abound. However, apart from witty drawings from *La Vie Parisienne* of 1885 depicting the various ways women eat asparagus, no hint is given of fellatio's existence. Yet in the centuries which Fuchs covers some depictions of this act must have been available for selection; indeed, there was extant contemporary material like Picasso's famous 1902 watercolour of his friend Isador Nonnel receiving fellatio in a Barcelona brothel. But whatever the reason may be, Fuchs and his publishers evidently felt that oral sex was not a predominant interest of their wealthy readers. If this was the erotica awash in Freud's Vienna, it is unsurprising that Freud brushes aside the probability that his women patients had been incited to their lust for fellatio by external stimulating information; rather, it is to an early internal stimulation that Freud ascribes the strength of the latent desire of some women.

Freud comments ironically that the use of the mouth as a sexual organ is regarded as a perversion if the lips or the tongue of one person are brought into contact with the genitals of another, but not if the mucus membranes of the lips of both of them come together. Yet, he suggests, both the kiss and fellatio have an 'innocent' origin. The mucus membrane of the lips and mouth is a primary erotic zone preserving the joys of sucking at the mother's breast:

> Intense activity of this erotogenic zone at an early age thus determines the subsequent presence of a somatic compliance of the part of the tract of the mucus membrane which begins at the lips. Thus, at a time when the sexual object proper, that is, the male organ, has already become known, circumstances may arise which once more increase the excitation of the oral zone, whose erotic character has been retained. It then needs very little creative power to substitute the sexual object of the moment (the penis) for the original object (the nipple) ... and to place the current sexual object in the situation in which gratification was originally obtained. So

we see that this...fantasy of sucking at a penis has the most innocent origin. It is a new version of what may be described as a pre-historic impression of sucking at the mother's or nurse's breast...

In our adult lives, we still long for the 'innocent' delights Freud describes. We never cease in our efforts to recapture the earliest pleasures we obtained while sucking at the breast, and these oral yearnings are subtly disguised. In the great talking shop of Westminster I was for 30 years daily compelled to endure a singular displacement of this desire, for so many of the garrulous bores in politics are victims, as we are, of their compulsive need for oral satisfaction. Of such people Karl Abraham, Freud's contemporary, once wrote:

> Their longing to seek gratification by way of sucking has changed to a need to give by way of the mouth, so that we find in them, besides a permanent longing to obtain everything, a constant need to communicate themselves orally to other people. This results in an obstinate urge to talk, connected in most cases with a feeling of overflowing. Persons of this kind have the impression that their fund of thought is inexhaustible, and they ascribe especial power of some unusual value to what they say.

The politicians' prolix contributions in the public realm tell us of their earliest private deprivations. Their oral discharges reveal to us an infancy where often a brusque or inadequate breast-feeding has left them dissatisfied and unassuaged; it is a handicap which they belatedly, and so deviously, strive to overcome. But far more overtly, the powerful urges of some women to suck the penis often speak of their early oral deprivation, of their excessively early weaning and, indeed, sometimes of their total lack of experience of the bliss which the breast, far more than the bottle, can provide.

Nowadays, despite all the pleadings of our paediatricians and child analysts urging the physical and emotional advantages bestowed by breast-feeding, children are nevertheless breast fed far less than previous generations. In the recent past, economic reasons determined that advantage was taken of this cheap nourishment; now economic reasons, the need for the mother to get back to work, play a considerable part in ensuring either that breast-feeding never commences or that it is available only for the shortest of times. More than one-third of babies born today receive no breast-feeding whatsoever; fewer than half the babies in the United Kingdom are breast-fed by the age of six weeks, the lowest rate in Europe. Inevitably, the baby girl who never gains the pleasures of oral sex at the breast will try to repair her loss as she grows up. Screaming young girls competitively and publicly offering a blow-job to Hugh Grant on his return from his fellatio adventures in California belong to the generation who have been short-changed in their nurturing. With contemporary capitalism colluding with New Labour to ensure that work has priority over mothering, and employment over welfare, it is unsurprising that some women, denied the nipple, turn for succour to the penis.

Teeny-boppers' public behaviour tells us that fellatio, one of the most intimate acts possible between man and woman, has been relegated to the commonplace. Yet even within my lifetime it was once felt to be so awesome and delicate, involving such complete commitment, that, while remaining unpractised by the bulk of the population ignorant of such sophisticated communicative sexual techniques, many a wealthy and privileged man, fearful of the potential meaningfulness of the act, went to the brothel, not to his wife's bedroom, to be thus pleasured. There they gave their money, not themselves.

This dichotomy between desire and tenderness, so embedded within the prevailing restrictive morality of my younger days, left these men incapable of achieving a fusion between their lustful and tender impulses. Women were angels or prostitutes. The Madonna-whore syndrome prevailed. Of course, love, with all its sweet bondages and mutualities, often prevailed among all classes, but in the generality the strangulation of affect induced by the conventional morality ensured that it would have been a rare event for fellatio to be proffered as a sacramental love token.

Now, however, our coarsened sensibilities have made fellatio the common coinage of casual sexual exchanges, and it appears to have become part of the standard flirtation rituals of our adolescents. Its ubiquity cannot simply be explained away as a tactic to circumvent a conjunction between penis and vagina, for its widespread practice preceded any awareness of Aids. At most the coming of Aids may have added to the number of its practitioners, although that seems improbable since the likely transmission of Aids through oral sex, as suggested by Swedish, Californian and Atlantia research, has been well-advertised. More, it would be no less simplistic to attribute solely to early oral deprivation, so common a feature of our working-mother culture, this widespread eagerness to suck and have the man ejaculate in this particular manner. That tells us something of its genesis but not of its elaborations, and they are many.

Even as the readiness of the male to participate in fellatio is not simply his wish to enjoy the physical excitations it arouses, so too the woman brings to oral coupling more than the acting out of the buried wish to obtain the juices denied to her at the breast. When Freud scrutinised the compulsive acting-out symptoms of his hysterics, he repeatedly emphasised that unravelling their problems required an understanding that the presenting symptoms had not one but several simultaneous and successive meanings. Such an understanding is certainly required if we are to appreciate the significance of fellatio within today's society where women, with considerable success, have rebelled against the submissive role formerly assigned to them.

The Depreciation of the Penis

It was my involvement in the in vitro controversies which commenced in the late 1970s that alerted me to the polysemous nature of fellatio, to its many meanings, to the challenge it can contain to male supremacy. In fellatio man is entirely at the mercy of the woman, utterly dependent upon her. Phallic supremacy is mocked and the woman can decide whether and when to grant the man satisfaction. Although, as some psychoanalytical clinicians have affirmed, the unconscious current operating when women revel in fellatio is the gaining of the delights of the worship or adoration of the phallic member, of male power, nevertheless, simultaneously and resentfully, it can be a powerful desire to be emancipated from such thralldom, to reverse the tables. To overthrow the god and become the goddess, the penis must be depreciated. It is unsurprising, when the man unconsciously is elevating himself to a phallic shrine and gaining much of his frisson from the degradation of the woman, that with the woman's unconscious motivation often being iconoclastic and depreciatory, mutual satisfaction is obtained only at surface level. The aftermath of acts of fellatio is not necessarily bathed in syndetic, mutually soothing moods; discerning therapists, explaining their clients' unhappiness, have often remarked on the subsequent quarrelsomeness of the participants with each other. Far from serving to unite each other, fellatio can be disruptive rather than connective. The fury of some of the women who since

9

the Lewinsky affair have made allegations against Clinton would suggest that, belatedly, they are releasing their unconscious resentments which they felt when voluntarily they were participants engaged in their worship of the god-president.

These days, articulate women in their 40s, write, often with misgivings, of how their rebellion as adolescents and undergraduates in the 1970s, before in vitro fertilisation arrived, then expressed itself in a depreciation of the penis. Clitoral orgasm had arrived, sales of dildos – the penis manqué – soared. The young feminist militants declared that a preference for mount-and-thrust sex was a confession of enjoyment in oppression. The joys of mutual masturbation between the sisters were affirmed, and the male organ made redundant. The published recollections of these '*Guardian* women' are those, no doubt, of only a minority of the girls up at university in the 1970s, but as a legislator I was ruefully to learn of the alarm that their protestations unwittingly aroused. Their rebellion came at a fraught time, the moment when, unknown to them, successful research into in vitro fertilisation was imminent. Soon the penis was no longer to be an absolute prerequisite for the perpetuation of the human race, and the awesome implications of that prospect was not one which, with Catholic ministers in key positions in the Labour Government of the 1970s and the back benches packed with male chauvinists, the House of Commons was prepared to face.

Unless reassured, it was predictable that the Commons macho man, already uneasily aware of being under feminist assault and terrified of the suggestion that he was dispensable, would overdeterminedly respond to what he felt was a subversion of his own virility. It was clear to me that wondrous possibilities were within the grasp of the scientists and doctors; the desperate needs of the infertile could perhaps be met, the anguish of miscarriages relieved, and some terrible inherited diseases conquered. But all these hopes could be dashed by the interventions of alarmed legislators unless there was in place a framework which contained and monitored the zeal of the researchers, and thus, no less important, contained the anxieties of a frightened legislature. But despite my importuning, the Government went into total denial rather than make any effort to evaluate and temper the social consequences of the new biology. It was not until July 1978 that, with some parliamentary cunning, I was at last able to waylay the Government and force them for the first time into a public response to my plea that the Government-appointed Advisory Genetic Manipulation Committee, then concerned with bugs and the supervision of the development recombinant DNA, should be enlarged to enable the ethical, legal and social aspects of the innovatory techniques to be reviewed.

However, Shirley Williams, the Secretary of State for Science, turned me down flat. No such committee would be appointed. Carrying all the theological prejudices that were to snarl up the in vitro fertilisation issue for years to come, she clearly felt that to set up such a body would implicitly sanction the in vitro fertilisation research already proceeding, work for which she had a decided distaste. It is futile to suggest to anti-abortionist fundamentalists that abortion involves the destruction of life in contrast to in vitro fertilisation which involves its creation; to them both are the devil's work and Shirley Williams, on the occasion of her refusal, was able to mask her allegiance to papal doctrine by claiming, quite correctly, that the Medical Research Council had informed her that it thoroughly disapproved of in vitro fertilisation research on human beings. In the face of lèse-majesté being shown to their penises, objectivity had totally deserted those sitting on the Medical Research Council.

The male Medical Research Council had found the insubordination intolerable; and the self-same fear it occasioned was to envelop the issue during the years of lonely campaigning in which, following Shirley Williams' refusal, I engaged. The actual arrival of test-tube babies did not assist me in my quest; on the contrary, the visibility of children born without copulation left the male establishment frozen with fear. Whitehall, the medical bureaucrats and the politicians were immobilised and, for the most part, the Church was rendered speechless, choked with rage at the blasphemy that the virgin birth could be replicated at will and the Holy Ghost relegated to the role of a laboratory assistant. As late as February 1982, the Prime Minister, Margaret Thatcher, gave me a dusty procrastinating reply when once again I urged the formation of a comprehensive inter-departmental and inter-disciplinary committee to review the unprecedented issues. I pressed the demand in the House of Commons in an adjournment debate in March 1982, and then for the first time the Government began to falter. Hesitatingly, it admitted the need for some enquiry. In July 1982 the Government announced the formation of a committee under the chairmanship of Dame Mary Warnock. It was given terms of reference – to consider the social, ethical and legal implications of developments relating to human fertilisation and embryology – which were almost exactly as I had demanded four years previously.

The committee, when it eventually reported, presented its balanced and pragmatic recommendations in cool dispassionate terms, but that was not how they were received. The bibliolaters and fundamentalists were soon at work, and the denunciations commenced. At one level the argument was no pristine colloquy; in vitro fertilisation may have been the miracle of the late twentieth century, but the musty debates were soon drenched in the vocabulary of medievalists for whom it was a re-enactment of the old struggle between religious zealots and science. But, at a deeper level, although initially not appreciated by the feminists, and not consciously understood even by most of the protagonists, a spectacular jousting was taking place. Feudal man had donned his armour, paying particular care to the placing of his cod-piece, and was not going to yield his dominant position.

It was Enoch Powell who emerged as the knight in shining armour eager to lead the battle against the emasculators. Powell had obtained, in the annual parliamentary ballot, a right of time to introduce a Private Members' Bill. His choice confirmed to the fundamentalists that God was on their side. Powell had no history or formal association with the fundamentalist lobbies. His religious and political views had indeed a different flavour, permeated as they were by the Manichaean fallacy – seeing the universe divided into good and bad – and the Warnock Report was seen by him as satanic, the dark side of the universal dualism.

In announcing and subsequently defending his intention to stop effective embryo research, Powell did not therefore rest his statements on religious conviction or, as he was too sage to suggest, on rationality. Unashamedly he asserted his 'instincts' had demanded his action. Displaying his responses a few inches upward from its source, he repetitively and powerfully affirmed his 'gut reaction'. Once again he was revealing his lack of confidence in his own heterosexual prowess. His prurient preoccupation with immigrant birth statistics and his notorious 'rivers of blood' speech were the reactions of a man envying, fearing and exaggerating the fecundity of blacks. What little store of virility he felt was within his possession was being taken away from him by in vitro fertilisation.

The conjunction of the great parliamentarian and the fundamentalists proved irresistible and Powell's Bill passed through the Commons' second reading by a huge majority, and was then bludgeoned through its committee stages. With the Medical Research Council now recanting, the alarmed medical and scientific community formed an alliance with a range of concerned women's organisations, feminist groups and societies concerned with childlessness and inherited disabilities to halt the Bill's progress, but they had come on to the scene too late. The Bill, unamended, reached the floor of the House for its final day.

Then serendipity intervened. A minor technical Bill which slightly amended the rule relating to the production of motor-car licences was due to precede consideration of Powell's Bill. It was anticipated that it would last but a few minutes, but I had other thoughts. As a penniless newly qualified solicitor, I had survived in the courts by doing road-traffic work farmed out to me by the prosecuting department of the local authority, and I retrieved that almost forgotten case-law knowledge and made a speech lasting hours on the little Bill – the longest speech in my parliamentary life. The fretting Deputy Speaker, despite pleas from Powell's supporters, could not halt me since I was, with the material in my hands, too experienced a parliamentarian to sway one jot from the Rules of Order. When Powell's Bill was finally reached, I had put down an amendment which the procedural rules required be called first. Having dallied with that amendment, despite Powell intervening to indicate his readiness to accept it as he tried desperately to save his Bill, my supporting colleagues had no difficulty in subsuming such little parliamentary time as was left to his Bill. For about twenty years, except when we addressed each other across the floor of the House, Powell and I never spoke; he never forgave me for the laughter in the Chamber when, repelled by his notorious 'rivers of blood' speech, I had declared that if there were fewer eunuchs in the land, there would be fewer

Enochs. When, as a result of my intervention, Powell's in vitro Bill ran out of time and thus fell my pact of animosity with Powell was well and truly sealed.

Yet Powell never accepted his defeat. Unto his last days, stricken with Parkinson's disease, still he heroically fought back, determined to affirm, despite in vitro fertilisation, the exclusiveness of the virgin birth. Rejected by his electorate and marooned in a bitter retirement, he continued to wage the battle away from Westminster, finding the ideal terrain in the Jewish Palestine of the first century.

Squandering his formidable intellect and his masterful command of Greek, he turned, obsessively, to a prolonged and detailed scrutiny of the New Testament and set out to upset the belief of the overwhelming majority of scholars that Mark's gospel was the first, and that it was upon that gospel that Matthew and Luke drew; this was utterly unacceptable to Powell for in Mark's gospel Jesus appears on the scene fully grown, and if its priority was accepted, then the annunciation and virgin birth recounted in the gospels of Matthew and Luke – but not in the writings of Paul, John and the rest of the writers of the New Testament – would be relegated to the realm of fanciful and mythological additions.

With Powell, in his political stances always perilously near messianic identification, it was an essential need for this extraordinarily mother-bound man to erase a human sire and to assert the divinity of a Jesus fathered by no one except God; sex and intercourse were thus banished from the tale, and the holy mother was to remain virginal, a state which unconsciously Powell doubtless wished upon his own mother.

It was indeed a tragedy that Powell, the great parliamentarian, should have ended his last years entangled in such a bizarre exercise; but it was the price he paid for having wrestled so unsuccessfully to come to terms with his own sexuality. He always reminded me of the Cathars, the courageous thirteenth century heretics of the Languedoc who, to become '*parfait*', advocated celibacy and suicide, both ideals negating the physical side of our nature. Powell's yearnings were congruent with those of the Cathars. On television he once declared his real desire was not to be a politician but to be a monk; but he failed to achieve celibacy, and not having achieved suicide, he felt guilty in living, more than once expressing his dismay that, unlike many of his comrades, he survived the war. Such life-negating not life-enhancing moods enveloped his politics, making them dangerous yet seductive. In the end he himself became entrapped by them; his last work, *The evolution of the gospels*, obsessive and manic, has an intellectual framework only fitfully able to contain near-madness. And so he was to die, not in glory but with a whimper.

Sex, Enoch Powell and
the Asylum Seekers

Powell's malign influence endures. Albeit in anaemic language which Powell would have scorned, William Hague, seeking to outflank Jack Straw, began early in 2000 to make demands for yet stricter controls over asylum-seekers. Emboldened by the electoral response of the local elections of May 2000 the Tory leader played the populist asylum-seekers card even as Powell did when the East African Asians were fleeing from Uganda. Although ending the political consensus which had prevailed among the main political parties since Edward Heath courageously threw Powell out of his cabinet, Hague, like Powell, disavowed the charge of racialism, claiming that all he sought was greater control of immigration to ensure that Britain was not perceived as a soft touch; he proffered the same apologia as did Powell who always maintained in his speeches that 'numbers were of the essence' not racialism.

No one can dispute that the end of the Cold War and the tragic turbulences in Africa created a huge logistic problem as millions were tempted from their homelands by economic advantage or are forcibly uprooted. But the hysteria in Britain about bogus asylum-seekers and illegal immigrants tells us that policies are not being determined by rational assessments but, rather, to a considerable extent, spring from the self-same ugly sources that moved Powell, to the approval of millions, to protest against the 'swamping' of

Britain by blacks. In fact, a cool appraisement of the demographic problems brewing in Britain may lead us to allow and even encourage mass immigration. People born in the post-war baby boom are ageing and some are beginning to retire. The resultant slow but steady shrinkage of the native-born labour force is clear in every advanced industrial society. This inexorable demographic change will make large-scale immigration inevitable eventually in every rich country, in order to support the vast cohorts of pensioners who will be retiring over the next thirty years. Britain, in the not so far distant future, will need immigration even as it was encouraged in the decades of labour shortage after World War II.

In the United States, doubtless because of a booming economy, with unemployment minimal and real wages rising, the Americans are belatedly realising that immigration can help to keep this virtuous circle spinning and do much to contain the latent demographic difficulties. While anti-immigration moods are inflamed by politicians in Britain, in America a pro-immigration movement has attracted support from across the ideological spectrum, from business to trade unions. American immigration policy, Anatole Kaletsky wrote in May 2000 in *The Times* was 'on the brink of a revolution'. An extraordinary coalition of political forces is promoting the idea of an amnesty which would grant US citizenship to an estimated 6,000,000 immigrants who have not only entered the country illegally but have worked there and lived off welfare state safety net benefits in defiance of the law. At the same time, Alan Greenspan, the venerated Chairman of the Reserve Board has insisted that the single most effective measure Congress could take to ensure economic expansion would be to 'uncap' the present immigration control.

In Britain, however, the immigration debate is confined to the vexatious and real problems of foreign beggars in the West End of London and the burdens on local authorities receiving asylum-seekers. Our timorous politicians fear to invite the electorate to contemplate the immigration which ere long must be accepted if we are to maintain our living standards; they lack the courage to face down the irrational passions that would be stirred by such an invitation. These were the emotions Powell stirred; a glance, therefore, however unwelcome, at their nature and at Powell's private travail, may be admonitory, for although it would perhaps be an overstatement to suggest the eloquent formulations advertising Powell's prejudices were paradigmatic, they certainly were not a caricature of the prejudices held by so many unfulfilled men and women in today's Britain. In frequent Commons debates when we agreed or disagreed, Powell and I addressed each other through the Speaker; but outside the Chamber, as we emerged from our almost adjacent offices, for twenty years we passed each other by never speaking. My quip about eunuchs and Enochs had pierced his carapace; he deeply resented my diagnosis of his condition, but it was uncomfortably correct.

His insistence that his alarums came solely from the concern of the consequences of the burgeoning birthrate of coloured immigrants was a sham. Powell's persistent fascination with the birthrates of those with darker skins than his own was not simply, as he maintained, a matter of numbers. It was essentially prurient; he feared the blacks' sexual and progenitive capacities. Men and women more confident and more comfortable in their sexuality do not forever act as calculating-machine voyeurs adding up the congresses of their fellow-citizens.

And Powell had particular reasons to doubt the strength of his own heterosexuality. I have little doubt that as a young man he had a German lover, and that that episodic homosexual experience bore down upon him all his life, leaving him with a stammering guilt-ridden sexuality, one envious and fearful of the fantasised sexual prowess that he projected upon the black man. In 1988, when the former Dean of Westminster interviewed him in connection with a book, Powell 'confessed' to his early homosexuality and read to the clergyman passages from his collection *First Poems* explaining the homosexual love behind the writing. Powell was not talking of some adolescent fumbling but of a more searing experience, and how traumatic that was can be observed when we learn how he responded to the loss of what he called his 'beloved country' – Germany – and thus his lover.

Powell was five years older than me; but as a provincial lad in my very early teens I was profoundly conscious, despite the attraction I already had to so much German literature, of the increasing menace of the rise of Nazism in Germany. That rise, however, passed over Powell's head as he became increasingly intoxicated with German *Kultur*; and this despite the fact that the scholarships he gained enabled him, as an undergraduate, to make numerous forays into Germany. His awakening only came when the Nazi regime was already well ensconced; then, when the Nazi gangsters fell out, and Rohm and other homosexual Brownshirt leaders were slaughtered, suddenly he woke up to the naked brutality of the regime. Powell was in Germany during the time when the Nazis were already espousing racialist doctrines and sadistically acting upon them. All this the young Powell ignored. It was not the Nazi execution of Social Democrats or their persecution of the Jews that shattered Powell's confidence in Germany; the precipitate was the assault upon the homosexual leadership. In characteristically histrionic tones he wrote of his dismay:

> I can still remember today how I sat for hours in a state of shock, shock which you experience when, around you you see the debris of a beautiful abode in which you have lived for a long time ... So it had all been illusion, all fantasy, all a self-created myth. Music, philosophy, poetry, science and the language itself - everything was demolished, broken to bits on the cliffs of a monstrous reality. The spiritual homeland had not been a spiritual homeland after all ... Overnight my spiritual homeland had disappeared and I was left only with my geographical homeland.

This is the language of a bereaved lover, not that of a disenchanted ideologue. Today bisexuality can be shrugged off, and the youthful homosexual activity of a politician can, fortunately, attract no serious public opprobrium – as has been well-demonstrated in the case of Michael Portillo. But Powell was of another generation, brought up when a different and more oppressive *zeitgeist* prevailed, with laws in place reflecting the most severe interpretations of the prohibitions of Leviticus; if official doctrine was defied, guilt and inhibition could be the consequence for the sinner; original sin was not an abstract doctrine but a reality for so many.

Powell defiantly made a bid to jettison his guilt, to free himself from God's injunctions which were so much in conflict with his private lifestyle and yearnings. As a young man he became a declared and committed atheist, and doubtless affirmed his disbelief with his customary display of dazzling logic. But disbelief and faith are not necessarily merely cerebral creatures; one can trace Powell's oscillations between godlessness and belief to the formative influences of his early familial life. For Powell was not born into a kingdom but, as his admiring biographer Roy Lewis tells us, into a family which was 'a republic of three persons' and within that republic, all his biographers agree, there was an intense alliance between the young Enoch and his school-teacher mother. The father played a decidedly lesser role, leaving his wife to shape the gifted child into a mental athlete; and to perform her task, the mother gave up teaching and made the child her single pupil.

Predictable consequences flowed from such an austere and intense family unit in which loyalty was not ceded to the father and the foundations of which rested upon a coalition of mother and child. The narcissism of the child can be excessively corroborated by the admiring mother and then, insufficiently mortified by a strong containing father, the child can be left to grow up permeated by a haughty grandiosity. This trait, although often successfully borne by Powell's formidable intellect, was nevertheless one of the least engaging elements in his make-up, and was a severe handicap throughout his political career; the elimination of the father in the early years of the child from any claim to priority can lead, in adolescence and later, to a pronounced bias against father-asserting philosophies or religions perceived as surrogates. God the Father was clearly not tolerable to Powell as a young man and in his atheism he denied Him priority, as his own father had been denied.

But God the Son was to prove another matter entirely. The isolation of the only child growing up in a literary, non-gregarious family, over-valuing the word and seemingly deficient in human relationships outside the books, could not be sustained. The atheist must walk and die in his own footsteps, his eternity linked to his work and his children, and although Powell once said: 'Unless one is alone one is unimportant', he lacked the resource to maintain that position. He turned to, and identified himself with, his Saviour, ready to emulate his Redeemer and to sacrifice himself for what he believed to be the true word. The political sophisticates who were astonished by Powell's renunciation in 1974 of his safe seat and power base in Wolverhampton, rather than fight under what he believed to be Heath's false banner, did not understand their man. He was acting out his needs; and lacking, as ever, subtlety or pretence, he made this explicit to those attuned to listen.

After briefly announcing his decision not to participate in what he described as 'a fraudulent election' he remained silent for two weeks, except for one public intervention and that was his little-noticed sermon entitled *The meaning of sacrifice; the Road to Calvary*. Powell went, with masochistic relish, on his way, enjoying every moment at the stations of his cross. To those who accused him of being a Judas, he retorted, with full justification, that he received no reward for his services. His critics misunderstood his role; his mimesis was no fringe part in the drama. His grandiosity, always teetering on the edge of omnipotence, insisted he was the central figure and as such he endured his political crucifixion. But it cannot be doubted that he went to his cross bearing not only the sins of the world but bearing his own sins, seeking redemption from his own guilts.

Those, like Powell, possessed of a profound belief in original sin can only too easily believe, at least unconsciously, that a special curse falls upon the sons of Ham; and such a view in extreme Protestant sects can have dire consequences. The practitioners of the theology of the Dutch Reformed Church made clear that the sons of Ham should pay the price for their alleged ancestors' mockery of Noah's nakedness; for many of the Boers the black was thus forever associated with wrong-doing and evil. Built into their religious beliefs were elaborate rationalisations to mask their antagonism and fear of the dark man's sexual endowment, a fear which found its ultimate expression in laws and taboos against miscegenation in apartheid South Africa made by white men to ward off the fantasised threat of blacks endowed with a more vigorous sexuality luring the white woman; and the prohibitions against sexual couplings between black and white reinforced the restraints of the white men. Burdened by their interpretation of the doctrine of original sin, torn by their ambivalences towards sex, feared as joy, suffered as agony, they needed the protection from temptation which anti-miscegenation laws and social conventions afforded them. Such attitudes and the motivations prompting them, find expression nowadays in the extraordinary antagonisms that can be aroused amongst too many when prominent sportsmen and celebrities break the taboo.

Unless, as white men and women, we are on guard against ourselves, all of us can stir the deep-seated biases whose constant presence within us is betrayed in our language and demeanour. None of us escape from describing the 'dark passions'; we do not speak of 'white as sin' but of 'black as sin'; sin can be thought of as black and sex as black and dirty. Even in our garb we often only faintly mortify our equations of sex and blackness. It is not extravagant to interpret the semiology of the pre-eminence of the 'little black dress' in every well-appointed wardrobe; the chic is not demure or innocent; it is flirtatious, subliminally bringing intimations of sensuousness.

The more Pauline emphases abound in Christian sects, the more the spirit and the flesh are severed, the more becomes the hostility to what are felt as threatening dark passions; thus the non-white man and the gypsy can be seen as visible containers of filth. When Hague, perceived in the May 2000 elections as playing the race card, assiduously attended, unlike former Tory leaders, gatherings of Christian fundamentalists, he found his natural constituency; it is amongst creeds with Puritanical credos that notions abound which can be speedily triggered into hostility against the dark-skinned.

When Powell dealt the race card he did not do so to garner votes and popularity; indeed, he was never happier than when his masochistic needs were assuaged by his becoming an object of widespread scorn. Hague has a different aim; his vulgar populism certainly finds resonances in the polling-booth among the sexually inadequate; but his advantage will only be temporary. In the end, in our irrevocably multi-racial society, if he pursues his present strategy it will end, as surely as it did for Enoch Powell, in his political destruction.

Manhood in Her Hands

My act of sabotage of Powell's anti-in vitro Bill received plaudits only from some of the women involved in the campaign to thwart Powell. By many it was sulkily received for, truth to tell, they were ambivalent in their involvement in a campaign to assist the rights of all women to motherhood. This particular campaign highlighted, and confirmed to me, the essential difference in typology existing among women's rights campaigners for there are too many among them whose ire is aroused by even a hint at women's procreative task. Even to suggest that wiser government can be created from the womb than can be fertilised by the penis arouses the protest that man wishes to 'condemn' them to the 'doom' of perpetual motherhood, and they regard as patronising and insulting the view that they could bring to our social inventions the same mood as women so often supply privately – to nurse and nourish, to care and tolerate, to reconcile and preserve. They are the women who scream that sexual harassment is at work if the suggestion is made that women can bring into public life some fullness, warmth and generosity, the psychic analogues to the woman's pregnancy, childbirth, lactation and the richly convex parts of her anatomy.

There are indeed two types of feminists: those who have fought their corner against male injustices in the interests of mother and child, and those who have a very different agenda which certainly does not proclaim mother and children first. The latter are

23

engaged in waging a sex war, and their feminism is a gendered form of ruthless individualism. These articulate sansculottes of the sexual revolution would want no peace settlement in our society even if all male-imposed injustices had been redressed. Their millenniarian goal is total female self-fulfilment free from societal encumbrances. It is, of course, a vanity, for they are endeavouring to recover the unattainable: many of the pathogenic elements driving these irridescent women to demand the impossible are to be found not necessarily in the present but in the earliest events of the mothering dyad, and one of the most significant of those events can be the denial of the bliss of the breast, resulting from inadequate mothering. When their intelligence matches the anger they feel at their primary frustrations, then they can become formidable proponents of their cause; and over the last few decades they have participated in many deserved victories against the grievous discriminations imposed upon them by a male-dominated society.

Yet despite all the advances, still they regard themselves as victims, and still their propagandising continues. Many of the turbulences within our present sexual mores are attributable to their activities, for as pace-setters and models they have influenced a whole generation of women, many of whom have become endowed with their discontents. Only in this context, and against this background, can we begin to understand the phenomenon in fin de siècle Britain of a widespread practice of casual fellatio, for in each act the woman can explicitly vent her anger and rejoice in triumphalism. This triumphalism, in practice, may, it is true, sometimes be ill-founded for the 'victory' can, perhaps unknown to them, go to the male enjoying the degradation of the woman. Indeed, there can sometimes, some psychoanalysts have affirmed, be considerable gains for the middle-aged, depression-prone male patient who seeks experience with a young woman for she, by submitting to giving a 'blow job', temporarily re-establishes for him a basic 'good ego feeling'. But empowerment, not therapy, is the predominant goal of the militant feminist.

That empowerment, so grievously delayed by a phallocentric society, now finds expression in bedroom and Oval Room as well as the boardroom, her partner's manhood literally in her hands and between her teeth. She alone determines the rhythms which formerly were the male prerogative that so often left her dissatisfied when the replete male insensitively turned away. In this enactment, however, there is no doubt in her mind as to who is in charge, who is the leading player and who, literally, has been assigned the bit part. Here, she imagines, the woman can have her cake and eat it; be the dominatrix and simultaneously gorge herself with the milk which an insufficiently caring mother had denied her.

Perhaps there has always been, and always will be, battles between the sexes, but in lasting relationships they are skirmishes, not relentless and unforgiving wars. The mortification of each individual's narcissism, the prerequisite for the sustaining of any partnership that is no façade but is passionate and not indifferent means that some accumulated resentments must flare up, some quarrels ensue, and then happily be followed by the sweetness of the reconciliations. Within such relationships fellatio can be the intimation of the delight postponed, a wooing preliminary to consummation, a draft manifesto of a declaration of an exclusive love soon to be finalised.

But this is not the fellatio of the conquering women of the White House seeking to hold to ransom the most powerful man on earth; nor is it the fellatio of the doctrinaire feminist now rebelling against the privileges of promiscuity arrogantly claimed as his preserve by yesterday's man. Her engagement in fellatio is no longueur; like fast food, it is quick service. Free of the encumbrances and disarrays of undressing, one zip and the philandering feminist has one more victory in the war she unconsciously wages both against man and her biology. For her, there is no acceptance of male domination or Freud's dictum that anatomy is destiny.

In fellatio the militant feminist is expressing her rebellion against the subjugation of sexuality under the order of procreation, and against the institutions which guarantee this order. The Pope, in defiance of the needs of the Third World, and against all humanity, continues to condemn the condom even as he cruelly condemns all homosexual acts – for he well understands the subversiveness of any sexual aid or act which prevents procreation. From his vantage point, any deviations from 'normal' expressions of sexuality is a threat, since it is an opposition against the continuance of the chain of representation, and thereby of paternal dominance. He is the supreme representative on earth, and as 'Papa Pope' the spilling of seed into the wrong orifice is a challenge to the legitimacy and continuance of his Church. His insight, but not his goal, is shared by psychoanalysts who sometimes describe the clinical perversions they encounter as attempts to prevent the reappearance of 'the dreaded father'.

In fellatio, therefore, the aggressive feminist finds a splendid battleground on which to wage her wars. Fellatio may not be as orgasmic for the female as for the male but the sado-masochistic satisfactions obtainable are various and highly charged. Feeling her own creativity demeaning, she mocks her vagina and simultaneously, as a Delilah, she ensures her partner is brought to a fruitless climax, one which can never bring paternity. The blows she directs against herself, and the blows against her partner, are all subsumed in the act of fellatio. As a bonus, by usurping his controlling machismo role, humiliatingly, she unconsciously achieves the ablation of the father, and wiping him out, punishes him for his faithlessness in choosing her mother, not her. And, greatest prize of all to the militant feminist, she can engage in the fantasy so often recorded by psychoanalysts in their hysteric patients of incorporating the envied male organ and thus becoming, by identification, a man.

And because of that defiance of the reality of her own anatomy – one in which she throws away the advantage of not having a penis – she can, in fellatio, truly gain only a Pyrrhic victory. It is not for nothing that in Greek legend Tiresias, who was transformed into a woman for seven years, asserted that woman had ten times more enjoyment than man. In Tiresias's comparison, it is the femininity of the woman that can give her an inexhaustible wealth of orgasms.

All attempts to circumscribe the feminine orgasm, to attempt to apply a single male model of sexual satisfaction, are suspect, for feminine orgasms are not exact or measurable. They are erratic, changing, elusive, unfolding, in a field with no exigencies, free from any demand that they keep to a precise form. Long ago, in 1895, Freud clearly perceived that as far as feminine sensuality is concerned, what he regarded as masculine virility was blurred and gave way to new oscillations and to new forms that escape the model represented by male sexuality. It was Melanie Klein who emphasised that the woman tends to attach a narcissism to her body as a whole – 'distributing it to a greater extent over the whole of her body' – whereas the man focuses his narcissism on his genitals.

All my personal experiences lead me, as I think it would to many who have been fortunate with their women, to accept the validity of the view recently presented by the Argentine psychoanalyst Alcira Mariam Alizade when she tells us:

> A woman can have a well-localised, sexologically measurable orgasm, with an abundant secretion that imitates semen. But to limit feminine pleasure to that form implies leaving aside a very great range of coition erogenous and affective phenomena in the unfolding of the wealth of her erotic potential.

It is unfortunate that many male sexologists have only too successfully induced women to deny a diffusion of sensuality which is their marvellous endowment and have encouraged them in an obsessional concern that 'success' or 'failure' in bed depends upon how well they imitate a man's ejaculation. The brutal fact is that men fear the erogenic overflowing which the more uninhibited woman releases, and Alizade cannot be gainsaid when she claims that the persistent attempt to accommodate the female of the species in the Procrustean bed of the male orgasm is a way of dominating and controlling her. The woman engaged in fellatio is being fooled if she imagines the man is fully under her control; she has fallen for the confidence trick and it is often not she but the man who is in the driving seat.

The Phallic Mother

According to Freud, penis envy is universal in woman and occupies a central position in her psychology. This interpretation of womankind's psychology inevitably leads to a negative view, a perspective of women as beings who are responding to the discovery of not having a penis, and are, in short, hommes manqués. However, even Freud's earliest followers demurred, believing Freud was attaching excessive importance to this differentiation between woman and man, and they stigmatised his approach as phallocentric. Today's women psychoanalysts are often even more severe in their criticisms, but although the classical psychoanalytical theory describing the sequacious path to be taken by a baby girl to achieve femininity, which includes circumventing penis envy, is much dented, the insights it affords in any scrutiny of the current ubiquity of the practice of fellatio have a special significance.

Those impatient that such a fussy scrutiny should be made of the simple act of a man sticking his cock in a woman's mouth may reflect that perhaps the physical act is essentially epiphenomenal, spume thrown up by the deeper movements of today's sociological and emotional tides which most certainly need charting if our society is not to go hopelessly adrift. However defective Freud's theory may be, as a navigational aid in our explorations, it has considerable value.

According to his theory, there are three conditions to be fulfilled before femininity can be achieved. The girl has to change her erotogenic zone from her clitoris to her vagina; she has to change her attachment from her mother to her father; and she has to revert from an active attitude towards her mother to a passive attitude to her father. According to Freud, the girl has to give up all her original essential sources of gratifications in order to achieve her metamorphosis into womanhood. She has to turn from masculinity to femininity. The only available libido to her is male; she is born a little man equipped with a 'male' organ, the clitoris, giving only male satisfaction. To become feminine she has to undergo psychic castration like the physical counterpart still practised in so many traditional cultures. Although present-day women analysts contest this developmental route to femininity that Freud assigns to women, they do not challenge the existence and force of penis envy: with the nerve endings in the vagina insufficient to make a move from the joys of the clitoris compellingly desirable, it is unsurprising that the pleasures of the small clitoris would lead to an unconscious desire to enhance those pleasures by having a larger clitoris – a penis. Indeed, analysts have often recorded that their hysteric patients engage in fantasies in which they incorporate the envied male organ and become, by identification, a male.

Attribution of such active expressions of sexuality to women often causes unease to men. I am sceptical of the claims made by some that female sexuality is usually more inhibited and masturbation less frequent or less open than in males. It has always been a stratagem by men to ward off their fears of female sexuality by idealising women, and simultaneously denying their right to sexual pleasure – a right that must remain a male monopoly. And they blot out the idea that their idealised women would 'sully' themselves by playing around their clitoridal area.

Sometimes, however, the artist can tell us what men fear to acknowledge. No painter has so engaged me as the early sixteenth-century Giorgione, pupil of Bellini and fellow student of Titian. Not many of the works he created in his short life are in existence now; the last one he painted was completed, after his death, by Titian. This is his famed Venus Pudica in the Dresden Art Gallery. The beautiful and peacefully stretched out sleeping nude was to inspire many generations of artists and, as the

Dresden catalogue claims, was one 'the likes of which had not been painted before'. Vasari has written that Giorgione was 'a very amorous man'; it was indeed the death of him, for while continuing a 'very pleasurable affair' with a woman smitten with the plague, he became dangerously infected and died. Some of the ironies of that fatal attraction are echoed in his alluring and dangerously self-absorbed Venus.

It was in unusual circumstances that in 1959 I first saw the beguiling painting. My demand in the Commons that we should stop feeding the paranoia of East Germany by refusing the Communist Government recognition infuriated my Labour leader, Hugh Gaitskell, the Cold War warrior, but it was, of course, more than acceptable to Walter Ulbricht, the East German dictator, who invited me and a few other colleagues sharing my view to meet him and his gangster colleagues in East Berlin. It was a bumpy encounter, but when Ulbricht, in a spurious display of openness, offered to show me around, I said I wished to see Dresden. It was mid-winter and the infrastructure between Berlin and Dresden, not helped by snowed-up roads, was chaotic; what is now a short road journey was then much more arduous. Ulbricht assumed that I wished, out of guilt, to see the beautiful city so needlessly destroyed. I felt no such guilt. The loss of life occasioned by the terrible bombing blunder was appalling, but such a terrible blunder came from a war precipitated by the Nazi regime supported by the overwhelming majority of Germans in East and West Germany. I spelled this out to Ulbricht so that he should know I did not wish to view the ruins of Dresden. I wished to see a Giorgione painting. The Philistine dictator was bemused by my insistence but laid on the facilities to ensure I was granted what he naturally regarded as a crackpot request.

The painting did not fail me, but totally seduced by the poetic harmony depicted between the human body and the backcloth landscape, captivated by the reiteration in the hills on the horizon with the contours of the naked Venus, and yielding to the evening calm which in golden hues envelops the picture, I misinterpreted the painting as a vision of an exquisitely beautiful woman passively dreaming. Forty years later, however, revisiting the painting in Dresden in 1998, I realised that, male-like, I had initially preferred to see the painting as an innocent idyll. Now I saw that it was no apotheosis of womankind. Lurking behind this extraordinary idealisation of Venus is a depiction of all man's ambivalences towards woman – his resentment of her power to attract him, his envy of her creativity, and his subliminal awareness that perhaps he is not her first love. And so, snidely, the painter releases his hostility by attempting to mock her, to degrade her. The naked woman's gesture, her hand resting on her genital area and a finger inserted into her vagina, is not a signal pointing to her femininity. On the contrary, it was a depiction of an active masturbatory act, and the magic stillness that falls upon the painting is not telling of a post-coital mood of a submissive woman but, rather, speaks of the quiet satisfaction gained from her active play on the clitoris.

Her eyes are closed, but her reverie is surely not suffused with a yearning for a young romantic man – though male presumptuousness would like to project such thoughts upon her. Indeed, unable to accept that the pleasure is unrelated to man, fanciful art historians, now compelled to acknowledge that the wondrous painting is a depiction of female masturbation, weaved stories derived from Ovid's *Metamorphoses*. They suggested that Venus was discovered by her husband Vulcan in flagrante delicto with Mars, who was compelled to flee and, faute de mieux, poor Venus was left to attain orgasm by herself. This farrago may soothe men's pride, but on gazing at the naked woman's countenance, it requires little imagination to divine that her love is not an adulterous one, it is a narcissistic one. It is a love of herself and then of one as near to herself as possible, a lesbian love, a homosexual love which in our society, despite the courageous crusading of butch lesbians, still remains for many a love that dare not speak its name.

Yet the clinical material assembled by some of Europe's contemporary women psychoanalysts leads them to conclude that the penis envy which Freud identified arises because women feel handicapped in the means available to them to express their homosexuality. The central place of a mother in a woman's life means that she is born, and continues to live, with a legacy of a homoerotic bond, and that female heterosexuality will always be accompanied by a strong homosexual undercurrent. These women analysts therefore regard the continuous female bisexuality of all women not so much as a consequence of a nostalgia for an inadequate clitoris which, to attain femininity, the woman has to give up, but rather as an ongoing homosexual longing for her first love, her mother.

Clearly, men have always found women's homosexuality threatening and have resented the intimacy of a mother and her girl-child. The Jewish god was indeed a jealous god for the myth tells us that men, not women, were created in 'his' image; women were a mere by-product of a man's rib. The Greeks depreciation of women's creative role was no less: Athene was taken from Zeus's head. In reality, in contrast to the myths, women can, in their daughters, recreate themselves, but the very closeness that can arise between mother and daughter brings its own hazards. It can, at its most benign, bring about the transmission of good mothering and move the daughter towards a joyful acceptance of her femininity and, in turn, her ultimate role. Other and less than good enough mothering can cause severe hiccups in the child's development; still she can remain frustrated, still wanting the active possession of her first love, a first love that in the child's unconscious, psychoanalysis tells us, was not the vaginal mother but a phallic mother. This belief is surely understandable, for if the daughter herself possesses a little penis why should not the mother have a bigger one?

It is against this background that the present eagerness of many young women to engage in fellatio should perhaps be seen. Their grandmothers, my contemporaries, for a short while during World War II took up work outside the home, and that undoubtedly led to some changes in the sexual mores of Britain. Yet when rapid demobilisation took place, with extraordinary little protest, most quit their employment and returned to their traditional roles. Societal pressures, the pill and feminist agitation brought their children, the mothers of the present generation, out of the kitchen, but many of them never successfully resolved the mother-work equation. They were never able to give enough of themselves to their daughters who, in turn, thus unassuaged in their active homosexual desires directed towards their mothers, find a particular satisfaction in the role-reversal fellatio offers when, as males, they can control their feminised partners unconsciously perceived as they saw their first too-often unrequited love, the phallic mother. Unlike male homosexuality, little has been written about female homosexuality, and the importance of the ongoing homosexual relationship between girl and mother which shadows all the adult heterosexuality of a woman is extraordinarily unremarked. In fellatio it shows itself in its most torrid form.

But even as we attribute buried female homosexual desires as part of the explanation of the current popularity of fellatio, we must nevertheless be on guard against casting modern women as the sole initiators, as predatory and deceiving Eves, tempting man to believe fellatio is only fun, a mere frolic. That would indeed be a misogynist reading of its widespread practice. Men are not unwilling and innocent victims. What then is the compulsive need existing today that compels so many men, in presidential style, to risk their whole manhood and place their trust in women who are often little more than strangers to them? Why in a contraceptive world, able to provide them with safe sex, do they choose as balm for their sexual itch a coupling so hazardous, so potentially dangerous to them? What, in short, is the nature of man's complicity?

The Abnegation of the Man

Man, engaged in fellatio, plays a passive role, his helplessness advertised to his partner and enjoyed by himself, but the quiescent physical expression found in the conjunction should not mislead us. Beyond his more overt and hesitant intimations, by way of verbal or body language, of his desire for the woman's administrations, is a highly active unconscious drive to precipitate the climactic occasion where he can luxuriate in total submission. When masochism takes over, the manipulative talents released to achieve its goal can be wondrous and sinister, and man, when seeking fellatio, by unconscious wooing of the woman, often uses them to the full. Masochistic seduction by a man of a woman can be replete with guile.

Masochism is certainly not a specific to woman, as was frequently brought home to me when, as a solicitor, I pursued monetary claims for men injured at work. In my experience it was often more difficult to succeed on the injured man's behalf when the accident really was the responsibility of his employers or fellow workmen than it was when he was unconsciously determinedly the agent of his own misfortune. The fluent and paranoiac capacity of the self-injured man to project guilt and responsibility on those around him is sometimes proof against all logic. I had one client whose so-called accident-proneness became a source of terror to his employers and their insurers when I established to the satisfaction of the court, on three occasions over a short span of years, that he was the victim and not the cause of the industrial accidents which befell him. My relish of his rationalisations, which remained undented and undaunted under all cross-examination, almost equalled the awe in which I held a woman client for whom I obtained three divorces on the grounds of cruelty by successive husbands. Unerringly she selected quiet men, married them, deftly provoked them to violence, and left them bewildered and shocked by the acts of aggression which she had managed to elicit and which she was able, through me, to catalogue against them. And among the professional criminals I defended almost invariably I found that their violences and robberies were unconscious provocations, invitations to retaliatory punishment; on being charged they protested their innocence but were furious with me if I obtained their acquittal, for I had then cheated them of their unacknowledged desire to be caged. Only when they lay passively, locked up in their stinking cells, did they write warmly to me, thanking me for my spirited defence which, happily for them, had failed to secure their release.

The behaviour of these burdened and wretched clients of mine would be no novelty to those doctors who have long since told us that a crippling neurosis which has defied every therapeutic effort may vanish if the patient loses all his money, or becomes involved in an unhappy marriage or is stricken by an organic disease. No-one can escape all suffering, and for some, only by substituting the satisfaction of another choice of suffering or deprivation will the existing painful pleasures be given up. But the options they then take are no permanent prophylactics; they are often no less self-destructive or ineffective than those presently endured. It is from this perspective that we should view the abnegation of the man in a casual act of fellatio.

Au fond, it is then a feint, not a positive expression of sexual desire. What appears to be an exhibitionist display to his partner of his manhood is a renunciation – simultaneously a renunciation of both his adult status and his gender. It is the attainment of, short of death, the ultimate mortification man can impose upon himself. In the casual encounter, the physical act itself is but a trivial libretto, inferior in quality, a clumsy accompaniment to the music of the underlying fantasy. Those greedy fantasies we have reluctantly been forced, by Freud's findings, to acknowledge are being simultaneously played out, for even as within our dreams we find a composite image which is invested with meaning and energy from a multiplicity of sources, so casual fellatio carries within the enactment to be not an adult but a helpless babe and, simultaneously, to be not a man but the suckling mother who he probably lacked. Clinton displays this syndrome at its most exotic, for he is the son of a mother who left him at birth for two years, and his compulsive search for fellatio tells us of his attempts to combat the desperate inner feelings of maternal abandonment which continuously assail him. Any causal explanations of human behaviour may always be liable to rebuttal, but I doubt if the link between casual mothering and casual fellatio is challengeable.

Even today, however, nearly 90 years after Freud explored the recorded fellatio fantasies of Leonardo da Vinci, and thus provided us with guidelines to an understanding of the phenomenon, still Freud's suggestions cause a frisson. Men are fearful to accept that buried within us, able to be triggered in particular by early family circumstances or societal conditions, is the lure of total helplessness, of freedom from responsibility, of the relief of total dependency, of, in short, emasculation. Da Vinci indeed appears to have totally abandoned adult sexuality; using his pencil as scalpel he literally anatomises the body, seeking to kill off his dangerous desires. To our advantage, his bid was only a partial success; the secret yearnings were transmuted, the fantasies contained within a unique creativity, suffusing his works of the Virgin and Child and his Mona Lisa with a mysterious magic. In his paintings fellatio becomes a hidden dynamic innuendo. With Clinton as the exemplar, today such subtle sublimations are absent; the fantasy now being widely acted out is reduced to an impermanent gymnastic, a symbol of our dissatisfactions, not of creativeness. Nevertheless, however transitory, the mortifications within fellatio, the self-abnegation, the forfeiture of gender, the relegation of the male from man to infant, is potentially not without its especial delights. In the agony of the renunciation of male adult genitality, for some there is a gain of a sinister ecstasy. In his feminisation the man revels, without formal conscious shaming acknowledgement, in his homosexuality; he adopts, in the act of fellatio, a feminine attitude but without a defined homosexual object-choice for, accommodating his secret guilty desire, his dominating controlling partner disguises her male psyche in the body of a woman. The man needs to have his desires so disguised: if unmasked, it would reveal the terrifying and terrible truth that his desire was incestuous, that the man to whom he wished to submit was not any man, but his first man, his father.

It is fashionable these days, particularly in some psycho-analytical circles, to depreciate the significance of the father in the shaping of an infant's development, and to believe our successes and failures can be traced to our earliest relationship with the mother. Sometimes, indeed, reading or hearing exponents so stressing the dyadic relationship, one wonders at their capacity to ignore the fact that children have two parents and usually grow up in close proximity to both and are confronted with the intimations of the parents' sexual life and their own exclusion from it.

Such father-elimination stances dodge the importance of bi-sexuality, out of which springs the ambivalence of the boy who initially not only resents his father's possession of the mother but wants him for himself. Freud tells us:

> The boy displays an affectionate feminine attitude to the father and a corresponding jealousy and hostility to his mother...Without taking bi-sexuality into account I think it would scarcely be possible to arrive at an understanding of the sexual manifestations that are actually to be observed in men and women...It may be that the ambivalence displayed in the relation to the parents can be attributed entirely to bisexuality and not...in consequence of rivalry.

Probably no sexual manifestation tells more of the early passionate desire of a son to be possessed by the father than fellatio. It is the belated vain attempt to gain the consummation denied to the son in his infancy. The impress of that first thwarted love affair marks all men; but that there should be today so widespread a nostalgia for a paradise never gained, that the early determining homosexual components in our nature should not now be constructively sublimated but are being so profitlessly squandered, tells us both of the emotional arrest of so many men fearful of meaningful adult genitality and of how stunted our society is becoming.

Fellatio, with its pretence that the man is engaged with the woman's mouth, masks the passive homosexual components involved, but it betokens too other male fears and in particular it quiets his castration anxieties for it begins with an exhibition of his proudly erect genital organ, and it can continue with the man watching the prowess of his penis as the woman kneels before him. When, as a young man, I defended peeping Toms in the magistrate courts, I learned that these perverse voyeurs of couples always identified in fantasy with one of the partners, or even with both. In fellatio the man too is a voyeur, observing while surrendering. One woman author in a recent widely circulated and vulgar sex manual, instructing her women readers in the acts of titillation, insists:

> Make sure he can watch. Men are erotic visualists and primarily aroused by what they can see, one reason why they're so into girlie mags. He'll want to see your face, maybe even hold your hair back. Don't close your eyes, keep them open. I hold eye contact with the man while I'm fellating him and make 'horney eyes' – narrow them sexily and make them smoulder.

But the author does not appreciate that even as he is watching the partner, there is no authentic merging of man and woman; here she is part-object and he is narcissistically celebrating the possession of his penis whilst avoiding the genital activity which is inhibited by castration fear; he is in the grip of an emotional paralysis, one from which he seeks to release himself by unconsciously denying the very existence of the whole vagina-endowed woman. He is striving to transform her into pure sensation, to reduce her to a form of fetish, a tactile layer, eliminating her as a feared real woman by plunging her into absolute anonymity.

In fellatio, the man makes the attempt to undo the shock of his first sighting of the vagina; the childish idea that the anatomical differences between boy and girl arises because the girl's penis has been cut off is never fully abandoned; and the fear that the parental punishment of castration will also fall upon him in reply to his sexual activities remains, reverberating beyond childhood.

But the strength of such continuing castration anxiety, an anxiety which Freud placed in the very centre of clinical psychoanalysis, depends upon how threatening the man's upbringing was, and how much love has tempered his fears of what he interprets as threats coming upon him from society. The phallus is an essential component of the male self-image and if a boy grows up feeling that it is under constant threat from an inhospitable and hostile environment, he, wanting shelter, will frenetically seek reassurance. Promiscuous fellatio is a desperate and pitiful attempt to gain such reassurance. With his fear preventing him from finding reassurance in the arms and vagina of the loved woman, often, with some desperation, he turns to fellatio. Timid contemporary man thus protects himself from the recall of the primal revelation of the distinction between man and penisless woman. It is a dodge to distance himself from castration anxieties which the vagina can excite, for the vagina is certainly not always to be assumed to be an object of desire. For man, it can also be the epicentre of his fears, fears that today are being fanned by unprecedented societal conditions.

Inadequate child-rearing, the threat felt by feminism and displacement of men by women in the employment field all combine to reduce many men, literally, to impotence. The extraordinary mushrooming of men's clinics now being so extensively advertised tell us how widespread is this impotence, and the phenomenal demand for Viagra reveals how uncertain is man's capacity, unaided by drugs, to enjoy genital sex. Fellatio can be seen as the fallback position of many men, the unsatisfactory halfway house between unattainable genital sex and total impotence; it is a register of the tensions accompanying the seismic shift in relations between man and woman brought about by changing patterns of work and family life within our society.

The hesitancy of so many of the present younger generation, lingering in fellatio, and so timidly advancing to vaginal sex which carries the threat that all, not a bit of oneself, must be given, is, in part, an endowment from parents who have fallen victims to the consumer society. The unit of two working parents perhaps brought a more just egalitarian family into existence, but it can enfeeble parental authority and while one can welcome the increasing absence of tyranny in the home, one cannot welcome the increasing absence of parents. With both their working parents seduced by commercial advertising into the illusion that only by surrounding themselves with yet more material objects could happiness be achieved, many within the present younger generation grew up in houses stuffed with consumer goods but empty or short of love. The parents, as real persons, were too often missing; there were no targets open to their children against whom they could rebel, no authority because it could not be pinned down to any person. The child never learned how to resist. His family unit too often was a sham and a totally unsatisfactory training ground. The advance from puberty to adulthood could not be taken: the love/hate relationships, the identification with the parents, all of which, if manhood and womanhood are to be achieved, must be worked through, became arrested. It is unsurprising therefore that we have now so many grown-ups who have the bodies of men and the feelings of pubescence.

A threat to growth in human personality has come from the excrescences of contemporary capitalism. A generation has reached, chronologically, adulthood but too often commercial forces keep them in bondage to perpetual puberty. Contemporary capitalism has in fact had considerable success in its attempts to create a fetishistic society: its technique, by way of manipulative advertising and by the sexualisation of films, magazines and fashions has been to stimulate an insatiable appetite for objects which have been falsely sexualised. The objects are all claimed to be absolutely necessary, promising eternal gratification and pleasure, and yet leave the purchasers unsatisfied, immediately yearning for more. They develop an attitude of striving towards ever greater satisfaction which dooms the individual so afflicted to a state identical in its essentials to that of the sexual pervert who is ever stuck at the preparatory stage of the sex act, and remains perpetually frustrated. By November 1998 the Henley Centre, invigilating consumer trends, found itself bewildered as shoppers moved with ever increasing speed from one product to another. The lifespan of a fashion becomes ever shorter; the acceleration leaves the manufacturer behind as the duped consumer finds himself cheated of the promised ultimate satisfaction and, thus frustrated, goes on to search for yet another object.

We now have a generation, many of whose parents were vague or absent, object- and status-seeking, failures as models, who left their pubescent children to be easy prey of the hired ad-men, the mercenaries of modern capitalism, to capture them and ensure that they became for life avid unassuaged consumers. Capitalism, to safeguard itself, has indeed found sophisticated techniques to exploit the instinctual urges of the masses and turned them into frenetic consumers whose unceasing demands will ensure that production goes on and profits go up. So often the object-pushers begin by hooking the vulnerable adolescent: on every television screen, film and hoarding, the addiction is cultivated through sexual exploitation and titillation. The bath soap, the branded drinks, the cigarette, the motor cars, the perfumes, the packaged tours, are all, by overt salacity or innuendo, eroticised; all are transformed into fetishes. In soothing and seductive tones all are held out as fore-pleasures which are the true ultimate delights.

Many of our present-day young men and women, as adolescents, submitted to these distorted emphases on fore-pleasures; their latent capacity for genuine inter-relationships, as distinct from narcissistic indulgence, has been seriously impaired, and their latent capacity for parental concern, damaged. Capacity for concern for the other, usually so absent in fellatio, is a maturational node, and if the environment is damaging, not facilitating, such capacity may never be obtained. Freud has warned us:

> The attainment of the normal sexual aim can clearly be endangered by the mechanism in which fore-pleasure is involved. The danger arises if at any time in the preparatory sexual processes the fore-pleasure turns out to be too great and the element of tension too small. The motive for proceeding further with the sexual process then disappears, the whole part is cut short, and the preparatory act in question takes the place of the normal sexual aim.

Advertisers use the commercial artist to clothe the offered product in symbols, so often oral, hoping the response coming from the viewers' stimulated erotogenic zone will take the form of a sale. But if the over-stimulated viewer lingers too long over his purchase he may become corrupted. In the end he may find that he is stunted; the component instincts ensconced in his more primitive erotogenic zones may have been inadequately subordinated under the primacy of the genitals. Even if he is able to copulate, he is unable to make love. He fucks but lacks concern, unable in intercourse – beyond the pleasure – to empathise with his partner. He can acquire objects, but cannot relate to a subject. He lacks a truly genital character. He possesses only what some German writers, blaming the manipulative nature of late capitalism, have described as the 'genital façade'. It is, of course, a burdensome façade. In fellatio, to the relief of the male participant, it can be temporarily discarded.

The Generative Fantasy

There are ahistorical fundamentalists, discomfited by any scrutiny of the physical expressions of sexuality, who would prefer to believe man's foreplay has remained unchanged since Adam, as a preliminary to the conception of Cain, wooed Eve on the perimeter of the Garden of Eden. But although the repertoire of the most acrobatic of sexual enthusiasts has indeed the same physical limitations as constrained the first man, the choreography of the performance is not necessarily fixed or determined just by invented personal caprice. Society can demand a heavy price for the indulgences, and it insists that rules and conventions which reflect the prevailing dominant ethos must be observed: the play must not be out of kilter with the prevailing societal moods.

We have constructed the Romans as the inventors of the 'orgy' but even in early imperial Italy, however hoi polloi may have behaved, an elite male morality prevailed which, if challenged, could bring nemesis even to an emperor. There were hang-ups which tell us much about the Roman society. Fellatio and cunnilingus were decidedly out – the elite man was never to be 'contaminated' by oral contact of genitalia, male or female. The elite man could act sexually as he wished provided he was never complicit to such contamination and so long as he never consented to be the 'victim' of anal penetration. Given the exercise of these inhibitions and observances of the status boundaries of the time, no opprobrium fell upon the elite man who penetrated female or male, young or old; it mattered not whether the penetrated partner was a boy or an adult man, whether the approach was from the front or rear. The repetitive motif found on extant red glazed vessels, on the painted walls of rich men's mansions and Pompeii's brothels, on the discs of terracotta lamps or metal gaming tokens was one of sexual domination.

Visual representations abound, showing hoi polloi chafing at the constraints of the elite; those excluded may have in their sex activities gone their own way, but these abandonments were the play of outsiders. No-one within the elite could maintain his status if he descended into orgies of threesomes and foursomes, of cunnilingus and fellatio, which are so often depicted in Roman artefacts. What investigation of Roman works of art demonstrates is that artists, patrons and viewers avidly sought imagery of all manner of sexual activities that the elite would in no circumstances have performed with his or her social equals. A member of the elite must always remain dominant, in control.

The openness of display of Roman sexuality was an openness of display of power founded on domination and slavery – the submissiveness inherent in a man's enjoyment of fellatio was intolerable to the elite Roman who evidently equated it with the pleasures of the passive homosexual which he found no less contemptible. The Roman sexual and public morality was indeed differently contoured from that which has come into existence in Britain at the end of the twentieth century. Two thousand years ago sadism prevailed in Rome and dominance and aggressiveness were celebrated; contrariwise, our sexual mores, reflecting our societal dilemmas, find 'New Man' desperately struggling, with little success, to contain the masochism threatening to overwhelm him.

Inadequate assessment has been made of the consequences to our sexual mores of the loss of empire. No schoolboy today enjoys the holiday which in my infant-school days, amidst much triumphalism and telling of the virility of the empire-builders, marked the officially declared annual Empire Day. Paul Veyne, the French authority on the manners of the ancient world, tells us that 'the cult of virility was the hidden part of the iceberg in ancient societies'. The corollary of that macho cult was a hatred and fear of any behaviour deemed to be effeminate – a mood which found more than faint echoes in imperialist Britain. The ultimate degradation of a man in Rome was his readiness to use his mouth in the interplay of fellatio and cunnilingus. Fundamentally, Veyne explains, 'sex has nothing to do with it', for the response was not a condemnation of homosexuality or heterosexual sex-play – it was a condemnation of passivity which was an intolerable offence. Participation in fellatio was therefore perceived:

> ...as something fantastically depraved...Apuleius describes bandits, and Suetonius even Nero, who abandoned themselves to fellatio, as people who indulged in vices whose pleasure lies in their very viciousness. Was not fellatio the basic form of self-humiliation? It gets a kick out of supinely giving pleasure to another, and servilely offers up any part of the body for another's enjoyment; sex has nothing to do with it.

Such Roman responses to fellation and passive homosexuality were not worlds apart from the attitudes towards passivity generally prevailing in my childhood. Now that 'Rule Britannia' can only be sung satirically, these over-determined attitudes have collapsed, and modern man's masochism is no longer thus held in check.

Much of this masochism engulfing the 'New Man', and which finds particular expression in contemporary fellation, appears to be what Freud has distinguished and chose to label as 'feminine', a form which although related to erotogenic masochism – where pleasure in pain is a prerequisite to sexual excitation – has its own particular expressions. It was not through Freud's female patients that he observed the infiltration of this 'female' masochism, but through male patients, often impotent. He found that in fantasy these were men who desired to be 'gagged, bound, painfully beaten, whipped, in some way maltreated, forced into unconditional obedience, dirtied and debased'. Such a masochist 'wants to be treated like a small and helpless child, but, particularly like a naughty child'; and when Freud studied the cases where the masochistic fantasies had been especially richly elaborated, he discovered that 'they placed the subject in a characteristically female situation; they signify, that is, being castrated, or copulated with, or giving birth to a baby'. But this regressive fantasy of Freud's masochistic patients of childish helplessness evidently brought with it a display of generative envy: the babe is by no means as 'innocent' as we may tend to romanticise, and a powerful concomitant of the child's earliest psychic life is envy. Indeed, the pessimistic psychoanalyst followers in Britain of Melanie Klein insist that envy is primarily innate and universal.

Personal experience has taught me not to dismiss Freud's emphases, for the envy of the male baby wanting to give birth can be reactivated in adult life, sometimes with droll consequences. Forty-three years ago, when my wife was heavily pregnant with our first child, I was suddenly seized with agonising stomach pains which my doctor, hurrying to the scene of the seizure, diagnosed as acute appendicitis, a diagnosis immediately confirmed by the junior doctors at the hospital to which an ambulance swiftly conveyed me. Arrangements were being made to take me into the operating theatre when I demurred and, despite my considerable discomfort, I insisted I wanted any operation to be done by a particular surgeon whose skills were known to me, but who was absent, although I knew it would be more than an hour before he could reach me. As I lay waiting, insight suddenly illuminated my condition. This was no flare-up of an appendix. I was experiencing a couvade, a mimetic ritual exercise known to me from my wartime experience in East Africa where I had learnt that among some tribes the husband, when the wife was about to give birth, retires to a separate hut and simulates and suffers the birth pains being suffered by his spouse. Insight gained, I immediately left my bed and, pain-free, quit the hospital shamefacedly attributing the episode to an excess of empathy on the part of a new husband with his wife. Retrospectively, I would now acknowledge there was an unconscious shadow side to my response: I was envious of her creativity.

These days it is the widespread practice for fathers, sometimes with a video camera to record the event in detail, to be present at the birth of their child. The motivations governing this comparatively new convention are, to say the least, problematic. Doubtless the insistence by a mother that the father, by witnessing her pains, should be punished for having precipitated her suffering, and the ready agreement of the man to be present, assuages some of the woman's sadism and some of the man's envy, voyeurism and masochism. However, old-fashioned women and men who, without exhibitionism, have enjoyed the quietude of their lifelong shared experiences, may query the propriety of heralding in the wondrous birth of a child by such a sado-masochistic cacophony.

That, however, modern man is so ready, and sometimes so eager, to participate in these birth charades which do not appear to have historical precedent in Britain perhaps tells us again how clumsy are his attempts to deal with his masochism. Yesteryear such social modes would have been regarded as pathological emanations little different from the birth fantasies Freud found enveloping his masochistic male pervert patients. Now, the deployment of fellation, with its unconscious repudiation of gender and adulthood as a means of recovering the male infant's fantasy of giving birth, appears, statistically, to be the norm. Only when the self-destructiveness that can be involved in the practice becomes dramatically overt, as when Clinton's masochism almost led to his political death, does it come under query.

But it is not only the United States of America which has publicised its incapacity to cope with the ever-present lure of masochistic desires which are irrevocably part of our nature and which, unless contained, can lead to suicidal behaviour in societies as in individuals. We have, in the Millennium Dome, ourselves advertised to the world our trepidations, our fears of the tug that may drag us back from the real external world to the dream-world of Freud's masochistic perverts where gender is non-existent and men can give birth to children. In the Dome we have moved dangerously near the abyss. Its interior was originally intended to be dominated by one androgynous figure: such a pathological retreat from heterosexuality proved, however, to be unsustainable and, yielding to protests, two figures were conceded to be the centrepiece, a vague 'abstract' woman and a castrated man, one without genitalia. The embrace between the two is tentative: no creative conception results from this caress, and so that there will be no misunderstanding of the message, the prize-winning logo chosen to be the symbol of the Millennium Dome tells us explicitly all about its ethos. A naked long-legged redhead with square shoulders and athletic form inspired, says the artist, by 'strong women like Boudicca' the warrior-queen, is to send the message to the world of the victory of the phallic woman in our new Britannia. No mother, no child, the logo tells us, is part of the 'millennium experience'.

Although the millennium is a celebration of the birth of a Jewish child 2,000 years ago, birth was banned by the Dome's sterile creators and their camp-followers. To introduce birth into the theme was too explosive: it would have brought into consciousness buried yearnings, the secret wishes of the envious males, especially those involved in the project who have a sexual orientation that bars them from full consummation of a heterosexual relationship and the joys of parenthood. On the brink, therefore, the regression halted; potency and hetero-sexuality are smudged or denied and we are invited to join in a paean to feminised and barren man, and to an ambiguous woman, who carries no child. In a temple that is essentially life-denying not life-affirming, we witness the triumph of institutionalised masochism, not the Christ-child.

Once, when great cathedrals were built, the dome of the edifice shared roots with some of the most basic elements in our lives. The word 'dome' indeed stems from the Latin domus, a house – not a house in the suburban sense but the house as protection. The Italian word for cathedral, duomo, emphasises that in essence, even as one's home is a spiritual place, so the Dome links the most powerful images of security with the eternal heavens.

But the great Dome has brought no such solace; no hint of domesticity or of the quiet profound love that can suffuse a house, transforming it into a home, is permitted now. This is a dome with sinister not benign intentions. The architectural correspondent of the *Guardian*, sensing its manipulativeness, described it as a 'disturbing symbol of social control' where 'the human spirit...can be reined in like a tethered pony'. Spirituality must not soar here; it is confined to a pathetic niche, entrapped in an airless and meaningless ecumenical chamber. No queue forms to enter this zone. And although the Dome may be stuffed with some of the latest technological toys, still it is as vacant as are born-again prophet politicians. In the end, when the Dome is sold off, contemporary capitalism will doubtless ensure that it becomes a temple of consumerism, and the nation will be invited to gorge themselves with the most modern of delights. Heralding its construction, Mandelson and Blair assured us 'Fun' enjoyed in 'a spirit of adventure', was the purpose of the Dome. On television Mandelson, before his enforced Cabinet departure, patronisingly spelled out to demurring workers of the north-east how a visit to the Dome will bring 'excitement' to them, providing a thrilling hiatus away from what he regards as the drudgery of their mundane routines. He is on a perpetual cruise, in tune with the disco but tone-deaf to the pleasures of domestic stillness, to the parental excitement of watching a child uttering his first sentences or taking his first steps. And all the games and all the ministering to the debasing needs of the populace will take place under a roof gutted of its primal meaningfulness, for the dome, featured so often in Christian and Moslem architecture, takes as its template the breast from which flows loving kindness. None will flow at Greenwich. Eros has no place here; this will be the domain of Thanatos. Here, in the shadow of this most suitable venue, amidst the chaos and dislocation produced by maladministration, when the midnight hour struck and the year 2000 began, thousands of young men and women, dosed with Ecstasy and amphetamines, 'chasing the dragon', frenetically danced, each alone, untouched, not held by a partner, gyrating around Britain's golden calf.

Our £180,000,000 Dome and the American constitutional crisis precipitated by an ejaculation come under the same rubric: in their several forms they are part of the theatre of the absurd which nations possessed by bouts of self-destructiveness are wont to stage. Too often the significance and importance of un-contained masochism in determining the nature of our society and its institutions is underestimated. Yet, if Freud's contention is right, and masochism is indeed older than sadism, then man's history of wars and of violent class struggles are part of the frantic attempts of man to ward off his yearning for the ultimate nirvana, and directing his erotically loaded aggressiveness outward, away from the interior life, for the little while man postpones the joys of his submission to death. The challenge Freud gave the twentieth century, illuminating the potency of sex in our lives, has been only superficially met. Gripped with panic, we dodge the awful implications of a hypothesis that a biologically determined instinct, bathed in an exciting sensuality, draws us to our nemesis, and that we can only advance a little the date of our masturbatory death by deflecting some of the force of this terrible instinct into sexually inspired cruelty against our fellow men.

It is easier to avoid than to accept these fearful implications, easier to regard the vast sale of punitive pornography as a minor titillation for the partially impotent and the ageing than a corroboration of a fundamental need of man for humiliation and ill-treatment as a pre-condition to the little death of tumescence. It is easier to view the self-mutilators in our prisons as freaks than as only slightly distorted mirror images of Everyman, and it is certainly more comfortable to find solace in myths than to acknowledge that the widespread practice of circumcision among African tribes, Jews and Moslems, and public school parents, is a symbolic castration reluctantly accepted as compensation for being denied the full consolation of self-immolation. Freud's assertions anger the facile optimists, conventional liberals and socialists who, believing man to be naturally good, prefer to sponsor evil illusions by which mankind can expect their lives to be beautified. It is, however, wiser to face and thus learn to temper, the Dionysian self-hate which can possess individuals and nations.

The force of this ebbing tide pulling us towards hopelessness into a slough of despondency and away from life is not to be underestimated. Too often, when pursuing my legislative ambitions, I felt its full tug and never more insistently than when, for the first time in the history of Parliament, I raised the issue of vasectomy during the second reading of an Abortion Bill debate in 1966. I had, on that occasion, scoffed at those colleagues of mine who appeared to be using their zeal for what they believed to be a law reform to wage the class struggle – the wealthy had abortions so why should the workers be denied them? I insisted there was no need to incite the workers to commit the folly of the hated bourgeoisie, and that it was droll to proffer abortion as a solution to the pregnant poverty-stricken wife who already had half-a-dozen children and was living in squalid overcrowded conditions. If she was aborted, the indifferent husband would, within months, undoubtedly impregnate her again; it would be more rational to sterilise the man. I suggested that the law relating to the performance of vasectomies, then ambiguous, should be clarified and, more, facilities for vasectomies should be made available in the health service. My suggestion was received coolly. The male members of the 1966 Parliament were tolerant only towards an assault being made on women's femininity. They had other views on what could be interpreted as an attack on maleness. As I spoke on the then unfamiliar subject of vasectomy, I was certainly conscious of how many members were wriggling in their seats.

But my comments when reported provoked a different response outside the House. The latent masochism embodied within the community and which can only too easily be activated became manifest and I felt its ensnaring pseudopodia reach out to me like slime. I was astonished to find myself deluged with approving letters from men in all parts of the country. I recalled the anathematisation by Justinian of the second-century martyr Origen; the synods' condemnation of the early heretic had not influenced twentieth-century semi-Christian England. My correspondents, judging by their fervour, had been gripped by Origen's heresy and wanted vasectomy as a penultimate step towards the self-inflicted sacrificium phalli followed by the great scholar. My post-bag had taught me the need to be wary. When, some years later, I co-operated with a colleague to put through the Vasectomy Act of 1972, I was able to ensure that the needed facility, so fateful and probably irreversible, would become in practice freely available only after skilled counselling to those with completed families who sought sterilisation as part of a voluntary programme for planned parenthood and not as part of a neurotic desire for self-abasement. I believed that it was necessary not to yield to the opportuning of those lonely unmarried men, often young, who formed a disturbing proportion of my correspondents and who, at no monetary expense to themselves, wished the State to end their fertility. They are the men who in these secular days cannot gain, through religion, the release of their boundless masochistic desires by contemplating the agony of the cross. Nothing short of themselves becoming sacrificial lambs would be satisfying.

Mechanical In Head and In Heart

These wretched lonely men, so afflicted with anomie, are not strangers to the human race: whole nations, as the tragedy of the German people's submission to Hitler illustrates, can become possessed of a masochistic desire to be sacrificial lambs.

Wilhelm Reich, the psychoanalyst whose deviations from orthodox Marxism and psychoanalysis resulted in him being expelled within a year from both the German Communist Party and the International Association of Psycho-Analysis, singularly understood the interplay between external societal conditions and the masochism burdening the individual which was to result in the phenomenon of the Nazi State.

His explorations of the dynamics of masochism, and his emphases on the disastrous consequences of a capitalist economic order that incited masochistic responses, angered Freud who extravagantly condemned Reich's contributions as written in the service of the German Communist Party. Although today we may regard some of Reich's observations as naïve and excessively idealistic, and although not a few of his assumptions were to be invalidated by later research, any survey of the current vogue for fellatio would be incomplete if we disregarded Reich's early work, before his genius crumbled into madness, for there, he singularly illuminated the destructive play that masochism can import into our sexual activities.

Reich's account of the ideal sexual act is remarkable for its explicitness which must have required considerable courage in the pre-Kinsey, pre-Masters & Johnson era in which it was written. He insists that psychic health depends upon what he describes as 'orgastic potency'. Such potency was not to be defined simply in terms of the capacity for erection, penetration and ejaculation (and mutatis mutandis for women); these capacities were, he maintained, only 'the indispensable prerequisites for orgastic potency'. True orgastic potency included these but involved much more. Above all, it involved:

> The capacity for surrender to the flow of biological energy without any inhibition, the capacity for complete discharge of all dammed-up sexual excitation through involuntary pleasurable contractions of the body, not just of the genitals.

The exercise of this capacity for surrender would exclude the presence of any trace of sadism in the male or of masochism in the female; nor would it include any sense of male prowess or smugness. Men to whom surrender means being 'feminine' are always, in Reich's view, 'orgastically disturbed'; and, most important, is that the 'surrender' is silent. The orgastically potent individuals never talk or laugh during the sexual act with the exception of uttering words of tenderness, since both talking and laughing indicate a serious lack of the capacity for surrender which requires an undivided absorption in the sensations of pleasure. He will have approved of the philosopher Wittgenstein's view that almost everything that is most important cannot be stated at all but only, at the very best, indicated by our use of language; he would certainly have regarded the hundreds of telephone sex chat-lines now in place as the excrescences of a morbid society ministering to the victims it has emotionally devastated.

For Reich, orgastic potency is the capacity to love body and soul, psychosomatically. It is a formulation that, as the psychiatrist Charles Rycroft has pointed out, is not dissimilar to that enunciated by D. H. Lawrence. Both men combined an intense and almost mystical belief in the prime importance of sex with a puritanical insistence that it should always be treated with high, if not dead, seriousness. Trivialisation of sex, Reich abhorred. Those who played their recreational sex games, lacking full orgastic potency, were the neurotics in our society, and they were many – an unsurprising affirmation, given Reich's high criteria. In particular, men and women who lack the capacity to totally 'surrender' are 'orgastically disturbed', and, he emphasises, none are more so than men to whom complete surrender is regarded as 'feminine' and demeaning.

We surely need to hesitate before dismissing the hectoring Reich and Lawrence as ranters, as absurd 1920 Romantics, ridiculously holistic when we see the dislocation in modern men's sexuality. When we uncomfortably know that Clinton may be more a paradigm than a caricature of that condition, then mockery of their idealism does not become us. Their demanding idealism is proffered as the antithesis of the poisonous doctrine offered by that most articulate of perverts, the man whose sadistic fantasies gave him the accolade of having his name perpetuated in every European language. The rules laid down by the Marquis de Sade's 'Code of Laws' in his *One Hundred and Twenty Days*, insist that all orifices must be interchangeable: vagina, mouth and anal passage are indistinguishable, and never in his perverse universe, lacking any notion of organisation, development or structure, is there an authentic personal relationship between two individuals. In his constant theme of sexual intercourse, the protagonists he depicts are engaged in group sex, men and women, children and old people, virgins and whores, nuns and bawds, mothers and sons, uncles and nephews, noblemen and rabble:

> All will be higgledy-piggedly, all will wallow, on the flagstones, on the earth, and, like animals, will interchange, will mix, will commit incest, adultery and sodomy.

Sade ended his life in an asylum but today his philosophy lives on in the contemporary French cinema now exporting to us its wares. The films are predicated on the belief that an entire generation has come into existence which identifies with love stories that reduce human relations to *triste chair* – sad flesh. These, of course, are films where acts of fellatio are commonplace; the erect penis has become less offensive as a dramatic prop than the smoking cigarette. The theme of sex without love has become the current inspiration in French film-making and there is no shortage of resonances to the theme this side of the Tunnel.

This anti-romanticism is a far cry from the romanticism which has at its source Freud's view that 'civilisation is a process in the service of Eros whose purpose is to combine single human individuals and after that families, the races, peoples and nations into one great unity, the unity of mankind', Freud believed that civilisation initially arose from 'genital love', the coming together of individuals, and late in his career he reconceptualised and expanded his emphasis on the significance of genital love:

> ...what psychoanalysis calls sexuality was by no means identical with the impulsion towards a union of the two sexes or towards producing a pleasurable sensation in the genitals; it had far more resemblance to the all-inclusive and all-embracing love of Plato's Symposium.

> ...In its origin, function and relation to sexual love, the Eros of the philosopher Plato coincides exactly with the love force, the libido of psychoanalysis.

The Eros of Plato, and thus of Freud, was the force described by Aristophanes in Plato's Symposium:

> The force which calls back the halves of our original nature; it tries to make one out of two and heal the wound of human nature... Eros is the name for our pursuit of wholeness, for our desire to be complete.

Freud, however, insisted that Eros was only one of the two cosmic principles which together make the world go around; the other was the death drive. Thanatos, the eternal adversary to Eros, bringing aggression and masochism, was ever at work seeking to subvert the bonding which could make us whole. Reich seems to have believed that Thanatos could be overcome, and that in authentic orgastic potency all traces of the sadism and masochism that Thanatos brought could be banished.

Today we may be bemused by Reich's optimism, but we should beware of being over-sophisticated, too readily brushing aside all the remarkable insights of his earlier works together with his later

undisciplined absurd and manic theories which were intimations of
his approaching paranoia. Fortunately, some of his early visions
have not remained becalmed. Although not formally acknowledged, not a few of his core ideas, thanks largely to the subsequent
expositions of the French anthropologist Georges Bataille,
resonate strongly in the work of the gifted French psychoanalyst
Laplanche, and nowadays the work of some of the Israeli women
psychoanalysts.

There is a congruence between Reich's evaluations of sexual
activity – in his stress on the huge gulf between those rutting
without attaining 'orgastic potency' and those who do – and the
fundamental distinctions Bataille makes between the 'animal' and
'normal' sexuality and what he regards as 'true' human sexuality
blessed with an eroticism, possessed of a profound desire and a
deep longing to return to continuity. This, Bataille proposes, is the
profound desire in us discontinuous beings which sends us on the
quest to re-establish the lost continuity from which we have been
severed, and so escape from our lonely separateness and fill the
gap between ourselves and all that is not.

No doubt there will be non-romantics, and those suspicious of
theses which idealise sex and so seek to exculpate guilt from
sexual behaviour, who will regard Bataille's elevation of the
potential significance of the sexual act with scepticism. It is tempting, of course, in reductionist mode, to reduce Bataille's
elaborations to little more than a disguise of the familiar
impossible wish of man to return to the womb from which he has
been expelled. But Bataille's presentation is certainly not
regressive. He saw eroticism as a device for carrying us forward
beyond the toll of our separate individuality:

> We find the state of affairs that binds us to our random and
> ephemeral individuality hard to bear... along with our tormenting
> desire that this evanescent individuality should last, there stands
> our obsession with a primal continuity linking us with
> everything...

> Through the activity of organs in a flow of coalescence and
> renewal, like the ebb and flow of waves surging into one another,
> the self is dispossessed.

Interpreting Bataille sympathetically, the Israeli analyst Ruth Stein commented:

> Though it is impossible to cross the borders and totally emerge with the other, the very conceiving of such a possibility enables one to look with the other human being into the abyss that lies between them, and to feel together the dizziness accruing from the joint looking. This to Bataille is essentially what arouses sexual excitement, what creates sexual ripples and shudders that transform plain 'animal sexuality' into eroticism, with its heightened mental and spiritual power

How mean and grudging prevailing sexual behaviour appears, imbued as it so often is with rote habits and fellatio, when matched against the transcendent possibilities of what Bataille described as 'an eroticism at white heat' which is 'the blind moment when eroticism attains its ultimate integrity'. What grubby squanderers we are if indeed homo sapiens has the capacity, through sex, to attain such fusion with the other and with the universe, that we waste our especial endowment in silly recreational sex.

Drawing considerably upon Laplanche's clinical explorations, Stein postulates that from our very beginnings, at the breast, we possess that especial endowment. Libidinal pleasure inheres in the slavering with which the infant drawing in the nourishment from the maternal breast deviates the organ-coupling into the production of surplus pleasure. Of its own force, the infant repeats and finds pleasurable acts that no longer draw in sustenance. This is the nature of the especial endowment we possess, the endowment of non-procreative sexuality. Such an interpretation of the genesis of non-procreative sexuality, treating it not as a mere by-product but one deserving of unbounded respect in its own right, is a far cry from the enticing notion that it is simply the psychic compensation which the individual organism receives for obeying the imperative of species production and that the reward is that we can do whatever we wish to exploit non-procreative sexuality. The French and Israeli psychoanalysts who proffer their interpretation are far more in tune with the moralistic assumptions of Reich and Bataille – and, indeed, of D. H. Lawrence, who preached the sanctity of sex and who fundamentally regarded sexual coupling as unworthy if it was not sacramental. This holy attitude towards sex will, understandably, not be acceptable to those sensitive to the whiff of incense and the odour of the chapel, but it is a noble reproach to those affecting a tolerant liberalism who, trivialising sex without qualms, accept its relegation to the gutter and to the White House.

In some respects Reich was a forerunner of those post-modernist sociologists who today lay such emphasis on the extent to which sexuality is being moulded and even constructed by social institutions. What most certainly cannot be brushed aside is Reich's Marxist insistence upon the role of the external factors, of the cultural oppression bearing down upon us which can so distort our sexual behaviour, and which Reich believed left us stunted, unable to attain the emancipation of orgastic potency. Indeed, he became an active member of the Communist Party because he saw capitalism as the agent of that dehumanising cultural oppression. We do not need to follow slavishly Reich's view, nor do we need to accept the strict constructionist stances of the formidable cultural historian Michel Foucault and his followers, who would seek to persuade us that the concept of sexuality itself is a cultural construction of recent Western capitalist bourgeois society, but we would certainly fail to understand present-day widely practised expressions of sexuality if we ignore the vicious influence of contemporary capitalism upon personal sexual conduct.

Since Reich's day, world capitalism and technological advance have still further, and devastatingly, estranged man from his work, leaving him, in his consequent loneliness, easy prey to severe depression, a condition said to afflict 5,000,000 of our fellow countrymen. And nowhere more than in the mining communities, still in existence when I was first elected to serve the people of a South Wales valley, did I find the antidote to the depressive work-related self-destructive moods. When electioneering I would go down the pits, and the miners, to tease me and to puncture my political pretensions, would steer me into the worst of the rat-holes in which they worked. As I crawled behind them to reach a coal-face, only my lack of height saved me from crippling dis-comfitures. But there in the darkness, alongside pneumoconiosis-ridden seams, amidst their raillery and laughter, the camaraderie, the libidinal bonding which Freud regarded as an essential if the discontents of civilisation were not to overwhelm us, was always in evidence. When the hazards of their occupation brought death, the whole pit immediately closed down and all the men marched together to carry the victim home.

And as in death so in life, the same ethos prevailed; in the mining villages celebrations and tragedies, births and sickness, successes and deprivations, were all shared. 'Communitarianism', and all the glib vocabulary now used in the banal exhortations coming from Islington Blairites, were unknown to them; they lived, not chatted about it. 'Only connect', the yearning of the cut-off homosexual novelist E. M. Forster, which has in recent years found such widespread resonances, was an emotion unknown to them; they needed no such exhortations, for their lives were ever connected with each other, bearing each other's burdens and sharing each other's joys. Their response to despairs was an antidote far less suspect and far more effective than that produced by the present-day collusion of greedy drug companies and anti-Freudian psychopharmaceutical analysts whose chemical engineering of personalities has led to a social over-reliance on powerful mood-altering medications.

By the time I retired from Parliament, thanks to Thatcher's hatchet-man, Ian McGregor, her appointed Coal Board boss, and to the provocations of the paranoid Scargill, there was only one pit left in my constituency – and that was converted into an underground museum. McGregor had a thick hide but once, at a rumbustious meeting held at the Commons with MPs of mining seats, I pierced his carapace. When the meeting was over, the guilty man pursued me, uninvited, to my Commons office, seeking to persuade me that my charge that his decision-making, and that of his ilk, was founded on the single-minded pursuit of profits untrammelled by any inhibiting social assessments, was unfounded. What he really wanted, and what he did not receive from me, was absolution. But his actions were unforgivable, going far beyond the closure of selected pits claimed to be uneconomic, for his brief was to deliver to Thatcher total 'victory' over the miners. Smashing the miners, however, meant more than the weakening of union power; it meant smashing the cement that kept whole communities together. For the Miners' Lodge was more than a defensive union branch; communality radiated through the Lodge to permeate the lives of my electorate. Initially the Miners' Lodge was the centre not only of industrial life, but of all political and social life as well. Local health schemes began there and blossomed in the National Health Service as Nye Bevan applied to the nation the lessons he had learned in the Monmouthshire Lodges. From the Lodges came the Miners' Institutes, their clubs and their libraries. Through the Lodge the miners acquired their own cinemas, their billiard halls and even a corporately owned brewery. The male-voice choirs and brass bands of Wales were all spin-offs from the Lodge. The sublimated homoerotic bindings, established in the hazardous work in the darkness of the pit, came above ground and gave life on the surface to a community – not a ramshackle society.

But even as pits were being closed at the top of my valley constituency and this communality was being eroded, a new town was being built at the bottom of the valley. This new town had the benefit of housing some of those who were brought up within the culture of the mining communities, and they brought their spiritual capital with them, mitigating to some extent, by their valiant efforts, the loneliness that can afflict so many of those living in new towns. Most of those new towns were peopled by men and women torn far away from their original surroundings, away from the intimacies of the terraced streets to live within the sanitised architecture of the new towns where space, not closeness, was the leitmotif. Grandparents and supportive extended families did not abide there. A condition, known to all our new towns, was endemic – it was called the 'New Town Blues'. Even in the harshest of times it was a disease unknown within the mining communities.

Unlike the residents in mining communities, where work provided a bonding leaving no man to feel he walked alone, the workers in the factories of the new towns so often found no relief in their workplaces from their depressive moods. More than 150 years ago Marx was already warning:

Owing to the extensive use of machinery and to the division of labour, the work of the proletarians has lost all original character and consequently all charm for the workman; he becomes an appendage of the machine, and it is only the most simple, the most monotonous and the most easily acquired knack that is required from him.

But Marx could not have anticipated the remarkable escalation in mechanisation and automation which brought about the triumph of the machine over man – of dead labour over living labour. When I took my motor component workers from my constituency to view the first robots installed at British Leyland's factory at Longbridge, I sensed that their wonder at the robots was tempered by their concern with the role of the 'robot-minders'. Robotics was isolating those men from their fellows and they told me that when they were, in effect, alone with their robots, they were lonely and missed the old fellowship of working in a group. Indeed, the foreman supervised his section of the factory on a bicycle, pedalling hundreds of yards from one worker to another. Our technology can thwart Eros's binding purpose, for in these large factories, so often men and women increasingly work alone, not libidinally bound to their fellow workers but chained to a machine. Soon, no doubt, they will be totally commanded by the computer; in 1987 a record number of robots were installed across the world and, as the price of robots falls relative to wages, robots will be even more widely used in still more areas – including services.

In his study of the culture of a large factory, the psychoanalyst Elliott Jaques explored the nature of the psychic defences often afforded by group organisations against the depressive anxieties of the individual; but many of the benign benefits that can arise out of factory-based group organisations are rapidly diminishing. When, before my RAF bounty enabled me to become a solicitor, I worked through my teens on the factory floor and acquired membership of the Transport & General Workers Union, I learned how civilising, not disrupting, are the libidinal ties to be found in an active trade union branch. The binding is not simply to fight employers for more pay and better conditions, but, albeit inarticulately, to give both courage and fun to workers who had to endure the dreary monotony of factory life. As in the RAF, comradeship could be real and supportive.

This threat of technology to such social bonding is now

awesome and increasingly the individual is incited to work from her or his own house. The office takes over the home, and so often the only link the employee has with others in the company is the computer. The employer so often treats the worker as a desiccated calculating machine, and his relationships with others becomes increasingly shrivelled. Work, once the cement binding so many of us together, now becomes a corrosive.

Rarely can a wall be built between the working life and the personal life; the isolation and the loneliness of the one seeps into the other. Work, where once Eros could triumph, is now the playground of Thanatos. The anomie and the destructiveness that can be occasioned envelops the man; his habititude at work prevails in his leisure. His sex life is confined to tumescence, and onanism and poverty-stricken fantasies become the means to attain a temporary homeostasis. The only advance from having masturbatory 'fun on the phone' is to lap-dancing restaurants and table-dancing clubs or, at most, simultaneous but not shared masturbation within fellation. The sadness of the workplace and the poignancy of lone self-pleasuring and non-related sex are as one in articulating our contemporary despair. Never has Thomas Carlyle's prophesy been more fulfilled: 'Men are grown mechanical in head and in heart, as well as in hand.'

The Onslaughts of Thanatos

In Roman times, even as they disported themselves in their extraordinary baths, the Romans placed in every corridor and dark corner of their bath complexes a statue of Priapus, the god of fertility and abundance, displaying one or two huge penises. With this they believed they could frighten off the dark destructive forces that lurked in every niche threatening to subvert confidence and bring about a collapse in their sexual powers.

We too seek to ward off similar depressive anxieties, but our sustaining gods taking over the apotropaic function of Priapus are Viagra and Prozac, and our obeisances to these deities can take the form of frenetic but trivial recreational sex. Fellatio, quintessentially non-reproductive sex, can be an integral part of such rituals.

But how frail a defence against despair such sexual behaviour can be was well illustrated to me when I once defended a murderer who while engaged, as was his wont, in bizarre perverse practices with his wife, suddenly, for no apparent reason, cut her up into shreds in the bathroom of their respectable suburban home. Courteously and gently he explained his savage conduct to me: 'It was absolutely necessary for me to kill her,' he said. 'If I had not killed her, I would have had no choice but to have killed myself.' And, for good measure, with the attendant prison officer fortunately within sight but, in accordance with the prison rules, out of hearing, he explained insistently that he had also killed a young man some years previously in the north of England for exactly the same reason. His mad frankness may have been unusual, but his motivation for murder was sadly orthodox.

The lure of self-destruction, the attraction of death, are often warded off only by turning outward the aggression which is threatening to destroy the assailant. The terrible injuries wreaked upon his wife was a measure of the destructiveness from which, at another's expense, he had just saved himself. Suicide or murder are often perceived as the only options, and the conscience, temporarily stilled though undeveloped, the deed balanced upon a razor's edge, becomes, by chance, murder not felo de se. The ultimate consummation may, however, only have been temporarily staved off, for one-third of the murderers of Britain commit suicide before being brought to trial, and many more make determined, though unsuccessful, attempts. Sometimes, indeed, it is done with a high sense of occasion, as I found on arriving at a prison for an interview with a client accused of murder who had so timed the appointment that he was able to receive me with a freshly cut throat and slashed wrists.

One of the checks to outbursts of aggression against oneself or another is to be found in the sexual perversions. The acts of the pervert are not what they seem to be, and in most cases they conceal their real nature rather than reveal it; for the perversions and the accompanying fantasies are in place as a shield to protect him from the consequences of the unconscious violences which seize him and which, if released, would destroy him and others.

Edward Glover, the doyen of the last generation of British psychoanalysts, asserted that the pervert's wayward behaviour is 'a defence against an over-charge of unconscious aggression and/or sadism'. When, under Glover's chairmanship and tutelage, I served for so many years on the Council of the Institute for the Scientific Treatment of Delinquency, I needed no persuasion from him to accept his view that perversions were indeed a defence against what he described as an over-charge of unconscious aggression. As a newly qualified solicitor, I had found myself not infrequently defending perverts who had offended against public order, and they had taught me what Glover explicated. I still recall my shock when, after successfully persuading the court to inflict a non-custodial sentence on a pervert and after, outside the court, having counselled him to confine his practices to the private domain, he peremptorily walked away from me, saying he could not do that for, if he stopped, he would kill someone. A few years later I heard that in another city he had been charged with attempted murder; his perversion, stifled or inadequately realised, had proved too frail to contain his violence.

Sometimes, when the violence becomes self-directed, the perversion becomes hopelessly and literally entangled as it struggles against the force taking the pervert to his death. Then we have tragedies like that which occurred in the last Parliament when an MP, not responding to the Whip, was eventually found, orange in mouth, oddly bedecked, hanging dead in his home, killed while seeking an orgasm. Those whose professions have taken them into inquests, as was frequently my lot, know that such suicides often fall within the purview of our coroners' courts.

To categorise fellatio, however, as a perversion and, from such a classification describe it simply as a dam against violent self-destructive desires, would be misleadingly reductive. Experienced clinicians are scrupulous in their distinction between what they call 'true perverts' and those – and that is all of us – who carry in our psyches only perverse elements, to a greater or lesser degree, which, unlike the true pervert, do not remain raw and wholly dominant in adult life. But that those elements, in particular circumstances, cultural and familial, can be alarmingly teased out, is evident in any viewing of the masochistic choreography displayed on the sexual scene of fin de siècle, twentieth-century, pornography-ridden Britain. Mishandling our aggression, fearful of the consequence of its release, our addiction to fellatio, using it as a barrier against the aggression which is in danger of turning round and overwhelming us, shows us fumbling only a little less disastrously than the wretched MP choked within the coils of the masochism which preceded his exit from life.

The churches, learned in the ecstasies of martyrdom, well understand this liaison of sex and inwardly directed aggression. Some of them, not too successfully, seek to disentangle such unseemly misalliances when they pronounce their sainthoods and beatitudes, lest they incite their followers into yearning for pleasures, reserved for saints, which for ordinary mortals must remain prohibited. They did not need Freud to tell them that 'the true masochist always turns his cheek whenever he has a choice of receiving a blow'; the dilemma of the churches, of course, is that the would-be suicide may welcome the delights of hell with which he is threatened.

Until 1961 the riposte of an enraged society, led by the churches fearful of the strength and, not least, the essential sensuality of suicide, remained firmly in place. Suicide and attempted suicide were criminal offences attracting a maximum sentence of life imprisonment. As a lawyer I had found nothing more demeaning in my professional life than to be compelled in open court, attended by ghoulish reporters, to plead for mercy for severely depressed women whose bungled suicide attempts had brought them into the court – not to hospitals and to psychiatrists. When I entered the House of Commons I joined Kenneth Robinson, the future Minister for Health, who had been agitating for changes in the law. He was an experienced operator and I a comparative newcomer, but I did what I could to support him. All our efforts, however, were met with strong resistance from the Home Office, then under Rab Butler. The Home Office insisted our proposals were too controversial, for some people would take the view that what in law is permissible is free from objection, and belief in the sanctity of life, and the duty of the State to uphold its responsibility to seek to preserve the life of every person, necessitated no weakening of our criminal law. The determination to harry the wretched man or woman who had fumbled the suicide, or had made the attempt as a dramatic plea for help, was hidden behind inimitable displays of self-righteous sententiousness.

Unlike Kenneth Robinson, I was not surprised that suicide should attract such hostility – what is termed 'schizoid suicide' is said to be the result of apathy towards real life which cannot be accepted any longer. All the available energy goes into a quiet but tenacious determination to fade out into oblivion. Such a depreciation of society is evidently felt to be quite intolerable and such lèse-majesté predictably has received punishment throughout the ages. More, depressive suicide, the result of angry destructive impulses, is too insufferable an insult to the puritans. The perpetrator not only has the pleasure of self-murder but, symbolically, the murder of someone else – such as the man for whom the suicide's lover has jilted him or, indeed, the faithless lover herself. And, to add to his trials, the suicide, at a deeper level, is often symbolically murdering the parental figures to whose behaviour can perhaps be traced his unhappiness.

In the end, however, fortunately, the mood moved in our favour. The committee appointed by the Archbishop of Canterbury eventually, cautiously, recommended that the offence of suicide should be abolished provided that a second-class burial service could be used in those cases of suicide oddly designated by the churchmen as 'manifestly selfish'. And then, ultimately, after long persuasion and the inevitably tardy reference for a review of the offence to the Criminal Law Review Committee, the judges came back with recommendations sufficiently tough upon the survivors of suicide pacts to enable the proposition, without loss of face, to be put to the House by way of a Government Bill that attempted suicide should no longer be a criminal offence. Then, reluctantly, after private badgering from Robinson and myself, the Government acceded and the Bill reached the statute book.

But removing the criminality from the act of suicide in no way stills the operation of the mechanism that can drive a man to his own destruction. Sometimes, when the life force is being overwhelmed, and the retreat to the dug-outs of perverse sexuality from which to continue the battle against Thanatos's onslaughts proves too shallow, then the last desperate bid is made to displace physical suicide, to endure a symbolic suicide rather than an actual suicide. In such moments of madness a man can destroy his whole life. The political suicide in Westminster of Ron Davies, the Secretary of State for Wales, is a tragic illustration of the phenomenon.

Not until his courageous statement to the House, in which while proffering his explanation for his Cabinet resignation he revealed the brutality he suffered as a child at the hands of his father, did I understand, when Labour was still in opposition, what had prompted him to mount a determined assault upon the whole of Labour's parliamentary establishment in the Whips' Office. It had puzzled me that a man of such considerable abilities, an obvious contender for Cabinet office if Labour returned to power, should covet the role of Chief Whip, a position attractive no doubt to an apparatchik but hardly one to match the creative abilities which he possesses and could be exercised in a ministry.

I had left the House by the time he began his campaign to supplant the existing Chief Whip but, perhaps thinking I may have influence over some Members to lend him support, at the 1989 Labour Party Conference he invited me to join him for dinner. He cogently explained to me why he wanted to take over our ramshackle Whips' Office and outlined his rational plans to improve its efficiency so that our MPs could be more effective in the House and play a more useful role in the coming general election. His criticisms of the negative role of the Whips' Office were entirely valid, and I did not discourage him in his endeavours to be elected to the post of Chief Whip; in the event, he gained a deserved substantial vote from his MP colleagues, although not enough to win.

Perhaps that event only postponed the catastrophe that was to come; for although on a conscious level his wish for the office was part of a genuine commitment to assist Labour to power, clearly unconscious factors were operating. The whipped boy wanted his revenge. To take away the power of the authoritarian surrogate father – our unsuspecting Chief Whip – was his aim. He would become the whipper, not the whipped; and he, having control over the secret recording of MPs' sexual and other peccadilloes maintained at that time in the Whips' Office, would know where everyone's bodies were buried and choose whether his would, or would not, be exhumed.

Unconsciously, in the most convoluted form, the sado-masochistic traits we all possess can be acted out in our working lives; but for some they cannot be so contained, and then they can overspill destructively into private life. Such are the burdened characters who, often clandestinely, seek out a partner who will submit to being whipped, or will act as dominatrix and whip them.

The force and cunning of the destructive death-wish, always operating within our society and within ourselves, are ignored at our peril; without vigilance it can obtain cruel victories. Hubris, inviting downfall, is not only the stuff of Greek tragedy. The lure of the death-wish that brought Davies to the darkness and anonymity of Clapham Common was well timed; it operated when, despite Blair's profound dislike of his lack of sycophancy and of his independence, he was nevertheless politically secure for, after a strenuous contest, he had just been elected by the Welsh Labour Movement to be the leader of the Welsh Assembly. He had reached the pinnacle of his political life, and never before in his life could he have fallen further. The opportunity for exquisite masochistic delight was irresistible, and recklessly, in what he accurately was to describe to the Commons as 'a moment of madness', he hurled himself into the abyss. His 'moment of madness' was one of a series of such moments; later Davies was courageously to declare publicly that he had entered into psychiatric therapy and fearlessly spelled out that he suffered from 'a compulsive disorder which causes me to seek out high-risk situations'. The timing of the Clapham high-risk incident meant that the Marquis de Sade himself, reciting the pleasurable techniques available to the masochist, could not have devised a more terrible scenario.

In his Commons' apology, Davies, with insight, expressly identified the link between his father's unjust brutality and his own predicament, and legitimately claimed that his political life had been determined by his father's violence by prompting him to fight against authoritarian injustices in the public weal. Unhappily for Davies, the aggression stored up as a child against the brutal father evidently could not be fully discharged benignly; unspent, it turned in on him and wrought the same havoc upon him as an adult as it had when he was a child. He was clearly trapped, as was Clinton, another victim of a violent father, into odd behavioural contortions in a bid to escape from his dilemma. To unravel, through prolonged and painful psychotherapy, the coils in which his father has entangled him will require Davies to be possessed of considerable stamina; I hope my fears that he lacks sufficient personal resource to succeed will prove groundless.

The political consequences of child abuse are, however, not only to be seen within the individual tragedies of a handful of prominent British and American politicians. In the twentieth century more people throughout the world have been murdered than in any previous century in the history of mankind, and no single factor has contributed more to the catastrophe than the violence suffered by three men at the hands of their fathers.

Mao, who was responsible for 30 million being sent to their deaths, was regularly whipped by his father, a brutal teacher who, through beatings, averred he would 'make a man' out of his son. Mao hardly ever admitted the full extent of the rage he must have felt against his father, a rage which he displaced so faithfully upon his 'enemies'. Stalin too, son of an alcoholic cobbler, was also whipped almost every day of his childhood; powerlessness as a child haunted him, and unconscious fears that such powerlessness could again recur resulted in his paranoid cast of mind. Fears of dangers that no longer existed but which were ever present in the tyrant's deranged mind led to the archipelago; unconsciously afraid to release his aggression against his father lest retaliatory action follow, he affected to the end an idealisation of his father even as he sought to rid himself of his valid hates by slaying so many of his innocent political 'comrades'.

And Hitler's childhood was no less dire than Stalin's. As a boy he was tormented, humiliated and mocked by his father without the slightest protection from his mother and, like Stalin, ever denied his true feelings towards his tormentor. He showed the syndromes familiar to those who have treated victims of child abuse; so often they show effects of the hatred of a parent that must remain unconscious not only because hating a father is strictly prohibited but also because it is in the interests of the child's self-preservation to maintain the illusion of having a good father. Only in the form of deflection on others was hatred permitted; in Hitler's case that unleashed hatred led to more than a million Jewish children being shot or thrown into gas ovens. That Hitler could find so many willing executioners to carry out his murders is undoubtedly to be explained, in part, by the child-rearing practices which prevailed in Germany and to which so large a section of Hitler's electorate had been subjected. I endeavoured in my book *Wotan My Enemy* (1994) to trace the nature and some of the sources and political consequences of the authoritarian family system, so often totally dominated by a bullying father, which was in place. The congruences between Hitler's brutalised childhood and the childhood of so many in Germany meant that many, not daring to discharge their repressed rage against the father, found relief in the alternative outlet Hitler proffered to them by way of the persecution of minorities.

How profound was the repression which Germans born in the beginning of the twentieth century suffered is chasteningly illustrated by any glance at the tracts of Dr Daniel Schreber, the guru to Germany's parents, whose influence was as malignant in his day as Spock's in the 1950s was benign, and as widespread. Some of his tracts ran to 40 editions, and all were directed to instructing parents in the systematic upbringing of infants from the very first day of life. When babies cry, he insisted, they should be taught to desist by the use of 'physically perceptible admonitions', assuring his readers that 'such a procedure is only necessary once, or at the most twice, and then one is master of the child for all time. From then on, one look, one single threatening gesture, will suffice to subjugate the child.' A newborn child was to be drilled from the very first day to obey. One latterday commentator has accurately written that in Schreber's works we are in the presence not of child-raising methods but of systematic instruction in child persecution. The persecuted child became, encouraged by Hitler's incitements, the persecuting adult.

When we recoil from a sadistic didactic like Schreber, when we look with horror at the dictator-monsters, when we are astonished by the bizarre practices of sexual perverts or the bewildering behavioural disorders of public figures, we must never never forget that the practitioners, casualties of their own childhood, are nevertheless members of the human race. All of them, with disastrous consequences, failed to handle constructively the aggressive endowment which is one of humanity's biological determinants. But the tragic force that triggered their vengeful assaults upon themselves or upon others not only operates within the most normal of loving desires but is also forever beckoning us to temptations to which none of us are totally immune. As Montaigne sagely commented, 'Each man bears the entire form of man's estate.'

Given, then, Everyman's biology, knowing the power of what Freud called an aggressive instinct, 'the derivative and the main representative of the death instinct,' and witnessing the appalling destruction it has caused in the wars and exterminations in the first part of our century, is it to be wondered that the peace which Britain has experienced for more than 50 years is becoming increasingly frustrating. The skirmishing of the Falklands and the Gulf wars proved an inadequate catharsis; aggression, never evaporating, dammed by peace, has changed its course and in its turnaround is now seeping into our contemporary society. The façade of 'Cool Britannia', where most are more prosperous than ever before, is well presented by our creative fashion designers, minimalist interior decorators and film-makers, but behind that exterior the floodwaters of blocked aggression are rising from the cellars, spreading a deadly damp throughout the societal structure. And even as we are fearful, insecure, striving desperately for yet more money and status, we live unhappily, lonely in a crowd. Technology brings increasingly the curse of isolation in factory and office and now presents our children with devices which, as the Chief Rabbi has commented, 'starve our children of the oxygen of togetherness'. Computer games, the Walkman and the Internet are all to be experienced in isolation and have led to teachers having to instruct children how to play together in the school playgrounds. In our own homes, we are isolating ourselves; a November 1998 survey found that people spent more time with their computer than with any other domestic activity, including cooking and eating. And so limited is the capacity of our adolescents to relate to each other that, as other surveys show, almost half the kids crowding the discos perform a partnerless dance of death, drugged to the hilt with mind-damaging Ecstasy. And our mounting divorce rates and increasing numbers of fatherless families all tell us the same sad tale of an incapacity to sustain a profound relationship. Promiscuous fellation, sex without even a token embrace, is but a distress symptom of our contemporary despair.

Freud taught us that the meaning of the evolution of civilisation is no longer obscure:

> It presents the struggle between Eros and death, between the instinct of life and the instinct of destruction, as it works itself out in the human species. This struggle is what all life essentially consists of and the evolution of civilisation may therefore be simply described as the struggle for life of the human species.

In the battle of these giants it is not difficult to perceive which of the adversaries is today, at least temporarily, gaining the upper hand. Such an overview is not that of a pessimistic old man enunciating an après moi le déluge Jeremiad; the dangerous malaise, the gutted life expressing itself in nihilism, impinges severely upon the sensibility of some of the most intelligent of our younger political observers. Robert Harris, Jeremy Paxman and Andrew Roberts all in various ways, when we marked the 80th anniversary of the ending of World War I, expressed anguish that they had been deprived of the opportunity to serve in a war. Speaking of my generation, Andrew Roberts wrote of his:

> ...profound sense of envy. Why should these men, simply through a chronological accident, have had the chance to serve their country so courageously, whereas our own generation has been consigned to live in an era that history will quickly forget? It is impossible not to feel a sense of nihilism about an age in which the biggest issues seems to be about interest rates and Ron Davies' nocturnal activities, rather than life and death, peace and war... It is hard to find much purpose in the modern era, shorn as it has been of sacrifice and danger.

These men are living in a world where a major conflict, a nuclear war, would mean the end of the human race, and thus inhibited, they are deprived of the traditional outlet for their aggressivity. Aggression stagnates, and in the resultant fetid atmosphere, masochism and despair thrive. The loss that these young men are feeling is what the Germans call *Grabenkameradschaft*, the comradeship which came up out of the trenches; now, with almost all my war-time comrades and all those with whom I found friendship in the war-time years dead, I feel all too keenly the wretchedness of walking alone. But in many ways that is the lot of so many of this younger generation, and having been brought up in a compounding Thatcherite ethos which lauded individualism and denied the very existence of the binding collective society, their stifled aggression, finding insufficient outlet in common endeavour – above all in war – makes their present sense of aloneness particularly poignant. The curse of this condition, endemic to many in the generation born in the mid- and late-'40s, is not confined to Britain and, elsewhere in Europe, the responses to its pains can find far more sinister expressions than in eloquent lamentations of the kind presented by Andrew Roberts. Nowhere, more recently, was this clearly spelled out than in the conduct of Germany's political leadership which, readily yielding to Anglo-American opportuning, so eagerly embraced the opportunity to become actively involved in the illegal Kosovo war. The

Chancellor, Gerhardt Schroder, Foreign Secretary and head of the Green Party Joschka Fischer, and Minister of Defence Rudolf Scharping, were born in 1944, 1948 and 1947 respectively; all belong to the post-WWII generation; all are men who grew up in the physically hard conditions of the time of the immediate post-war years when large areas of Germany were in rubble, food supplies were scarce and there were victims to be mourned in almost every family; a scrutiny of their personal biographies tells us that in addition to these grim burdens, all of them suffered within their families or their schools severe and sometimes abusive treatment from authoritarian regimes.

The utter helplessness they felt as children was to be echoed and repeated when, as students, they became part of 'generation '68' and were to find that all their protests against the conservative establishment during their rebellion and during the '70s were to come to naught. The authorities had the whip hand and the lasting experience they were fated to endure was of political impotence. They, as politicians, could find no adequate relief for their aggression or any outlet for their need to avenge their humiliations; but aggression, like sex, cannot be extinguished. Fischer extravagantly endeavoured to outlaw his aggression, becoming for a decade an absolute pacifist eschewing all violence; but this attempt, like those of his colleagues who were to become the German war cabinet in the Kosovo war, was a failure; when finally, thirty years after the 1968 events, the much-longed for opportunity was there, these men found it irresistible and whooped in triumph at finding that with NATO approval they could, although largely vicariously, participate in the Balkan war.

In an interview about the Rambouillet negotiations, before the war had escalated, the swaggering Fischer boasted: 'I had to decide about the question of war or peace'; and, indeed, he did make his lamentable contribution. It was particularly the Germans who arranged the peace negotiations in Rambouillet in such a way that they inevitably ended in a deadlock. By trying to force the signature of the proposed treaty by military threats, and by giving an ultimation, the NATO members themselves created the situation of 'no alternative' which they then used to explain their later bombing campaign. It is impossible then, now we wish to exculpate modern Germany and its modern democracy from

Hitler's evils, not to feel an unease when we see, as we did in 1999, subterranean forces that can still be triggered off. The Nazi inheritance is not easily jettisoned.

In Britain the dammed-up barrier against the release of aggression in war has also had it consequences. Here so often high flyers, successful career-wise and surrounded by material possessions that would have, at their age, been beyond the wildest dreams of their fathers and grandfathers, are nevertheless wracked with an irrational anxiety that is gnawing them to shreds – and this is a manifestation of the repressed aggression. Freud, who was engaged throughout his whole life in exploring the sources of the angst which he found in so many complex forms in his patients, concluded that repression was the most significant operant in producing neurotic anxiety. The fearful, over-determined neurotic response of the war-deprived generation to trivial setbacks make those whose stoicism was forged in past privations and in war mock their absurd tremulousness as they seek counselling and compensation if they fall down and graze their knees. Their never-ending workouts, and the ever-proliferating gymnasiums ministering to them, their obsessional jogging, make visible their fear that death stalks them every minute of the day and can be warded off only by incessant health-bestowing exercises. They are, alas, engaged in thaumaturgy, not therapy, but there is no shortage of expensive health farms ready to provide them with perennial youth.

Their grandfathers, more nobly but less elisively, and certainly more disastrously, with the aid of the societal values then prevailing, dealt with the destructive masochism that possessed them, as it does every generation, with a terrible abandon: they yielded to it. At the outset of World War I, the image of the soldier was that of the Christian knight, not so much a warrior but rather a willing 'sacrifice' prepared to lay down his life for his king, his country, his womenfolk. By the millions, that image was lived up to, leading to greater casualties than had ever before, or since, been suffered by Britain.

The lesson had been learned; when the time came for my generation to don our uniforms, we did so with a sigh. It was the suicide of Hitler we desired, and effected, not our own self-immolation. In the interplay of destructive and bonding forces that must accompany every war, in 'our' war, a justifiable war against the evils of Nazism, Eros triumphed and the biorhythm of the nation continued to the same beat in the immediate austere war years. We shared, rationing was totally accepted and, showing our continuing concern for each other, we created the Welfare State. But Thatcherism brought the apotheosis of competitive individualism and derision of the egalitarian values embedded within an authentic communitarianism. Within this political environment, little altered by Blair's Government, a delighted Thanatos stalks, snapping the bonds tying us together.

Political scientists who are zealous empiricists, and all those over-dependent on focus groups and opinion polls, will, of course, chafe at capacious interpretations of our contemporary dilemmas which use Freud's figurative vocabulary. There are indeed hazards if we lapse into reification, the process of treating concepts as though they were things, of abstract nouns as though they were concrete nouns – but when we use the language of mythology, and speak of Eros and Thanatos, we are talking not of conscious processes but of unconscious processes. If we do not use a figurative language to describe those processes that occur deep inside of us and of the societies we inhabit, then not only could we never describe those processes at all, but we could never even become aware of them.

On the eleventh hour of the eleventh day of the eleventh month in 1998, we witnessed a nation strangely moved by those processes. After so many repressed amnesiacal years the nation, with little chiding, came to a standstill, and for three minutes once again, in silence, in street, supermarket, office and factory, in remembrance contemplated the slaying and the sacrifices endured in two world wars. All of us, together, faced and mourned the death of millions, seeking to alleviate our remorse, our guilt as survivors, and, in unison, bound ourselves into our common humanity. This was an affirmation of loss, temporarily triumphant in what Freud called 'the inborn conflict arising from ambivalence, of the eternal struggle between the trends of life and death'. Our political quest, vain as it may be, should surely be each year to extend such a three minutes to 365 days. Will Hutton, former editor-in-chief of the *Observer*, eloquently expressed our need to be possessed by such an aspiration:

Love, perhaps the most intoxicating and life-giving human experience, is at heart about the reward from the reciprocity of regard; to love and have the love returned is the ultimate human exchange, whether between mother and child or between lovers. This expectation and need for reciprocity is a more generalised human need...it is at the core of our conception of social capital without which our societies begin to become unhinged.

In 1998 the lineaments of such love were clearly distinguished at Omagh when after Thanatos had over-reached himself, and after the carnage, the divided communities came together to seal their bonding on the anniversary of the crucifixion, a bonding that was to presage the coming into existence of an All-Party Executive of a Northern Ireland Assembly. And it was in 1998 too that we could comfort ourselves that although we live in seasons when the hinges of our society creak ominously, nevertheless hope was not to be extinguished, and our quest may not be impossible. Before that year was out we knew that in a few years there will be looking down upon us a new star, brighter than any other in the firmament. Sixteen nations had come together to launch a space-ship; the Russians had built and launched the first module; the USA had funded it and then sent up a linking second component appropriately named 'Unity'. Man had at last released his aggression not for mutual destruction but in the service of all mankind to conquer the universe. The possibility, but not the certainty, came into existence that with wisdom we may yet navigate our politics aligned to the beneficiencies of the new star now circling our precarious world.

The Sin of Tristesse

Freud's 'poetic' interpretations of our civilisation and its discontents discomfits some of his followers in Britain; they evidently feel more at ease within a more empirical 'scientific' tradition, and they distance themselves from Freud's late presentation that violence is an externalisation of a death instinct. In their often dedicated clinical work when they attempt to lever out the savageries which violent patients direct against themselves or others, they claim to find corroboration of Freud's earlier thinking when he linked aggression to an 'ego instinct' in the service of self-preservation. Following that lead, they consider our violences are evoked by any threat to what they describe as 'psychic homeostasis', a concept borrowed from its physiological counterpart, the tendency of organisms to maintain themselves in a constant state.

These clinicians, from their work with violent criminals or suicidal patients, provide us with startling insights which have a special relevance today: with technology accelerating as never before, we are destabilised and in a desperate attempt to maintain our equilibrium we lash out wildly. From this vantage point, our self-inflicted flagellations and our resulting societal despair and pain can be interpreted as a biological imperative, a frantic survival tactic; external reality is too threatening and we have retreated. Our personal behavioural disorders, of which fellatio is one of many, may, from this perspective, be seen as maladaptions to a bewildering and unceasing flux of the external environment.

The communications revolution has disorientated us. From the time when I was a boy and my father brought home a cat's whiskers wireless and placed on my head the crackling headphones, to the time when with casual insouciance, in a digital age, we speak to men on the moon has involved too many changes in too short a span to be endurable. Many of my generation have become displaced persons, strangers in an alien land, and so many of the middle-aged feel ditched, left behind, unable to catch up with the younger generation now in the driving seat. Our marvellously rapid advance in science and technology has become a threatening Golem with whom we fear a direct confrontation for he is our creation, a dark twin with whom we are so bound that his slaying would be our suicide. Instead, in a bid to end the destabilising tensions man-made science has precipitated, we desperately use other techniques and seek to escape from our predicament by releasing our rage masochistically. We punish ourselves for our own hubris, and thus flaying ourselves, we, and our personal relationships, are left in tatters.

And now we are supplementing such maladapted efforts to feel safe, to achieve homeostasis within a destabilising environment, by inventing a terrifying schizoid response. We are now aspiring to exorcise our fears of our technological inventions not by dismantling them, but by enhancing them in order to enable us to enjoy the illusion that we may release our aggression without fear of retribution. Igor Ivanov, the Russian Foreign Minister, wrote to Kofi Annan, the United Nations Secretary-General, in October 1998, warning that the effect of new information weapons 'may be comparable to that of weapons of mass destruction'. Ivanov was not exaggerating. He is clearly aware that what is being described as information warfare – 'cyber warfare' – is now within contemplation by the powers. Secret army research departments in America and Russia are racing to perfect 'logic bombs' and computer viruses designed to create havoc in an enemy country by destroying computer networks, controlling weapon systems, finance of transactions, and even traffic. A 1998 United States defence department report described how an attack might unfold. It starts with an unexplained power black-out in a large city. Telephone systems across the country become paralysed. Freight and passenger trains collide. Civilian air-traffic control systems go haywire. Malfunctioning pipe-line flow mechanisms trigger oil refinery blasts. 'Logic bombs' can disable the financial system, disrupting money transfers and causing stocks to plunge on world exchanges. 'An information war has no front line,' said the study. By October 1999 George Tenet, the US Director of Intelligence, claiming the need to ward off the threat of cyber-terrorism, was warning: 'We face a growing cyber threat, the threat from so-called weapons of mass disruption. Potential targets are not only government computers but the lifelines that we all take for granted – our power grids and our water and transportation system.'

The forebodings that such particular grim possibilities bring are not yet part of the general consciousness and do not yet weigh down upon all in our society. But few, more than half a century after Hiroshima, have not buried within themselves an awareness that apocalyptic prognostications are no longer the ravings of cranks, and that rational assessments of the future – given man's history of never-ending warfare – may well mean that the end of the world is nigh. But dire prophetic warnings have always been unwelcome and from the earliest post-war years I have found how widespread is the resistance to acknowledging the existence of the nuclear threat. 'Campaigns for nuclear disarmament,' Michael Foot has written, 'show a familiar pattern; they may rise suddenly to the highest pitch of excitement, but then relapse into a seeming slothfulness, as appears to be the situation now.'

But even at times of 'the highest pitch of excitement', the mass of the population turn their backs rather than face the hazards the atomic age has brought. I recall vividly a protest meeting which Bertrand Russell and I addressed in Cardiff in 1961, in a week in the middle of the Cuban crisis, when Soviet ships carrying the nuclear warheads were within hours of a confrontation with a blockading United States navy. That meeting was taking place in the most dangerous moment this world had ever known, yet in a hall that contained less than 1,000 places there were empty seats. A pop concert would have packed in more. And when Michael Foot and I led protest marches in Wales, although they attracted not a few fellow demonstrators, it would be a conceit to pretend our attempts to stir the prevailing sloth were greeted by most people with any enthusiasm.

We who declared ourselves peacemongers were seen as disturbers of the peace, for a demand to rid ourselves of nuclear weapons is subversive. It challenges the preferred belief – illusory though it is – that no further adaptive adjustment is needed to cope with man's aggression, that to possess the bombs means no threat to our stability exists, for no-one dare attack us. By throwing doubts upon this stubbornly held faith, my electorate in 1983 was to severely punish me. It has been reported, probably correctly, that I have fought more local and national elections – 17 in all – than any man now alive, but in the 1983 election, provocatively emphasising Labour's then manifesto commitment to nuclear disarmament, and by deliberately activating and participating in educative CND meetings in my constituency, an electorate already disturbed by my opposition to Thatcher's Falklands War, gave me my most punishing campaign. As I canvassed every doorstep, defence, not the more usual local matters, was the issue and, respectfully but firmly, my case was rejected; it was disturbing the statis which they wanted to be left untouched. Without the bomb, they would feel naked and afraid. To carry bad tidings to an electorate eager to be sustained by illusions brings woe to the messengers. My voters had generously tolerated, with only occasional rumbles, my sponsorships of so many unpopular causes, so many reforming laws impinging upon human relationships, but this was a step too far. When the election result was declared, my majority, for the first time, after so many years, slumped below 10,000.

My personal setback was reflected in the national poll. Labour's manifesto commitment to nuclear disarmament proved indeed to be a suicide note, and with the campaigners dispirited, the issue became muted. For years, the passionate controversies once stirred have been stilled. As a nation we have exhibited a symptom analogous to one well known to psychiatrists, that of 'avoidance behaviour', which they meet when they strive to treat post-traumatic stress disorders. But the nuclear threat is not banished by not talking about it; the stresses it causes as it hovers around us are not dissipated by denial of their existence. We cannot live with a constant threat of annihilation; by repressing our awareness of the dangers we guarantee our becoming an anxious society possessed by a pessimism, the cause of which we lack the courage to confront.

Now, doubtless occasioned by the spread of nuclear capacity to countries dominated by psychopathological, or indeed psychotic, leaders, those of us still alive who first raised the alarums find we have improbable allies. Robert McNamara, formerly the United States' Secretary of Defence, is now a nuclear disarmer as passionate as any Aldermaston marcher; and an even more newly dedicated disarmer is General George B. Butler, former Commander of the United States Strategic Air Command, and the man who would have had to pass on the orders from the President. He now says: 'It is simply wrong, morally speaking, for any mortal to be invested with the authority to call into question the survival of the human race.' Such a 'mortal' is Clinton, a man who, while telephoning senators, enjoyed being sexually pleasured. It is unnerving to ask whether the man, while being jerked off by a Monica Lewinsky to heighten his pleasure, or to distract attention from his antics, or through inadvertence, could, by a jerk of his own, press the doomsday button.

Man, never free from guilt, has always been haunted by the fears that his hubris would bring about his total destruction. The last attempt, at Babel, to reach the heavens, brought retribution to the arrogant engineers of the land of Shi-nar and in these days of carcinogenic climate changes, the storms and ocean upheavals heralding floods to come, now lend to the story of Noah a sinister significance. To our misfortune we lack the confidence of the biblical chronicler that God will honour His covenant, and that the rainbow will emerge out of the darkness; for now, when there is in place, as never before in the evolution of man from the primeval slime, a threatening external environment which can destroy all organic life on our planet, we are intimidated. The atactic responses on display in our personal behavioural disorders show us seeking to camouflage our fears. In fact, we have lost our nerve and are submitting to, not overcoming, the catabolic forces now ascendant in our external environment.

In many respects the defeatism at work is a post-Holocaust and post-nuclear bomb phenomenon. Even after the slaughter of the World War I, a belief in the inevitability of progress, though tempered, was still being sustained; it was not only Marxists who believed that, with a determined push, Utopia could be reached. A benign historicism still pervaded for a short time much of the intellectual climate of Western Europe.

Indeed, as a young man, it was biology, not history, that buoyed up my belief in the future of mankind; and like not a few of my more politically precocious peers, we were seduced into a faith that pronounced that the teleology to be found in the evolution of man moved man's spirit in his societal affairs. There existed an imbrication between a biological purposedness which explained homo sapiens' ascent out of the primordial swamps and made attainable to man a harmony in the conduct of his political strategies. In short, it was biology, not God, that was on our side.

No-one fanned our political idealism more than the now-forgotten Italian professor of biological philosophy, Eugenio Rignano, whose works were translated into all the West European languages. Turning now to the yellowed pages in his work *The Nature of Life*, published in English in 1930, I see from my inscription that I carried it, with a very few other books, in my kit-bag when I was in the RAF in the Middle East in 1944. Maybe its weight has contributed to the degenerative arthritis that afflicts my back in my old age, but at the time it gave me hope.

Although their conclusions widely differ, Rignano's hypothesis had as its starting point what some of today's psychoanalysts use in their interpretations: both place considerable emphasis on the phenomenon of homeostasis, the inherent tendency of organisms to maintain their stability, to respond to and attempt to overcome a threatening environment by an adaptation to keep themselves in a constant harmonious state. For Rignano, this capacity is a key to understanding the evolution of homo sapiens; recklessly he transposed the successful struggle in the organic world for existence to account for the emergence of man to society. Man could ensure the struggle for life which had brought him to the pinnacle would be replaced by a collective harmonious life. Today Rignano's grandiloquent language no longer intoxicates – we see his belief in a benevolent teleology overloaded and his biological and sociological syntheses flawed and chasteningly over-optimistic. But in the thirties he was providing the young with a 'scientific' validation for their idealism; it is perhaps pertinent that it should be recalled that for some of my generation it was not only communism that was to be the god that failed.

At the very time Rignano from his professorial chair in Milan was beckoning us to his Eden, Freud, the biologist in Vienna, was warning us that the fruit in those Arcadian orchards was worm-ridden. He saw the force of the instinctual urges that could bind man into a harmonious unity, but he saw too, in 1930, before the Holocaust and before the bomb, the dangers that other forces were bringing:

> The fateful question for the human species seems to me to be whether and to what extent their cultural development will succeed in mastering the disturbance of their communal life by the human instinct of aggression and self-destruction. It may be that in this respect precisely the present time deserves a special interest. Men have gained control over the forces of nature to such an extent that with their help they would have no difficulty in exterminating one another to the last man. They know this, and hence comes a large part of their current unrest, their unhappiness and their mood of anxiety.

Over 60 years after what Freud, with studied irony, called 'this special time', our inventiveness has moved on from the crude technology of the gas chambers to the United States' press-button detonator that within one minute can release 4,000 nuclear missiles that could exterminate not only Jews but all mankind. We indeed now live in very special times, and to add to our woes, it is millennium time. The date may, historically, be awry but on and around the year 2000, although we may seek to banish its significance from consciousness, despite the comforting zodiac interpreters and the soothing medical correspondents filling our newspapers, it is a time when nevertheless we tremble in our mortality.

Faith in the nearness of the Second Advent and the establishment of a reign of a glory on earth no longer prevails in Western society, but not all the old apprehensions clustered around the Great Anticipation – the fear that the last terrible battle with the enemies of God was impending, the conviction that all of us would be judged, that we were about to be embroiled in the terrors of the last days, that the Four Horsemen of the Apocalypse were riding dangerously close – have been expelled. The imagery and vocabulary which express our forebodings may have changed but the same anxieties, in secular form, are pervasive in supposedly post-Christian and materialistic Britain.

We may try to repress our fears of a menacing apocalyptic disaster into our unconscious, but it surfaces, and, not prepared to acknowledge the causation, we find ourselves enveloped in melancholy. The study by Demos, the independent think-tank, in December 1998 tells us that the people of Bangladesh, one of the poorest countries in the world, get far more happiness from their meagre incomes than the British do from their relatively large ones. The Bangladeshi starve while we desperately endeavour to allay our anxieties, consuming more and more comfort food, so that now 60 per cent of men in Britain are obese – and that despite fatness being a social, physical and economic handicap. Will Hutton has pointed out:

> The fat are generally unhealthier, with lower life expectancy. They are held in lower social esteem, and earn less than their thinner peers. Their relationships are less successful. Even juries give them longer sentences.

Our gargantuan appetites, stimulated by the burgeoning range of supermarket products, tells how in adulthood we seek compensation for an initial lack of breast-feeding, and the fast-food fashion is not only dictated by our new working habits but also comes about through our lack of initial confidence that should have been established at the breast. Now, consequently, we need to gobble our food speedily. My generation were taught that Gladstone masticated his food at least 30 times before swallowing, and now I note when I sit at the table with the younger generations that they finish their meal – such is their anxiety that it may be taken away from them – before I have barely commenced. The researchers of Demon concluded – a shade too portentously, for some of us believe they are stating the obvious – that 'although Britons are rich compared with many other countries, many suffer from an emotional poverty caused by consumerism and the destruction of communities'. With what sounds suspiciously like the whine of a grievance from the dependency generation, one of the academics who worked on the report complains, 'We are seduced by an economic juggernaut and our personal needs are not being met.' Unwittingly, but correctly, in using the metaphor of Juggernaut, the title of the Hindu god Vishnu, who relentlessly with inhuman force destroys blindly anyone that comes in its way, the researcher stumbles upon dark forces that bear down upon man's affairs and wrecks his personal relationships.

In Britain, a depressed country that has still not mourned through its loss of empire and lacks the confidence of a firm national identity, a will to resist is specially lacking, but to attempt the almost impossible task of setting out a political agenda that can withstand and overcome the havoc-making demons assailing us, to turn them round, subjugate them so that they become our mercenaries, is a duty we owe to our grandchildren lest they become the last generation on earth.

To shirk that duty would be the Great Sin. It is not within the list of seven deadly sins which, from the ninth century onward, have been used in questioning in the confessional – 'what a man is compelled to confess to God' – but it was there on the list of John Cassiam, the great agitator and codifier of the fifth century, and it was there, combined with acidie, when the formal codification of sins was pronounced in the sixth century by St Gregory. It is the sin of tristesse, weakly and variously translated as dejection or wilful sadness. But it is more, it is despair, and that is the temptation to which the committed – and, in particular, the authentic politician – must never, never yield.

Masochism Transmuted

It is incontestable that potential disasters on the scale now threatening are without precedent: our self-destructive follies, our bombs, our precipitation of cancer-bringing climatic changes, our untempered greed bringing the crisis in global capitalism, all taking place in millennarian days, could be presented as auguries announcing the coming of the Last Days. But Europe has had almost unbelievably terrible days before this and if, over-awed by what our own destructiveness can bring upon us, we blot out as irrelevant the responses made by Europe to past calamities, we leave ourselves untutored in the arts of warding off, or overcoming, catastrophe. There can be no hope of developing a politics of prevention informed by depth psychology to save us from ultimate disaster if we do not view, and attempt to understand, the convolutions and therapies, some effective, some cunning cozenage, used in times past by the people of Europe to withstand total ruination.

The twentieth century, dire as it has been, cannot claim to have achieved a higher rate of mortality than ever known before – that unwelcome accolade goes to the fourteenth century. When bubonic fever struck Europe in 1348, the rate of mortality from the Black Death plague was incomparably the greatest catastrophe that has befallen Europe over the last thousand years – far greater than the two world wars of the twentieth century together. Between 1348 and 1349 about one-third of the total population perished.

The plague was interpreted, in normal medieval fashion, as a divine chastisement for the transgressions of a sinful world. The manner in which the populace sought to divert this chastisement can bring, if we penetrate the outward forms taken by its protective techniques, illumination to the psycho-dynamics operating today as we both create and wrestle with predicaments which our own hubris and self-destructiveness have now brought upon us.

So often in the Middle Ages and beyond when disasters occurred the populace ignored the actual calendar, did not wait on our 2000 AD, and hastened the arrival of the millennium. Already in 1348 people were interpreting earthquakes in Carinthia and Italy as 'messianic woes' which were to usher in the Last Days; and the uniquely appalling catastrophe of the Black Death was then interpreted in the same sense.

The experience of overwhelming insecurity, disorientation and anxiety had the effect of raising eschatological excitement among the masses to fever pitch. They did not attempt, as we do, to dance away millennarian anxieties in a Dome, absurdly attempting to smother them in an infantile festival of fun; their response was flagellant processions in which the participants took their place in what they believed was the world-shattering, world-transforming drama of the Last Days unfolding in all its terror and exultation. For a mystic thirty-three and a half days, in memory of the number of years which, according to traditional calculation, were spent by Christ on earth, the flagellant, living in a world of chialistic fantasy, would whip himself for hours, scourging himself with sharp spikes, some with flesh-tearing hooks. He stopped only when, bleeding from head to foot, he was too exhausted to continue in the grim self-torture which he had inflicted in the hope of inducing a judging and punishing God to put away His wrath, to forgive him his sins, to spare him the greater chastisements which would otherwise be his in this life and the next.

But the flagellant was striving not only to save himself. He was possessed with a more intoxicating prospect – that of belonging to an élite of self-immolating redeemers, men charged with the redemptive mission which would assure not only their own survival but that of all mankind. His penance was an imitato Christi.

Embedded within the credo of almost all the varying flagellant sects, in one form or another, were the same beliefs so fiercely held in the previous century when, for a while, the year 1260 was held to be the apocalyptic year when the Third Age was to reach its fulfilment. Then, as later, amidst plague, famine and war, multitudes believed at various cruel times that the dawning of the Age of the Holy Spirit was imminent, and soon they would be in a world where all men would be living in peace, observing voluntary poverty and wrapped in contemplative bliss. To accelerate its arrival, by their outrageous self-torture, the flagellants are perhaps Europe's most instructive exemplars of belief in the use of masochism to bring about wondrous changes in the condition of man on earth.

For a Jew to acknowledge nobility informed their eschatology is not easy, for the flagellants played an important part in the great massacre of European Jewry which accompanied the Black Death – the greatest ever slaughter before the Holocaust. By the time the flagellants had finished their burning and drowning of all the Jews they could find, there were indeed very few left in Germany or the Low Countries. It could have been of no comfort to the innocent victims to have been told of the purity of the motivations of many of their slaughterers, but the frenzied murderers did believe they were clearing the way for the Second Coming and 'because they thought to please God in that way'. And in the same mood, with anarchic force, they took on the princes and bishops, all of whom they saw as obstacles to the coming into being of a paradisical world; only by a coalition of ecclesiastical and secular powers, backed by a papal bull outlawing them, were they eventually vanquished.

Before we draw back aghast at the self-mutilations of these flagellants, and treat them as savages living in a remote time, we surely should ask whether we can claim superiority in the handling of our mashochism. They had a vision at the service of which they placed their masochism; lacking the vision and focus possessed by the flagellants, our masochism takes more dreadful forms. We prepare our self-destruction, ready to destroy our planet by the development of germ and chemical warfare, by the destruction of our rainforests and our climate, and build up our stocks of nuclear bombs and missiles. What masochism remains unspent and free-floating drifts into our personal relationships, mortifying our flesh and leaving us flinching at the very thought of full and authentic consummation between man and woman.

But if there are those repelled by the notion that a renewed society, more holistic, less fragmented than ours, may be helped to attainment by using as exemplars frenzied flagellants, then they may find more acceptable lessons to be learned from the more gentle medieval responses to catastrophes, responses which demonstrate how the masochism endemic to mankind can be marvellously transmuted. One of the most staggering demonstrations of the deployment of masochism in the service of mankind, and which humiliatingly tells us how bungled are our own present efforts to temper its destructiveness, is to be found in France in Colmar. There stands Mathis Grünewald's early sixteenth-century Issenheim altarpiece, one of Europe's greatest religious paintings and one which was deliberately conceived as a therapy for plague victims. It contains the most harrowing image of the crucifixion in Western art.

Psychotherapy did not begin with Freud. The altar, a polyptych, was commissioned by patrons of the mendicant order of Antonites founded in 1080 who had always dedicated themselves to the care of the sufferers of the various sicknesses which successive plagues brought. As a first stage of the healing programme, before the victims were brought into the hospital to be fed, the patients were required to contemplate Grünewald's image and only then were deemed to be sufficiently receptive to receive medical treatment. It was a psychological purging, for it was believed that the patient's spiritual well-being was a prerequisite to the regaining of physical strength. And, above all, the image upon which they gazed, and which is the most haunting part of the altarpiece, is the crucifixion where there is no circumspection in the painter's portrayal of the agony of Christ.

The art correspondent of *The Times*, Richard Cork, after a visit to the altar in 1998, vividly described the scene:

> Gruunewald makes no attempt to dilute the awfulness of the event...exhausted by pain and degradation, this haggard figure hangs down with such terminal heaviness that his shoulders are wrenched from their sockets. Hammered nails tear at his palms.

Although his fingers stab in protest, he can do nothing to arrest the relentless process of deterioration. With head lolling forward, and mouth open because he no longer retains the strength to keep it shut, the defeated Christ is in a death agony almost too gruesome to scrutinise. Blood oozes from the gangrenous feet, the one skewered hideously on the other by a gleaming bolt.

His sweaty pallor proves that the end is close, but nothing is going to hasten the last excruciating moments of his torture. Pitched against the dark void unalleviated by signs of divine intervention, he is condemned to writhe until his body seems unable to withstand any more punishment.

The Christ is depicted alone and isolated, the Virgin and the anguished Mary Magdalene unable to help, yet the sores erupting all over His body tell the plague-stricken viewers that they are not alone in their predicament, and, by identifying themselves with the battered and festering body of Christ, they must have gained immense reassurance, and an emancipation from the humiliating stigma attached to their condition. And to comfort them further Grünewald presents another panel, an astounding one of the resurrection, stressing the miraculous exhilaration of life after death, a dazzling purified apparition that, although Christ holds up His hands still bearing the red marks of His wounds, now they cause Him no pain. It is unsurprising that this great ensemble of panels has resonated in so many creative works in the twentieth century, from the novels of Nobel Prize-winning Elias Canetti to the symphony and opera of the German composer Hindemith. It is the most convincing representation Europe has of the belief that the Passion can turn around masochism and bring boundless hope.

But masochism, anchored to the Passion, can yield not only a political programme for a future Utopia, as it did for the flagellants, or act both as prophylactic and healing balm for troubled souls and bodies, as it did in the Issenheim altar, it can bring too a wondrous beauty where least expected. We tend to associate the rococo style with playfulness and exquisite gracefulness, with gaiety and charm, yet I believe, as do not a few others, that rococo is found at its most captivating not in charming palaces of Naples or Versailles but in the Wies pilgrimage church of the 'scourged Saviour' in Bavaria. Only in some of the churches in Vilnius in Lithuania have I found such unity of apparent lightness and grace with profound spirituality.

The legend that lies behind the construction of this church tells of a figure of a scourged Saviour that was put together in 1730 from various older parts to serve in a Good Friday procession. So piteous, however, was its appearance that the congregants' grief was too great to be tolerated, and it was for years put aside in an attic of a monastery where, some 50 years later, tears were said to be seen in the eyes of the Christ, an event which precipitated a great pilgrimage from all over Europe and ultimately to a church being built to house the miraculous image.

The image of the Christ is a striking contrast to the joyous and riotous rococo fresco paintings and the dancing stucco which engulfs it; no happier place exists on earth and today each year, although few come from Britain, it is visited by more than a million people. To believers, doubtless, as was intended, it is seen as a glorious gateway to heaven, a present alleviation of their burdens and, through Christ's agony, an intimation of the joys to come in the hereafter.

This conversion of masochism into an architecture of almost delirious happiness, like its transmutation by the flagellants into a meaningful social programme and like the Issenheim altar's healing alchemy, was predicated on faith, on absolute belief in the Passion. Jews, not reared in such belief, chose a more terrible fate; they did not deal with their masochism by identifying with the crucified Christ. Rather, they took upon themselves the role of the sacrificial lamb and in their own sufferings they sustained the belief that their agonies would lead in the end to man's redemption, and all mankind's return to Zion. But in Christian Europe, for centuries man's masochism was tempered by trust in the cross; now it is almost absent in our society. Most youngsters in Britain today would be likely to speculate that the Passion was the name of a pop group.

The collapse of faith has not come suddenly, and its consequence was not the immediate release of masochism to wreak havoc unchecked and unrestrained. Until recently the spirit of self-sacrifice found its outlet in constructive secular modes, but now, like manned trench warfare, these too are vanishing, leaving our self-destructiveness to flood our political landscape and our personal lives.

In my lifetime, the martyrdom of the saints which over the centuries recharged the benign consequences of identification with the crucified Christ, has not retained its hold, but no secular vehicle more effectively took over the sacrificial ethos embedded in Christian concern for humanity than the British Labour Movement. Our marching song for nearly a hundred years has been the self-declared hymn, 'The Red Flag', a declaration of faith to be maintained even unto death:

> Come dungeons dark or gallows grim,
> This song shall be our parting hymn.

It has been a call to us to be ready to become martyrs for our socialist cause:

> The people's flag is deepest red;
> It shrouded oft our martyred dead,
> And ere their limbs grew stiff and cold,
> Their heart's blood dyed its every fold.
> Then raise the scarlet standard high!
> Within its shade we'll live or die.
> Tho' cowards flinch and traitors sneer,
> We'll keep the red flag flying here.

The song has been sung with fervour at hundreds of Labour and trade union meetings and rallies. It is still sung at Labour Party conferences – but not, it is certain, for much longer, as the political thieves who under Blair have stolen the soul of the party find it an encumbrance and offensive to Woking Man. And, with its fading away, derided as absurdly anachronistic, a vacuum has arisen as personal aspiration is lauded, and dedication and self-sacrifice for others increasingly finds no place in a managerial Labour Party devoid of doctrine and with no aim beyond striving to be inoffensive to Middle England.

For my generation and the one preceding, the hymn was meaningful, never an historic period piece. I recall when as a young man in the RAF in the Middle East, the army military police descended upon the unit in which I was serving, arrested me for my political activities, and bundled me into a truck to take me down to Suez Port with the intention of my being sent to isolation upon an arid island in the Persian Gulf, that in the lurching truck, crossing the Nile Delta, unconsciously and comfortingly I was humming to myself the familiar and sustaining song.

Arrest, imprisonment and victimisation were experiences suffered by so many of those who shaped the early Labour movement – even the most respectable socialist agitators, like Arthur Jenkins, the father of Roy Jenkins, who before his death represented my constituency in the Commons, could find himself imprisoned for a short period as a consequence of involvement in what was deemed to be a riot. And it was the common lot of those who fought for the cause in factory or pit to be dismissed and refused work for years by any employer. For them, and those reared in yesterday's political and industrial struggles, singing 'The Red Flag' was no piece of hyperbolic self-dramatisation. Politics then was not, as now, a career choice; it was a dedication involving sacrifice, not the gain of pelf and place. The deliberate de-politicisation that Blair incites means that for the first time in Britain's history we are living in a land almost devoid of religious faith and of secular ideology. No effective container is in existence, as hitherto there always has been, to hold our masochism, and as a consequence we are severely stricken. Thanatos's toxins enter uncontrolled into the body politic, and our present febrile personal relationships between man and woman, parent and child, spell out to us how little immunity we have to the resulting infections.

The Sado-Masochistic Charge

The unsparing and relentless publicising of the marriage and divorce of the Foreign Secretary raises questions about the propriety of adding to the clamour by proffering the relationship between the Cooks, despite it being so obviously fraught with an invasive and unspent masochism, as an illustration, paradigm or caricature of the condition in contemporary Britain of marriage or partnership between two working adults.

When, after so prolonged a struggle, I successfully sponsored the Divorce Act of 1969 which ended the doctrine of the matrimonial offence and made marriage breakdown the only ground for divorce, I unwisely believed that with the severe constraints upon the media reporting of the details of a divorce hearing, all the Act left to the press was the right to publish the fact that a marriage breakdown had occurred and that the court had granted a divorce. But soon prurience overcame the right to privacy, and finding a hole in the legislation, the press commenced the practice of also publishing the facts upon which the breakdown had been established in the court, whether adultery, desertion or cruelty. Concerned in particular for the children of a marriage who endured the school playground taunts that followed when their mother's adultery or father's cruelty was so unnecessarily blazoned abroad, I asked Lord Hailsham, the Lord Chancellor, if this reporting practice could not be ended. The Lord Chancellor told me:

The reading public is entitled to know the facts and form its own judgement. I am not prepared myself to argue whether such judgements as they do form are right or wrong. I personally believe that the general rule should be that proceedings in court should be public and published, and the inconvenience of the parties by being exposed to publicity must be secondary to the right of the public to know the facts.

Ironically, Hailsham's reply in itself poses the dilemma as to whether the same rights of privacy should be extended to politicians as to the private individual; as to whether their decision-making should be shielded, so that they should not suffer probings of the unconscious or conscious motivations behind their decisions. This decision of Hailsham's, although he so vigorously presented it as a matter of principle, in fact reeked of his personal prejudices. The pains of his notorious war-time divorce never left him, and repeatedly on the many occasions over the years I attended upon him, seeking to gain his help to modify existing divorce laws covering maintenance and custody questions, I encountered those personal prejudices.

As Captain Quintin Hogg, while serving in the Middle East, he was unexpectedly given the opportunity to have a short leave. He returned to London, let himself into his house, and found his wife in the arms of a Free French officer. I do not believe the narcissistic wound which he then suffered was ever healed. The divorce case was fully reported, and the faithless wife 'exposed' to the general public and, not least, to those serving overseas where, certainly in the RAF in the Middle East, it had its resonances. Many married men carried around their necks, along with their identity disks, what was described as the 'Blighty key', upon which they rested their hope that one day they would return and be able to enter again into their homes. When Hogg's divorce was reported, many wisely threw away their key, eschewing such sudden entries and opting for the belief that ignorance was bliss. Hogg's insistence that the guilty party should be 'exposed to publicity' bears all the marks of a man still desirous that the public should know who is an 'innocent' party and who should be pilloried.

Hogg, in failing, probably through lack of insight, to acknowledge the bias which informed his decision, was following the usual practice of politicians. The protective carapace of the practising politician assuming the affectation of undiluted commitment to principle and community and dismissing the ad hominem argument as a vulgar irrelevance in no way invalidating his manifesto, is, however, paper thin – and the electorate know it. Indeed, the politician, urged on by his grooming spin doctors, and drawn by his narcissism to television, has paradoxically colluded to ensure that he is judged by his 'personality' even as he wanly and unconvincingly complains that he wants the public to direct their attention only to his proffered policies. Blair, on populist morning chat-shows, tells of his good relations with his children, with his father-in-law, of his lack of bossiness in his home – all trivia giving carefully designed glimpses of his sweetness – but he vigorously complains if then we insist upon monitoring the man behind the smile.

Most politicians' complaints of this sort should be brushed aside. The drives generated by the psychological needs of the politicians so often invade and distort the panaceas they offer to their electorates, and if more objective assessments of policies are to be made, assessments must be made of the men and women who expound them. It follows, when political decision-making can have such fateful consequences for the nation, that the elected politician cannot claim the same right of privacy which must be afforded to electors. In my judgement, the only issue – but one fraught with difficulties – is not whether the intermeshing of the interior life of the politician with his public activities should be exempt from scrutiny, but how we can ensure that that scrutiny is genuinely in the public interest and not appalling scavenging. This is not easily achieved. Since all biography is autobiography, the critic who denies the privacy the politician claims exposes himself and is almost bound to endure the taunts of those who would attack his credentials. Before delving into another's interior life the critic therefore needs, ideally, through introspective work into his own personal resource, to face painful insights into his own motivation before daring to be judgemental of others. With such complexities surrounding the issues, it is unsurprising that in Britain we have been less than successful in our efforts to set the boundaries by the creation of the Press Complaints Commission to curb the excess of the gutter tabloids without destroying the freedom of information. Whether the self-discipline of the press enables this to come about remains to be seen.

Our pragmatic approach is, however, very different from the route taken in the United States. This route has provoked some of their most thoughtful academics, not least the philosopher of law Thomas Nagel, in despair with the shameful farce of the trial of Clinton, to affirm that the public space of politics is designed for the pursuit and resolution of public issues and that it cannot handle the intrusions of incendiary private matter that result when politicians are denied the right to present a merely public face.

This sweeping response, a plea to insulate the politician from surveillance of his private and interior life, is essentially an attempt to contain the consequences that have occurred in the United States where the general loosening of inhibitions in recent decades has on the one hand led to greater tolerance towards variations in sexual life and, on the other hand, led to the collapse of protections of privacy for any figure in whose sexual life the public might take a prurient interest. Even more than in Britain, permissiveness, the conscious investment in the ideals of sexual freedom, has not led to the stilling of the savagery, puritanical but unconscious, that operates beneath the veneer. In the United States what looked initially like a growth of freedom has culminated in the reconstitution of the public pillory.

Not the least of the contributory causes to this mêlée which led to the obscene spectacle of the Clinton trial was the excessive reliance placed by Americans upon the constitution and the law, both of which are so ill equipped to cope with the questions raised by Clinton's private behaviour. The involvement of the Supreme Court in refusing to allow Paula Jones's law suit to be deferred until the end of Clinton's term of office, the approval given by the panel of Washington federal judges to the obsessional puritanical prosecutor to extend his initial investigation to the president's sex life, the morass of laws in place governing sexuality including sexual harassment, the existence of the independent prosecutor's statute and, indeed, the impeachment procedures themselves, all tell us that we are fortunate to be without a written constitution in this country so that our courts are given the prime task of interpreting laws made by Parliament, not of making their own. Our pragmatic approach is certainly imperfect and much remains to be done to disengage prurience from needed scrutiny in the public interest, but we have not impaled ourselves upon iron fences built around rigid statutes and overtly structured constitutions.

In the Robin Cook affair, however, most considerations of the boundaries which a society should set between a right of privacy and that of a public interest are inappropriate. Margaret Cook herself, in her sulphurous book, has erased all such boundaries and has, she claims, 'bared her soul'. In a catalogue of Robin Cook's years of misbehaviour, telling of what she calls his 'tendency to self-destruct', she wallows in her own misery and suffering. From the very beginning of the relationship to the very end, both were unfaithful to each other, and both ruthlessly inflicted wounds upon each other as a preliminary to their reconciling embraces.

Some of her bitter probings of her partner's weaknesses are doubtless to be discounted – Robin Cook was certainly no alcoholic. I spoke to him in the House and witnessed his brilliant parliamentary forays too often to be so persuaded. He certainly never followed the disastrous examples of his Labour Foreign Secretary predecessor George Brown, whose public rumbustious-ness was notorious, or that of Michael Stewart with his excessive silent drinking while, and after, defending Britain's support for America's war against Vietnam.

Unhappily, however, other personal criticisms Margaret Cook makes are undoubtedly well founded, not least Cook's insensitivity to the opinions and feelings of those around him. As his biographer puts it: 'He fails to register to the presence of others.' In 1986, aware as I was of his growing unpopularity in the Parliamentary Labour Party, and of the envy his superior ability – which he never disguised – prompted among many of his colleagues, I became concerned that in the approaching election by MPs of the shadow cabinet, he would lose his place and that Labour would be deprived of its most effective frontbench spokesman. I drew him aside and warned him of the danger; he was astonished, blissfully unaware of the hazard. My warning, and his attempts to retrieve the situation, came too late: his vote shrank substantially, and he was not re-elected by his peers.

The most wounding allegation, however, that Margaret Cook

makes against him is that he acknowledged that he had, because of his ambition, 'sold his soul' to New Labour. For those knowing, as Margaret Cook says, that 'his intelligence and ability were unmatched at Westminster', the dismay that his defection from the role of upholder of traditional Labour values against Blairism is in itself a 'public interest' justification, perhaps the only justification, to seek to explicate further his anguished marriage. Disenchanted and dismayed Labour activists and their sympathisers, seeing headlines, as in *The Times* of January 1999 'Cook hits back with praise for Labour leaders', witness his unconvincing attempt to rebut his former wife's 'sold his soul' allegation, and with little or no disguise thus see him bringing his private marriage altercations into the public arena. Dedicated followers, bewildered by their lost leader, upon whom they rested so much of their hopes, are surely entitled to understand that the debacle comes not from flaws in their own convictions but in the blemishes of the man who they saw as equipped to be the leader of Britain's Left.

In all marriages, except those totally dead – and sometimes even in those – sado-masochistic patterns are woven into our bondings. We punish our partners and are punished by them, sometimes in subtle exchanges and sometimes far more overtly. However, the Cooks' public presentation of their marriage, setting out in excruciating detail with all diffidences abandoned, surely gives us a florid example of a marriage of long duration which was always kept alive by the sado-masochistic charges continuously triggered by one or other of the partners. Infidelities were inflicted upon the other and then, in order to ensure the maximum degree of torment was aroused, each recounted to the other, apparently in a mixture of triumph and remorse, their waywardness. Each of these highly intelligent people, as an expression of indifference amounting to contempt, refused to take any interest whatsoever in the work and professional activities of their partner.

The catalogue of continuous slights Margaret Cook claims to have suffered understandably prompted Edwina Currie, in reviewing Cook's book, to ask the question: 'Why did she stay so long?' But the answer is clear: the pains propped up the love and without them the marriage would have collapsed. In my younger years, when practising in the magistrates' matrimonial court, I found so often that in violent disputes between steelworker husbands and their wives that it was only when the beating stopped that the marriage could be said to have irrevocably broken down. Margaret Cook has averred that but for the intervention of Blair's lackey spin doctors, more concerned with presenting a suitable story for public consumption than stabilising the marriage, they would probably still be together. She is perhaps right, and they would then no doubt have continued to torture each other 'til death did them part. That indeed would have left Robin Cook untarnished and uncompromised, not needing Blair's patronage to survive, able to have been unyielding and to use his considerable talents to defend Labour's traditional values.

Cook's failure has brought profound disappointment to many and, in particular, to stalwarts in the Labour Party, and that cannot be diminished. Perhaps the bitterness felt by them, because of their perception of Cook as a defector, may however be tempered by some understanding of his interior life, of the unconscious forces that appear to have led the most able of Labour's front-bench spokesmen to become so politically entrapped. Such an empathic mode may help to prevent their dedicated political enthusiasm, as they declare their wish to put Labour back into 'New Labour', from turning into cynicism.

Certainly such an approach, any attempt to explore Robin Cook's psyche, might well show that some, but not all, of the dilemmas with which he finds himself entangled come from the prevailing zeitgeist which has excluded the Passion. Cook's total repudiation of Christianity and its core container of masochism – identification with the suffering Christ – although claimed by him to have been reached by intellectual appraisal in his first year at university and not by a 'sort of Damascene non-conversion' was nevertheless too violent a break with his past to be regarded so cerebrally.

He had come to university but a few months before with the intention of entering the Church as a minister, and he commenced his English degree, as a preliminary to taking a Divinity degree. His whole upbringing as an only son within an intense and closely knit family had taken place in a mortified ascetic Protestant household, one enveloped in a severe and austere Christianity. During his primary schooldays he unfailingly accompanied, every Sunday, his parents to church and was a prizewinner in the recitation competition of the catechism and gladly linked himself to the task of planting nasturtiums all the way round his church on wet and windy Sunday afternoons. In the duties and observances of a Scottish Presbyterian ethos, his childhood and adolescence were well provided with socially approved rituals possessed of a sponge-like porosity, well able to absorb much of young Cook's masochism.

A few terms after his entry into university, evidently endeavouring to shake off the dominance of his father's creed and practice, in the flat his ever and over-protective father had just bought for him, came the great rebellion: he denounced the God-father and 'came to the view that there was no God and since then I have been a signed-up and conforming atheist'. The abruptness seems more like a delayed Oedipal response than, as he has claimed, the consequence of considered rationalist exploration. In throwing away his Christianity he, however, disposed of more than an oppressively caring father – he left himself bereft of the vehicle which lightened the masochistic load which this man carries.

He sought to find less demanding alternative and smoother routes, ones where he could ease his burden and where, without shame, he could openly carry his considerable ambitions. With partial insight he has described the immediate consequence of his bid to emancipate himself from the God-father: 'What then happened psychologically inside me is that my commitment to the Church of Scotland as a minister of religion transferred itself into the Labour Party and socialism.'

Although as a home the traditional Labour Party has been a more ramshackle structure than the Church, nevertheless it has, with its emphases on the motifs of the subjugation of self in the interests of the community, always been a lure for many of the more masochistically inclined, a haven from which they can work to alleviate the sufferings of the disadvantaged. In itself, therefore, Cook's switch from God to Party is unexceptional, although it does provide a neat illustration of the therapeutic lineaments that can be sought, not always as successfully as in religion, within an institutionalised secular ideology, the collapse of which may release unspent masochism that can destroy personal relationships. Judging by the corrosive letters and infidelities ostentatiously endured by the Cooks in their student courtship days, Robin Cook's conversion to atheism was a less than successful attempt to displace masochism from religion to ideology. That, however, may be due more to the particular quality and quantity of the masochism woven into Cook's character rather than to any lack of potential available within the ethos of a socialist party to enable selflessness to overcome egoism. The imperfect canalisation of Cook's masochism within a political faith should not mislead us; rather, in the Cooks' marriage we see, as in a fun-fair mirror, an exaggerated image of a general condition, one prone to afflict so many relationships between man and woman in a faithless non-ideological society.

Self-disgust Into Spirituality

I doubt if there is any place on earth where the fierce force and courage of a masochistic leader can sear one more than at Ephesus, the city dedicated to the celebration of sexuality. Here, amidst the temples and shrines built to acclaim fertility first in the name of Cybele and later to her successors, Artemis and Diana, came the great adventurer, one of the most extraordinary men ever produced by my people: Paul of Tarsus, the myth-maker and founder of Christianity, the harshest disparager of the flesh that the Western world has ever known. And down those marble roads, unintimidated by the grand temples affirming the joys of sex, the zealot declaimed against the turpitude of the worshippers, subverting their confidence as he inflamed the dormant guilts that forever lurk beneath the ecstasy of the reveller. He was the great converter of self-disgust into spirituality, and his message, resonating down the centuries, has so often in British history found a response amongst political leaders, miserably discomfited by their own sexuality. Repeatedly, Paul's utterances have been echoed in their speeches and underlined in their conduct:

> I know that nothing good lodges in me – in my unspiritual nature...I bruise my own body and make it know its master...in this present body we do indeed groan...we know that as long as we are at home in the body we are exiles from the Lord...we are not better than pots of earthenware to contain this treasure.

Paul's words may have often given them some temporary solace but he could not save them; to gain relief from their own agonies these men, often in bizarre manner, needed publicly to exhibit them and to be their own missionaries. From Lord Chancellor Thomas More always, literally, wearing a hair-shirt under his gorgeous robes and zealously provoking his own martyrdom, down to Gladstone, returning to Downing Street from his rescue work among prostitutes, in order to scourge himself for his lascivious thoughts and masturbatory antics while circulating among them, we witness masochistic leaders enmeshing their private travail into the public weal. In my lifetime the politician who provided a surfeit of clinical material telling of the role and dangers of masochistic leadership was the hero of my adolescence – Stafford Cripps, who was to become Labour's Chancellor of the Exchequer in the 1945 Government. It took time and my own maturation in the war for me to become wary of such leadership. I did not know Cripps personally – he belonged to an older generation – but his influence upon me as a boy and youth came about because I attended so many of his evangelising meetings. In those early days my admiration of him was boundless; his role as a great lawyer, playing Robin Hood as he plundered his rich clients to aid the poor, fuelled my own ambitions, and his expulsion in 1939 from the Labour Party precipitated the one occasion in my life when, disenchanted for a while, my commitment to the Labour movement faltered. Yet, after the war, on my return to Wales from the RAF, I clashed with him at conferences on more than one occasion, and I formed a distaste for his sickly religiosity and his clear enjoyment of the austere economic policies he was imposing.

His self-righteous Christianity, his Messianic belief that he was chosen and had a special line to God, infuriated his Cabinet colleagues. Ben Pimlott, in his monumental biography of Hugh Dalton, has described Cripps as a 'dazzling, destructive and uncompromising personality' and in the immediate post-war years, it was the destructiveness which I sensed, a destructiveness which ultimately he was to turn in on himself. In anorexic mood he imposed upon himself a diet of strict and ill-balanced vegetarianism, excluding the cyanocobalamin present in liver, kidney, milk, eggs and mussels, which he evidently needed. The element was further exhausted by the detoxification of cyanide in tobacco smoke, for Cripps at conferences was a chain-smoker, ringing the changes with cigarettes and pipe tobacco and, in the evenings, with cigars too. There can be little doubt that the troubles of his spinal vertebrae which led to his death stemmed from nutritional insufficiencies. It was said that the tireless Chancellor of the Exchequer had sacrificed his health for the sake of the nation but that was only a partial truth. His yearning for sacrifice was morbid, and in the sealed envelope which on his death he left for his wife he made this explicit: 'I want my effort to live on and to inspire others to work for the eventual salvation of mankind which we all look for.' Politicians are healthier and more effective if they are more modest in objectives. Whatever may have been the value in first-century Palestine of the redeemers in present-day Westminster they, if possessed of the brilliance of Cripps, can become a menace to themselves and to the nation. Cripps was certainly a menace to me, and I did not easily escape from his aura.

Thanatos does not skip a generation; relentlessly he continues to make his selection. Before answering the question as to whether our present Foreign Secretary qualifies to enter the pantheon of Britain's masochistic leaders, a glance at an exact Westminster contemporary of mine, whose qualifications cannot be disputed, may, by bringing into high relief the required attributes, help to give a reply.

Thanatos's Intermediary

Few of Britain's modern ascetic political missionaries exhibited the masochistic syndrome more explicitly – the extraordinary capacity to allow masochism to dictate public policy – than Keith Joseph, the harbinger of Thatcherism, whose yearning for punishment in small and big matters sometimes seemed boundless. His public recantations became notorious and earned him the soubriquet of the 'Mad Monk'. These mea culpa attitudes became particularly familiar to me since, for nearly 30 years, he was my regular, punctilious and scrupulous pair, each week arranging, as far as our Whips would permit, our absences from the House to meet our outside political and social commitments. If through inadvertence, forgetfulness or sudden change of parliamentary business, by error some of us nevertheless recorded our votes, Joseph was, until the last days of 1987 when both of us quit the Commons, disproportionately grieved and always determined to accept responsibility for the minor contretemps. Since he so evidently enjoyed blaming himself, and was so well-meaning a man, I rarely denied him the pleasure.

He fitted appositely into Carl Jung's typology, exhibiting almost all the characteristics which Jung labelled as belonging to the introverted thinking type. These are men forever intellectualising, over-valuing thought processes, searching for intellectual solutions for what are properly emotional problems. Their thought processes can become highly libidinised, and their

107

predominant mode of self-expression is not in relation to other people but in the world of thought. Ideas tend to become substitutes for feelings, and intellectual values for emotional values. They are doubtless splendid Fellows of All Souls, as Keith Joseph was, but they make imperfect politicians for, always faltering in any attempt to communicate with others, they are forever creating misunderstandings and then, with an air of bewilderment, apologising for their gaffes.

It is certainly no Procrustean caprice to fit Joseph into Jung's 'thinking type'; he possessed all the vulnerabilities that Jung claimed clung to such personalities. However subtle their intellectual propositions may be, there can be an astonishing infantilism displayed in their personal relationships. Jung observed:

> If he should ever chance to be understood, he is credulously liable to over-estimate. Ambitious women have only to understand how advantage may be taken of this uncritical attitude...to make an easy prey of him. He lets himself be brutalised and exploited in the ignominious way, if only he can be left undisturbed in his ideas.

Of such stuff are the Keith Josephs of this world made. Who but a high-minded intellectual of Keith Joseph's calibre could have so absurdly told us how stricken he was by Thatcher: 'My eyes light up at the sight of her, even though she is hitting me about the head, so to speak.' Doubtless his eyes lit up because his goddess hit him over the head, but not all of us pine for such masochistic pleasures. Joseph never stopped preaching that the nation needed 're-moralising'; we must repent, he told us, for if we do not 'the nation moves towards degeneration'. And, like all old-time evangelists, first he would induce guilt and shame – acknowledgement of sin was the prerequisite to rebirth. 'The worship of instinct, of spontaneity, the rejection of self-discipline is not progress ...' Then, abandoning the burden of intellectual rigour, the academic – in an orgy of self-indulgence and to the surprise of many – offered us the inspiration of the second of his femmes fatales. 'Let us take inspiration from that admirable woman Mary Whitehouse...a shining example of what one woman can do. She has mobilised and given fresh heart to many...' The banality of

Whitehouse and her lashing of Britain's concupiscence appeared irresistible to the guilt-laden, submissive Joseph.

His unconquered fear of what he, like Whitehouse, perceived as Britain's concupiscence, was to cost him the leadership of his party. Like Enoch Powell, whose fears of the fecundity of the blacks led him to make his self-destructive 'rivers of blood' speech, Joseph interpolated within one of his famed 'cycle of deprivation' speeches a fatal aside, one in which he revealed his yearning for the eugenic policy that could contain what he saw as the threatening sexual and progenitive capacity of too many in the working class.

Before Joseph – in October 1974, as Shadow Home Secretary – made that speech, he had discussed its contents with me, an unusual gesture on his part, since rarely did we include in our perfunctory exchanges any mention of policy. On this occasion, well aware of my heavy involvement in family law and illegitimacy issues, he wanted to plunder what he regarded as my expertise. I willingly encouraged him to make a speech which I understood was to take further his ideas on the cycle of deprivation, and would be designed to save the children of deprived and disadvantaged families, to break the concatenation of circumstances and events which so often led inexorably to those children becoming problem adults. There was, of course, no hint in our discussions of the dangerous eugenic element which when introduced into his speech brought down upon him a storm of condemnation. Blissfully unaware of the terrifying implications of his intended assertion that, to prevent 'national degeneration', something must be done to arrest the high birth rates of those falling into classes four and five, he did not even mention this explosive elaboration to me. When, a few days after the well-publicised and widely resented speech, I privately admonished him for having so sabotaged his own well-intentioned efforts, he ruefully accepted my reproach. I sensed he took pleasure in my reprimand, as he took pleasure in the public opprobrium that was falling upon him.

Indeed, if Joseph thought he was not receiving sufficient punishment for his gaffes, he would pre-empt his critics, insisting his mistakes were unforgiveable. As the minister responsible for the accursed high-rise council flats, he was later to wallow in his blunder, never missing an opportunity to confess publicly his error. Unfortunately, the buildings could not be dismantled as easily as his original support for them. Joseph may have enjoyed his lamentations but they brought little comfort to those attempting to live in them.

Keith Joseph was often described as a John the Baptist heralding Thatcher, a description that doubtless was congenial to those who, at least unconsciously, endowed Margaret Thatcher with the powers of a deity. But, although Joseph was indeed Thatcher's creature, a no less revealing comparison would be one made with Paul, whose repudiation of sensuousness made him a vulnerable candidate for a dramatic conversion. Sudden revelations of the truth and extravagant repudiations of past sins are usually associated with religious, not political, experience. But Keith Joseph illustrated how masochistic politicians can take the road to Damascus. The outcome of inner struggle can find political as well as religious expression; for in each case conversion is a bid to still unacceptable illicit passions.

Joseph himself pinpointed his blindingly dazzling conversion: 'It was only in April 1974 that I was converted to Conservatism. I had thought that I was a Conservative but now I see I wasn't one at all.' He had found the true light and the way and it is a fact that in conversations at that time he compared himself with a prophet coming down from the mountain. There was an Old Testament ring to his cries of woe from the wilderness as he urged repentance from the wicked ways of socialism and beat his breast for his own part in what he had belatedly discovered to be the betrayal of the ark of the Conservative covenant.

Even as Paul denounced the Torah as shit, so, in similar terms, did Joseph denounce past Conservative Governments with which he had been associated, and declared: 'The reality is that for 30 years Conservative Governments did not consider it practicable to reverse the vast bulk of accumulated detritus of socialism.'

The public consequences of Joseph's conversion were far-reaching. His suffering and agonising were unloaded on to the nation, and many in the Conservative Party and in the nation were ready to accept them and to hearken to the self-proclaimed prophet, for there were confusions abroad and it was in such seasons that those who claim new visions and certainties are given deference. In more confident times, the political fanatic, the psychopathic and severely paranoid leader is treated with disdain, or confined to a mental hospital. The ravings of Hitler would, in a healthier society, have qualified him for the madhouse, not the leadership of Germany. But even in Britain's milder political climate, where our crises are happily not as severe as those of the Weimar Republic and our leaders not so aberrant, there are, nevertheless, societal conditions which give rare opportunities to the prophet-politician. Joseph's economic theories, although apparently sophisticated and rational, were full of his psychological prejudices.

The critique of post-war Conservatism that Joseph developed in 1974, and which became the blueprint for Thatcher's Governments, is replete with Joseph's self-chastisement. He preached that stern monetarist doctrines were needed, cuts should be ruthlessly made in welfare expenditure, spendthrift policies and departments should be outlawed, unemployment should be endured and the feeling must be shed that 'somehow the lean and tight-lipped muster of men in the 1930 dole queues were at least partly our fault'. Only through suffering can a nation ultimately find strength and joy. The Centre for Policy Studies, set up in 1974 by Joseph and Thatcher to serve as their 'think-tank', was less cerebral than claimed; instead, by way of highly refined rationalisations, Joseph's masochism was institutionalised. And with such backing, when the battle for the Conservative leadership came, Joseph – the sole frontbencher at the time to give Thatcher full support – found that the bewildered backbench peasants were ready to respond to his masochistic pleas. And together, with exquisite relief, they submitted to She; and She, proclaiming the apotheosis of individualism, and that there was no such thing as society, made narcissism a societal virtue, every man or woman for him or herself and never for each other. With the well-meaning and naïve Joseph as the tool and intermediary of Thanatos, self-love and not true love became the official doctrine in the land.

Playing to Lose

One generation before Wilhelm Reich, the pioneer psychoanalyst Otto Gross, with whom Jung had mutual analyses, laid down emphases stressing that a dialectical inter-dependence existed between individual change on the one hand and collective political change on the other. His affirmation that 'the psychology of the unconscious is the philosophy of the revolution' was too radical an insight to be tolerated by his more orthodox professional psychoanalyst colleagues, who so often preferred the safety of the consulting room to explorations which could lead them into a scrutiny of external turbulent societal conditions. But though the temptation may be to treat politics as mere epiphenomena, to challenge the primacy of politics, to neutralise politics by reducing them almost to a psychological category, the impinging zeitgeist cannot be so disengaged from the individual. No clearer example of this entanglement is available in our national lottery gambling-ridden society than in the conduct of one of our most eminent racing tipsters, our own Foreign Secretary.

Visiting Newmarket Heath on a fine summer morning can certainly be rewarding: the smell of the grass, the sound of larks singing, the rhythmic drumming of hoofs on the turf, the touch of a satin pelt, and the liberating sight of horses galloping through breast-high mists are delights, but these joys are but the surface aspect of the sport of kings. Although I understand, without necessarily any censoriousness on my part, Robin Cook's expressed belief that the most exciting sights and noises he knows are 'the colour and noise of a large field coming into a steeple-chase fence, which is a tremendous spectacle', I am ever aware that beneath the aristocratic pretensions of the oligarchic self-perpetuating Jockey Club and the Ascot fashion parades lies the huge murky and ruthless gambling industry, an industry that is always poised to exploit the frailties of working people.

It is indeed an irony that a Labour tipster Foreign Secretary – one who extraordinarily and unsuccessfully fought his civil servants after his appointment to retain the right to continue his racing column in the *Glasgow Herald* – should have had as a predecessor Labour's first and distinguished Foreign Secretary, Arthur Henderson, a man who fully understood how the working class could become the prey of bookmakers. Repeatedly, to trade union audiences, Henderson insisted that 'gambling is a greater foe to Labour than all the forces of capitalism'. His was not then an idiosyncratic view, and it may not well be now as anachronistic an opinion as appears at first sight. Baldwin, the Conservative Prime Minister, also knew the vulnerability of the working-class. When the egregious railway workers' leader J. H. Thomas, a Cabinet minister in three governments, two Labour and one Tory – exchanged budget tips with a millionaire Tory MP and Fred Bates, the owner of two racing newspapers, in return for racing tips, behaviour which ultimately led to a judicial enquiry, Baldwin contemptuously and patronisingly commented: 'Thomas is a terrific gambler who most likely let his tongue wag when he was in his cups – the two weaknesses of his class.' Macmillan certainly knew the workers had to be protected from themselves. When he introduced premium bonds, he was careful to ensure that the lottery was to be a gamble on only the interest and not on the capital investment. This was his defence when Harold Wilson, following Labour's traditional stance which Cook almost clownishly has deserted, bitterly attacked what he saw as an ugly encouragement of gambling.

Suspicion of gambling in the Labour movement was well in place in 1958 when I became an MP. My constituency management committee almost shame-facedly asked me for a dispensation to permit them to run a little raffle at our meetings, something outlawed by the previous member, a dispensation which, when granted, in those more deferential days, was gratefully received. These hesitations to institutionalise chance in any form stemmed not only from the convictions of the Nonconformist chapels in my valley or the Henderson belief that gambling was a capitalist trap, luring workers away from the class struggle to dreams of wealth; it was because, deep down, more by intuition than rational assessment, gambling was held to have a menacing satanic quality.

In these seasons of a twice-weekly national lottery, ever more casinos, and well-designed, comfortable betting shops, such responses may appear to be quirky, but what in fact is quirky is that Cook, the hope of the Labour activists seeking to ward off Blairite Thatcherism and believed to be so much in tune with Labour's traditional values, should always, in this respect, have been so out of kilter with the predominant mood, one which certainly prevailed in Scottish Labour circles. Indeed, it was in July 1968 that, with the aid in particular of Scottish MPs, I was able in Commons debates to savage a tentative proposal to hold a national lottery put forward by the Treasury Minister, Harold Lever, one of the most intelligent MPs in the Commons during my parliamentary lifetime, and one whose friendship I so much enjoyed. Lever, an incorrigible gambler himself, was taken aback by the force of the opposition his proposal aroused among so many of his colleagues, who regarded his suggestion as an audacious affront to all the principles they held. I endeavoured to put a case against the national lottery that was based not on the religious principles that informed other opponents of the scheme, but on rationality:

> As I have listened in past years to those who have come to me professionally in difficulty as a consequence of gambling – the embezzling clerk, the falsifying trade union official, or the fraudulent bank manager – I have heard them explaining how they thought their luck would change. I have always glimpsed a world of their absurd magic; pick up a pin, wear a charm, touch a dwarf, or see the moon through glass, see a magpie, three parrots or so many crows.
>
> I do not mock at those who find real life so bewildering, or so painful, that they must escape to gambling; I do not mock at those who are disenchanted and disappointed with life so that perforce they must dream of wealth and riches, vainly hoping that by lottery

or ballot their impoverished life may perhaps at some time be magically transformed by some external gain or fortune. I do not mock at them. I do not bring to this problem some of the puritanical zeal which has informed some of the speeches we have heard, nor do I choose, as some Honourable Members have, to quote theology, because I have not forgotten that one of the Apostles himself was chosen by lot. But, by very different means, I come to the same conclusion as they do.

In this House we seek to govern by rational argument and rational discussion. We try. We do not necessarily succeed. We try to lead people from irrationality and prejudice and our task all the time in our legislation is to defy those who pessimistically believe that the perplexity and helplessness of the human race is such that it cannot be remedied, that we are the playthings of gods, of chance, or luck, or fate...The voice of reason, of the intellect, is very soft, it has to be endlessly repeated, has many rebuffs, but although it has a soft voice, fortunately the voice of reason is one which does not rest until it has obtained a hearing.

It is true that people cannot be bludgeoned into hearing it. It is true that we cannot end gambling by legislation. We cannot force the community into rationality, but surely our role should be to contain it, to curtail it and certainly not to activate it as an act of State so that we spread and create more superstition and more irrationality. I do not regard this debate at all as one between those who are puritans and the permissive. As a humanist and a rationalist, I find the idea of a national lottery as no less repugnant than those Nonconformists in my constituency who have written to me urging opposition to the proposal.

And I reproached Lever and Labour MPs supporting the proposal:

When today's Labour members stand their philosophy on its head, I am bound to query the spectacle. Socialism surely has something to do with the redistribution of wealth, with the community taking unearned income from the undeserving and deploying, according to determined priorities, the money for the benefit of the whole community. Is not that what socialism is supposed to be about? The national lottery is the very antithesis of this. It would collect money from all the community; it would hand over a substantial proportion of the proceeds – unearned, untaxed, undeserved – to a newly created capitalist. Then it would use the balance under the guise of hypothecation for causes which succeeded in jumping the queue.

In the Parliament of 1974 our arguments held sway and the proposal of the lottery was ditched by the government. The prohibition against a public lottery made by Parliament in 1826, because, as one contemporary commentator declared, 'of all depraving institutions it had the largest share in debasing society', remained in place. But the shrewd commentator William Hone was correct in his prophecy that 'after all, perhaps, the monster is only scotched not killed'. It was to be resuscitated only when Thatcherism had insinuated itself into the psyche of the nation.

My views on gambling were not founded on my experiences as a punter – these were limited. Like many of us living within the South Wales working-class culture of the depression years of the thirties, in my late teens I attended for a season the local greyhound track, a venue much disapproved of by the chapel and respectable Welshmen. My attendance was as much part of my entrance into manhood as had been my bar mitzvah at 13. Although I claimed to have won more than I lost, my interest flagged after a year and on Saturday nights I switched to girls. That interest was more sustained and it was not until the post-war years that my attention again turned to gambling; but this time I was a solicitor, not a punter.

For some years before I went into the House, I became increasingly professionally involved with one of Britain's largest bookmakers and football pools promoters. The ageing owner lived and worked near me and so, by an accident of geography and his increasing reluctance to travel to London lawyers, he sought me out. He was a great collector; he wanted to collect me too. But my insisting upon my independent status and refusing his offers to put me on his payroll whetted his appetite and I found him forever seeking me out for legal guidance. My close contact with him for some years gave me a vantage point from which to observe and understand Britain's shoddy and vast gambling industry and, indeed, its ramifications in Africa, and meant that with this acquired knowledge of the gambling industry, I came into the House with a no less censorious attitude towards gambling than that held by the most severe Nonconformist chapels in my constituency. I can recall that I revealed my prejudices for the first but not the last time during the debates on the Betting & Gaming Bill in 1959 when, to replace the illegal street runners, the opening of betting shops under severe restrictions was given the go-ahead by the government. At that time, turning to the pages of Hansard, I see how prissily I spoke:

> Listening to the Home Secretary giving the amount spent each year upon gambling, it was chastening to think that in our society so many people find so little excitement in life and so little zest that they can gain a thrill only by this type of activity...I think a more mature democracy would be seeking means to stimulate the imagination of people so that they dream other dreams than that of winning on a horse race.

> Although some of us professionally engage sometimes in the farcical proceedings under the existing betting and gaming laws, and even though we want an effort to be made to provide a rationale for the betting and gaming laws, I can only agree to support this scheme if the effort will not lead to further stimulation of gambling and will not make it still easier for gambling promoters to make still vaster fortunes out of the cupidity and credulousness of the most feckless sections of the community.

I spoke thus because I was aware of the evasions, cheatings and the exploitation of the credulous embedded within the gambling industry, but it was not simply the stress and disruption it sometimes brought into the family life of working people that I regretted. More objectionable was the manner in which the glamorisation of racing facilitated and legitimised the demeaning of men and women who by accepting the invitation to dream their dreams of gain, lost their adulthood. The considerable clinical material to which I had gained access in my professional work validated so many of the hypotheses in the psychoanalytical literature on gambling with which I was acquainted.

Because I had thus been made so aware of the causality of compulsive gambling habits, on learning of Cook's role as a tipster, I had misgivings whether he could fulfil the expectations placed upon him as the able and leading standard bearer of the Left. His racing column was not to be regarded merely as a money-earner supplementing his parliamentary salary; he was paid only a piffling £100 a week for his work and, after he became Foreign Secretary, he speedily waived the sum entirely in a bid to circumvent the ministerial rules which could otherwise have prevented him from continuing to publish his racing prophecies. Money was certainly not the real spur to his persistence; there were deeper motivations.

I know not whether he followed his own advice and laid bets on the horses he commended; it would, however, be unusual for a tipster to do otherwise. Although it is clearly possible that Cook's betting was sometimes only vicarious, I doubt whether he was by any means wholly abstemious. He was always ambivalent about gambling and in his student days although, until exams approached, he would spend much of his time after the pubs closed with his 'gang' whom he would help supply 'booze and crisps' as they all gathered to play, with stakes, poker, rummy and canasta, he evidently liked to be the voyeur at these games. A participant recalls that although 'some of us would risk what was for us at the time a lot of money...he had a more Puritan streak and didn't like to gamble'. The father's influence was then evidently more powerful – indeed, it has never wholly been cast off and Margaret Cook has written that if his father had still been alive, he would never have dared to have left her – but one suspects that in later life he was both participant and observer.

Of course, Cook had the wit to know the folly of excessive gambling:

> As for racing itself, the risk is exciting but anyone who thinks he can make lots of money from betting requires counselling. You should never put on more than you can afford to lose without regret.

But I suspect he did not always follow his own precept any more than did his followers listening to his advice on the form of horses, the going, the distance and the experience of the jockeys. He did not seem to grasp how droll it was that a man should warn of the follies of gambling and simultaneously incite his readers to bet on 'winners'.

Cook's preoccupation disconcerted civil servants. On his first day as Foreign Secretary, he insisted that an hour be set aside in the afternoon to allow him to watch the 2000 Guineas at Newmarket, the first Classic of the flat-racing season. And his preoccupations certainly disconcerted some Labour activists: he could, and did, address brilliantly an annual general constituency meeting and then, in the middle of the subsequent mayoral reception, ignore and upset everyone by going off to a corner to file his racing report.

This pattern of behaviour cannot simply be dismissed as a boyish enthusiasm or a hobby, and it is more unnerving in a senior politician when what is being presented is akin to that most dangerous of symptoms characterising the compulsive gambler – the unconscious desire to lose. For strange as it may seem to a more detached outside observer whose gambling may be confined to a flutter on the Derby or a church bazaar raffle, the real addict, as every bookmaker enjoying his prey knows, plays to lose, not to win. This unconscious desire to lose money can be a warning indication of how profound may be a masochistic wish to be punished and left bereft. Cook, his former wife tells us, in his daily life could 'crazily' lose 'significant sums of money' through 'carelessness':

> He was crazily careless about money and possessions. I was once correctly quoted as saying that if he ever became Chancellor of the Exchequer – his ambition – I'd advise my friends to emigrate. He never carried a wallet, stuffing notes and coins in his back pocket and frequently losing significant sums.

Risk-taking aimed at loss, gambling to lose, is a phenomenon explored in some revealing and startling asides within Freud's essay 'Dostoyevsky and Parricide'. Freud found the causality of Dostoyevsky's compulsive habits in a particular variation of the Oedipus complex; it was a variation which probably plays a part in all our lives but it was one which, because of Dostoyevsky's particular experiences as an infant, had a shattering impact on his adult life. Freud emphasised how when the child is in his Oedipal phase – in intense rivalry with his father and resenting the father's possession of the mother – he not only has parricidal wishes against his 'rival' but simultaneously has the desire to be the father's love-object. This bisexuality, prompting the boy's wish to become both his mother's lover and to be taken by his father to displace the wife, can, in adverse external circumstances, bring about intolerable dilemmas which often reach into adulthood.

The boy fears that his wish to slay the father may bring him the retaliation of castration; at the same time he fears submission as a feminine love-object will bring about the same result. The ideal resolution of these dilemmas may never be possible, but most of us, from fear of castration, in the interests of preserving our masculinity, give up the wish to possess our mother and to slay the father, and confine both impulses – hatred of the father and being in love with the father – to the unconscious. There, albeit imperfectly, they remain repressed but still prompting in all of us a feeling of guilt and a need for expiation. Freud finds, however, that in those whose bisexual disposition has caused them especially to fear the consequences of their feminine attitudes, a pathogenic intensification of their feelings of guilt arises. In adulthood such boys are prone to attempt to relieve their guilt by placing themselves at the mercy of fate and demanding that it provides a means of resolving their impossible dilemmas.

For, in the Freudian view, gambling is in essence provocation of fate, forcing it to take decisions for or against the individual. With every throw of the dice, with every turn of the card, with every spin of the wheel, the question being asked over and over again reflects the earlier Oedipal dilemmas: am I omnipotent, able by my secret wishes to kill my father, and have I, if he is in fact dead, killed him? And simultaneously – since formal logic is not part of the unconscious – am I the beloved of my father? He loves me, he loves me not. If the gambler wins, he receives affirmative answers to all his questions. He is the killer and the beloved. But in either case he must pay the price of emasculation, a totally unacceptable and terrifying conclusion. So, to remain intact, the compulsive gambler never desists; he is determined to continue until he loses in order to survive. Only by losing does he gain relief from his guilt as killer and lover for then he obtains the punishment he deserves for his parricidal and incestuous wishes.

During the years that I observed my bookmaker client supplying these masochistic needs to thousands of customers, it was clear that although the punters, to maintain their psychic equilibrium, were determined to lose their money, the thrills that they had en route were sustaining them. Those joyless thrills were paralleled by Freud to masturbation. Indeed, Dostoyevsky himself described the tremulous excitement which losing afforded him and pointed out that the punishment of total loss at the end of a losing run led to orgasm. Thus the psychic masochist pursues his lonely path, producing pleasure out of displeasure. It is a solitary journey; onanism, as non-related fellatio, turns its back on human relationships. There is no more lonely and sadder place than the silent, crowded gambling room of a fashionable, luxuriously appointed London casino; to enter one is to enter a lavish mausoleum.

A man who is a victim of such a temperament can, away from the betting shop, displace his unconscious wish to lose; it can play a significant part in his working life. He may want to take risks that unconsciously he knows will lead to failure. One of the interesting but disquieting features of Cook's interest in horse racing is his disdain for flat racing – the National Hunt jump racing is his first love. 'I think jump jockeys are still the bravest people I know. To turn up every day and know that one in every ten races you are going to take a crashing fall is an amazing form of courage and commitment.' In the events that have taken place since his appointment as Foreign Secretary, to the dismay of his well-wishers, he seems to have been emulating his heroes on an off day, and be quite determined to ride for a fall. To the glee of his political opponents, who fear his intelligence and superior debating skills, one political blunder follows another. Sometimes his refusal, as he rides ahead, to see the most obvious dangers littering the course is an invitation to the inevitable disaster.

It is disquieting that, as we have become increasingly involved in the Balkans imbroglio, we have a risk-taking Foreign Secretary, too eager to gamble. With a reclusive and depressive Serbian leader emerging from a family haunted by a death-wish – both Milosevic's parents separately, and after an interval of some years, committed suicide – and with an American draft-dodging President endeavouring to overcome his pusillanimity by an over-determined display of bellicosity, to have in place a British Foreign Secretary with a temperament that is unconsciously attracted to hazardous decision-making, is discomfiting.

Lacking insight into his own masochism, Cook has been no less insensitive to that possessing Milosevic. Upon the Serbian psyche is embossed the legend of the heroic Prince Lazar, killed and defeated fighting against the Turks in the Battle of Kosovo in the fourteenth century. Milosevic identifies himself with Lazar, who has long assumed Christ-like proportions in Serbia's history and epic poetry. The sick attractions of defeat and martyrdom compounded the Kosovo tragedy, and although it would be extravagant to suggest that Cook's masochism matches that of a suicidal Milosevic, nevertheless I believe that the traits with which he is possessed may well taint his capacity to contribute to a resolution which could mitigate, not increase, the sufferings of the Balkans.

Although, unlike Blair, Cook is no historical illiterate, with his temperament totally overcoming his intelligence and his earlier social conditioning, he recklessly incited Europe and the United States of America to gamble upon victory in an unwinnable war, one that was illegal by any international rules of law, where the whole ritual of Western humanitarianism was a sham, a cover for the exploitation of foreign affairs for domestic ends. 'Humanitarian intervention,' Simon Jenkins commented in *The Times* in November 1999, 'is a code for political and military meddling in the internal affairs of sovereign states – and damn the consequences.' The losses sustained in this gamble in which Cook so enthusiastically participated should bring him a rare masochistic delight. 'What began as humanitarian action in Yugoslavia,' Simon Jenkins went on, 'has so far cost eleven billion dollars in warfare alone. A further $60 billion of cost (according to *The Economist* Intelligence Unit) has been inflicted by the NATO intervention; that does not include the blocking of the Danube. At the end more people are displaced than at the start. If the Balkans is the outcome of "not standing idly by", God stands for idleness.'

It has been urged that some of the troubles Cook has brought upon himself arise from mere peccadilloes and that the storms around his head are the puffings of humiliated opponents and, indeed, envious colleagues resenting his superior ability; unhappily, such an assessment is too often unsound. His conflict, for example, with the Select Committee on Foreign Affairs in the spring of 1999 revealed a purblindness on his part which I believe can only be fully explained in terms of this need to bring down hot coals upon his head. With a divided and ineffective Opposition in place, Select Committees have an especial place today to invigilate government departments and their chiefs. They can, as I am well aware from my own experience as chairman of a Select Committee, be an absolute necessity to curb the abuse of power and misdemeanours of the Executive. For a minister and his officials to collude with a fifth columnist informer on the Committee in order to subvert its uncomfortable findings is, in my book at least, an outrageous attack upon the principle of open government of which Cook was once a doughty exponent. That a man of Cook's wit should have placed himself in so vulnerable and foreseeable position, one which would, almost inevitably, be discovered, is not the mark of a fool or a wicked man; unconsciously, out of his own control, he invites his troubles.

Certainly his clear failure to live up to his firm initial declaration, on his appointment as Foreign Secretary, that henceforth Britain would follow an ethical foreign policy, a failure which was attacked so scathingly in August 1999 by the Select Committee on Foreign Affairs and described as 'deplorable, scandalous, and disgraceful', is an illustration of his penchant to invite political punishment. No less an example of this penchant, after he had in opposition enhanced his reputation by savagely attacking the Tories over a cover-up in the 'arms to Iraq' affair, was his issuing of a gagging order through the courts against a businessman when the previous gagging by the Tories against the same man had prompted him so vigorously to comment: 'None of these businessmen would have been convicted if ministers had not abused their power by placing gagging orders before the courts. Ministers must not be allowed to protect themselves from embarrassment at the expense of the course of justice.' I do not think this man, believed to be the most idealistic of politicians, has simply and suddenly turned cynical; Cook's voltes face which have so affronted his former admirers and attracted so much deserved criticism are, far more probably, the consequence of his failure to handle his own masochism.

There is indeed little qualitative difference between the masochism which cunningly finds expression in provoking political punishment and that which is assuaged by the blows of lost bets on a horse race. Before, however, bestowing pity on the tragic compulsive dilemmas of the addicted gambler, we should spare some for ourselves. The gambler is vividly uncovering for us the determinedly infantile experience which Freud spelled out as producing his psychopathology, but his drive is only a caricature of the motivational forces operating on all of us who are less avid players. Writing of these forces, Freud observed: 'Infantile reactions from the Oedipus complex such as these may disappear if reality gives them no nourishment.' Contrariwise, the appetite grows if they are well fed. It was my awareness of how easily our dormant passions may descend into grim self-destructiveness that caused me, during the passage of that Betting & Gaming Act of 1960, to want to make the betting shops that were being set up as austere as possible. I wanted them to lack the accoutrements, amenities and advertising displays that would lure customers into continuous betting and, not without some success, sought to have them nudged away into unattractive side streets. The oracular nature of gambling makes it as impossible to ban as prostitution. But, rightly, we do not encourage the siting of luxurious brothels in our High Streets, even though in some respects fornication may sometimes be a more maturational experience for the purchasing practitioner than gambling.

With Thatcher, in her privatisation zeal encouraging millions to play the market, inciting the nation into the belief that to hold a share certificate was to possess a winning lottery ticket, the change in the ethos governing the House was chasteningly illustrated in 1986 when all the wise restraints imposed in 1960 were, to the satisfaction of the national bookmakers supporting the Tory Party, swept away by way of a Statutory Instrument. The betting shops were given the right to become attractive centres with all amenities including television beamed in not just from the BBC and Channel Four, but also from a bookmaker-owned special satellite covering all the horse and greyhound racing meetings throughout the day. Now the working-class punters were spurred on by the accompanying excited commentaries into an orgy of gambling. The class battle had indeed been won: gambling in luxurious casinos was no longer to be the prerogative of the rich, and boys coming from the working or lower middle classes, like Norman Tebbit, could without any adverse comment move effortlessly from the chairmanship of the Conservative Party to the directorship of a company controlling one of the largest bookmaking chains in the country.

Nowadays, the way having been left open for the creation of a national lottery, each Saturday and Wednesday night the nation is glued to the television dreaming of the impossible lottery win. Is it really all harmless fun, or is it a morbid symptom of a decomposing society? Is not government by hazard, the determination of options and priorities by lottery not by considered rational choice or taxation, placing us in that same category of governments as we may place the Scythians, Turks, Ancient Germans and all those peoples whom we know from Ezekiel and Nebuchadnezzar were governed by various sorts of magic? Is it becoming that we enter the 21st century by following the example in Ancient Greece where people would flock to oracles to seek guidance in public affairs or by imitating the Romans who often had government by bibliomancy. The national lottery is a State proclamation, one institutionalising the same type of primitive thinking.

That this has come about tells how sparse are the moralists and rationalists in Parliament today, and how the risk-takers, always significant among politicians, have had their way. During the years I was in the Commons I was so often to learn that there were politicians who were compulsive risk-takers forever wooing failure, persistently gambling with fate, sometimes within the political arena, sometimes by way of a concealed but scandalous private life, sometimes by direct wagering, and sometimes by using all three routes to find their date with destiny. Of course, few have the political talents of a Charles James Fox, Britain's first Foreign Secretary and a forerunner of Robin Cook, who in the eighteenth century lost £140,000 in three years and, although an expert whist player who invariably won at the game, always preferred to play hazard, a game of pure chance, complaining that whist afforded him no excitement. Fox's tenure of office was, as one could anticipate from his psychological disposition, short-lived. He soon provoked his own resignation and spent the rest of his life as a loser, in Opposition – a condition which doubtless was more satisfying for him than enduring the penalties of success. There are always in the House of Commons not a few who continue the tradition of Fox's days when gambling was the principal activity of the political clubs.

Each of the two most weighty of Tory MPs whose talents I admired and with whom I had a stimulating relationship –

Reginald Maudling and Edward du Cann – nearly became Prime Ministers. Both, in turn, possessed by fantasies of obtaining vast wealth, recklessly gambled in doubtful financial adventures that brought about their political deaths. They, I believe, unconsciously courted their nemesis; but they only killed off their political aspirations. However, the greatest gambler of all those I encountered in the Commons, a man whose friendly overtures I mocked, was the disgusting, pitiful, impossible farceur, Robert Maxwell. He regularly wagered thousands of pounds of his own money, and of others, on the single spin of a roulette wheel and, predictably, could purge himself only by encompassing his own obliteration. No punishment he could inflict upon himself could suffice, short of actual death. He was no loss to the nation but the political death of a rare civilised politician like Maudling tells us how much a political party and the nation can lose when leaders, however brilliant, cannot free themselves from the coils of their own masochism.

It may appear over the top, and certainly it is spitting against the wind, to group the self-destructive gambling of the political leader, or the compulsive conduct of the punter haunting the betting shop, with that of a woman with a featureless life having a twice-a-week flutter of excitement by way of a couple of national lottery tickets. But the very financial success of the lottery indicates how easy it is to incite gambling and how it can pervade, as it has, the whole ethos of a society; within that ethos, in the spring of 2000, thousands of small investors were lured into the City casino to gamble their savings in disastrous dot com flotations. What, however, makes the national lottery so repellent is that by masquerading as a charity it seeks to disguise its role as an inciter to gain, greed and primitive thinking. It pollutes some of the most beautiful of the theological virtues than can enter into the language and the practice of secular politics – that of charity. The virtues of faith, hope and charity have a chronology and conjunction that is meaningful. Faith comes first, strong or weak, depending in the last analysis upon the quality of trust established by the mother ministering to the infant need; without faith, based on trust, there can be little hope, for, denied experience of good relationships in the past, there can be small expectation of a benign future. And, no less, without the experience of primal reciprocity, true charity, translated in the modern Bible as love – which gives, and hence receives – cannot be evoked.

If it be thought that I am extravagantly over-sensitive to forces, like the national lottery, that can sully those virtues, it is because I am aware, as were those contemporaries who joined me in delaying the lottery's coming, that these were the virtues which informed the early socialists who founded the British Labour, Trade Union and Co-Operative movements. Their inspirational strengths remain available to those with the courage to ignore the raillery of those who would expel affect wrapped in those virtues from politics. Impatient with and fearful of a delve into their emotions, they would reduce politics to a branch of arid economics and command that attention be given only to the ideational crust of politics. Their resultant discourses, with the emotions ebbed, high and dry, become banal doctrines or clichés. The politics of passion spurred on by the old virtues are of another order; and those who dare to practise them know that social movements take their whole shape and force, as the Labour Movement historically did, from their constitutive and binding affects.

The menace of our national lottery lies in its capacity to snap the conjunction between faith, hope and charity. True charity is not to be found imprinted upon national lottery tickets; we see it at its best on Red Nose Day, when all, children and adults in happy moods, know and feel that they are giving without hope of gain to a specific named charity with which they are establishing a life-enhancing reciprocity. The national lottery is draining this capacity to give and receive love. Tony Blair may chatter about creating a 'giving age' around the millennium but the reality is that the national lottery ensures that we are giving less. Individual donations have dramatically slumped; within the last four years the median monthly gift, ironing out the effect of big gifts, has slumped by over 50 per cent. Despite the expectations of an increase in private giving to mark the millennium, such donations still lag far behind levels of six years ago.

Those who legitimately claim that the national lottery has given considerable funding to many smaller charities entirely miss the point. My experience as chairman of a small charity taught me how significant is the direct link between a specified donor and a specified donee, and how the whole process is diminished if an anonymous intermediary comes between them. When the intermediary is inherently tainted with hopes of personal advantage, as is a national lottery player, an act of charity loses all its reciprocal capacity to reward giver and receiver. The old theological virtue of charity was not in place as a mere additive to the cement binding a society; it was the actual cement itself and Freud, always laying emphasis upon Eros as the force that could bind mankind, was repeating in secular terms an old truth. Now, in the national lottery, Thanatos insinuates himself among the intermediaries, ensuring that an act of charity, of love, can in our society be a corrosive not a coagulant.

Long ago Karl Marx demonstrated that money, by acting as the intermediary of exchange between people, can usurp the mediating activity of human social action, and so when man endows money with the role of intermediary between himself and others, he himself is an exile, a dehumanised being. Man alone, Marx insisted, should be the intermediary between men and by giving this function to money he makes himself a slave. In our fevered world of tipster foreign secretaries and national lotteries, Marx's admonition painfully resonates.

Labor or Amor?

Can we learn to love again? Or are we so enslaved by work and status, so desperate for acknowledgement of achievement, that love must be forfeited? Our libidinal energy is finite; Freud always reminded us that 'since man does not have unlimited quantities of psychic energy at his disposal, he has to accomplish his tasks by making an expedient distribution of his libido'. Lured by the baubles proffered by contemporary capitalism, have we fatally and irrevocably shifted our energies, withdrawn our investment in human relationships, and chosen to chase, narcissistically and frenetically, today's shoddy prizes – a pursuit which leaves us so drained that our sexuality can no longer flower into love but yields only half-hearted fucking, rutting and undemanding non-reciprocal fellatio and pornography?

In 1999, an investigation into attendances at private health clinics revealed that the sexual behaviour of so many people in economically successful regions was far more awry than in poorer areas, that high-flying businessmen might be big in the boardroom but were lost in the bedroom; that more than 90 per cent of the high-earners (those with incomes in the £80,000-£100,000 bracket) gave the same reason for their attendance – 'sexual difficulties'. A *Guardian* editorial sagely commented:

> ... sex is a litmus test for society's emotional health. Satisfactory sex means sufficient leisure time, physical intimacy, relaxation and

happiness. There is, then, a serious question here about the rationale for economic growth. If a successful economy depends on squashed leisure time, stressed-out workers and loss of sexual joy, maybe we should be asking: is it worth it?

The *Guardian* editorial question was tentative. The answer is unequivocal. The imbalances that can arise in society when the right to be lazy is denied, when indolence is deemed criminal, when the still Sunday is abolished, when work in itself becomes so extravagantly over-valued that the whole fabric of our welfare state is subverted as government harasses the disabled, the widows, the sick and the single mother, coercing them into employment, are contributing hugely to our present personal predicaments. When Freud discussed the significance of work for the economics of the libido, he claimed:

> No other technique for the conduct of life attaches the individual so firmly to reality as laying emphasis on work; for his work at least gives him a secure place in a portion of reality, in the human community. The possibility it offers of displacing a large amount of libidinal components, whether narcissistic, aggressive or even erotic...on to the human relations connected with it lends it a value by no means second to what it enjoys as something indispensable for the preservation and justification of existence in society...And yet, as a path to happiness, work is not highly prized by men. They do not strive after it as they do after other possibilities of satisfaction. The great majority of people only work under the stress of necessity, and this natural human aversion to work raises most difficult social problems.

Those social problems are today exacerbated. For the over-whelming majority the possibility of displacing in work a large amount of the aggressive and erotic-libidinal components diminishes; technology ensures that work becomes increasingly isolating, not binding, fraught with insecurities, increasingly fragmented, unrewarding, endured rather than enjoyed. In work our frustrations and consequent anger increases and inflames rather than displaces aggression, and the work is loveless.

Yet there can be no let-up. The mortgage must be paid, the car or cars must be gleaming, IKEA must be visited. Self-esteem is no longer gained by loving and being loved; work becomes the defining characteristic of social worth. From the tyranny of work there is little escape. There are no days of rest, no holy days, only holidays where the victims of this work cult, carrying mobile phones, laptops and pagers to lock them into their offices, desperately seek a temporary homeostasis through sex tours in Thailand, après-ski, with the emphasis on après, in St Moritz, or raves in Benidorm. There is time only for fucks and fellatio, not for love-making, for that would be too demanding, too selfless, requiring above all else the cultivation of intimacy.

Of course, there have been other eras besides our own when brutalised relationships widely prevailed. Classicists tell us that husbands of the ancient world rarely remained faithful, lavishing far more affection on young boys or on the prostitutes known as the hetaerae than on their wives. When men copulated with their wives they tended, apparently, to prefer anal intercourse, or coitus a tergo, vaginal penetration from behind. This arrangement precluded much intimacy during sex and certainly eliminated any facing contact between the participants: the men had a good view of their wives' buttocks, whereas the women looked at nothing whatsoever. One classical scholar, Professor Eva Keuls, has provided us with a compelling account of how much women suffered in a climate dominated by the figure of Zeus, a philandering scallywag whom Keuls has branded as a master rapist. Zeus has long since been dethroned and women are no longer ready to be so contemptuously marginalised. They would certainly be unlikely to tolerate a regime such as prevailed in Rome where, the historian Gibbon tells us, during the first two centuries of the Empire, only Claudius, of all the rulers, never cheated on his wives by taking a male lover to bed.

But the emancipation of today's women from such male domination is surely illusory, for they have exchanged an explicit master to become the bondswomen of more subtle manipulators. Technology, contemporary capitalism and its mercenaries, the advertising and media industries, together with many of the more militant feminists, have combined to ensure that they remain in service. Work has ensnared them. Now, with women outnumbering men in employment, 'liberation' has, for the vast majority of women living within an average family, meant low-paid, part-time jobs; they feel that to survive with self-respect they must maintain a lifestyle which makes a second wage imperative. These 'liberated' women are living within a tedious and stress-making ethos far removed from that depicted by the glossy magazine images of the successful working woman. Worse, far worse, so often they are following the destructive example of many a modern male who is diffident about parenthood but obsessive about work. So many of these women, aided by the pill, allow themselves to be tricked into the belief that work, not their capacity to mother and to love, defines their social worth, and their casual, undemanding promiscuities are an almost inevitable consequence of such false doctrines.

But after the nights of staccato sex and attendances at hen parties featuring male strippers, there is the morning after when they feel compelled to return to their joyless work, and that compulsion comes not only from economic necessity or social aspirations but also from guilt, a guilt which overhangs all humanity's relation to work, and which particular societal pressures can inflict, as it does today. For the derivation of work from the sin of Adam and Eve expresses a profound psychological truth: the expulsion from bountiful indolent Eden left mankind, in order to survive, condemned to work. As Emil Durkheim, the founding father of sociology, told us more than a century ago: 'Work is still for most men a punishment and a scourge.' Today that unconscious search for punishment by many of Britain's womenfolk, as they seek to expiate their guilt in the workplace, is exploited by a contemporary capitalism, not blind to their masochism, as never before. Many women are not 'free', libidinous swingers within a permissive society; they are victims, and in these godless days, with no institutions or beliefs in place to assist them, their burden is unrelieved.

Yet I have seen in my lifetime women who, far more successfully than so many of today's striving young women, dealt with the imperative that work imposes: they worked at home, not in office, shop or workshop. When I came to the Commons, in my constituency, then a coal-mining seat, women who worked outside the home were suspect, and acquiescent men who encouraged or accepted the notion of a working wife were despised by the mining community. But the influence of those 'mams' of the South Wales valleys was nevertheless all-pervasive – they were free of the self-doubts which afflict so many women today and who define their self-worth in quite different terms.

Without washing machines, dryers or dishwashers, without bathrooms or running hot water, they received into their spotless homes their menfolk from the deep pits. With no pit-head baths then in existence, the miners were covered with coal-dust and wives readily filled the tin baths and tenderly washed away the grime of toil. On Mondays, the wash days, the miner's wife spent her time at her scrubbing board and cheerfully hung out the clothes on the lines in the cramped backyard. But she certainly did not feel exploited or oppressed, for the division of the duties and responsibilities between husband and wife were unambiguously defined. She was the queen of the household and the treasurer. She had no need to engage in a battle for 'equality'. When pay-day came the miner came home from the pits and pushed his unopened wage packet into the apron pocket of his waiting wife, sitting outside the terraced home, and accepted without demur what she would then give back to him as pocket money; she managed the finances of the household.

In turn, the husband was totally kept out of the kitchen. Cooking and washing up were not within his province, but parenthood was most certainly shared. The macho miner, in between shifts while his wife was engaged in her considerable chores, would take the baby wrapped comfortingly around him in a shawl, Welsh fashion, and join his mates similarly encumbered at the street corners where, amidst their talk of whippets, rugby and local Lodge politics, the babies slumbered on. The carping within so many marriages today as to who should do what as overworked women return home to face fatigued husbands and domestic chores was unknown. There were, of course, drunken husbands and domestic violence marring the ideal of the family life prevailing in the coalfields. But community pressures and disapproval operated severely upon miscreants who did not conform.

It is no doubt possible to interpret the allocation of specific roles to the women of yesterday's South Wales valleys as a validation of the dogmatic insistence of militant feminists that most differences between men and women are culturally imposed.

But to conclude this would indeed be misleading and unhelpful in any search for combining the gains in opportunities made by women in recent years with a realistic respect for their distinctive sexual, familial and emotional lives.

The gender-feminists, who see women as a besieged political class united in hostility against males holding on to their patriarchal privileges and powers, predicate much of their theories on the basis that all women want to work away from their homes and that housebound mothers are frustrated women who want to be in paid employment even if they have young children but are denied their wish by lack of childcare facilities. But the miners' wives were not sullen, bitter women longing to break the 'chains' of domesticity. They did not wail against the inescapable fact that the woman bears the child and the man does not. Motherhood is regarded as a burden, if not a curse, by too many of the women in academia or journalism – women who enjoy to a considerable extent the luxury of controlling their time, working hours and energy, and often are in relationships with men who play the role of the so-called New Man because they themselves are in such occupations. Too often under the guise of equality, gender-feminists want to foist upon other women what is no more than their own chosen lifestyle.

I believe the overwhelming majority of women today have far more in common with the emotional responses and experiences enjoyed by the wives of the last generation of miners than with Islington woman boasting that she has a New Man in tow around the house. That her relationships often become fraught and lack durability is unsurprising, for most men, however much they consciously repudiate the norms of traditional male behaviour, are as keen to assume a role which is unconsciously felt as feminine as would be an agoraphobic to take a stroll from a space shuttle.

The tragedy is that the agenda of the gender-feminists runs through so much of current British welfare policy. It is certainly one of the galvanising forces behind the Blairite 'new deal' concept which, by incitement and coercion, augments our cheap part-time labour force and forces so many women out of the home into the willing maws of devouring employers. The vigorous analytical polemic of Melanie Phillips against Gordon Brown's 1998 budget, which enshrined Government policy, grasps the dangers of which our bachelor Chancellor seems blissfully unaware. Her conclusions on the thrust of the budget have weight:

> It collapses men's role as family breadwinner, which is to be imposed upon women instead, while mothers looking after their own children are to be devalued and discouraged...It will keep women dependent upon the State which now merely changes its role from surrogate male breadwinner to a new surrogate function as a female carer, looking after children while mothers are pushed out to work...The intention is precisely to undermine the male breadwinner and trash hands-on motherhood. Full-time mothering is now to be viewed with contempt...Women are to be manoeuvred into work even when they are nursing their babies... The State will pay strangers to look after children. This reflects the myth that children are generally better off in substitute care than with their families.

Phillips' general view is supported by the 1999 research findings of the Government's own Women's Unit, which told disconcerted ministers that women believe that mothers who want to stay at home to look after their children are not valued by New Labour. The findings certainly do not show approval for the heavy ministerial emphases placed on the work ethic as the foundation of a revived Welfare State, nor the acceptance of the Chancellor's repeated contention that work is the best route for women to take to gain self-reliance. Ministerial sources, wishing to quash any idea that government policies would be seriously modified by the findings, put out indignant denials that the Government would even consider paying women to stay at home or back a wages-for-housework campaign – and so placated the gender-feminists.

The fact is that the gender-feminists on the back benches supporting Government policies, making an apotheosis of work and, explicitly or implicitly, affirming that no woman can really be 'alive' without employment, are helping to create a destructive zeitgeist carrying the view that what Beveridge considered 'the vital unpaid service' of mothers caring for their own children is now of no value whatsoever. But what hope can there be of adults knowing how to love if their capacity for love is never awakened, if it was impaired by a conflict-ridden mother, doubtful of, if not despising, her own motherhood. It may well be that to ensure the perpetuation of the species there is imprinted on our genes a directional capacity driving us to copulation; but although we too belong to the animal kingdom, homo sapiens, to ensure the survival of the species, relies less on his genes than other animals, and it is only nurture, not nature, than can ensure that within sexual intercourse we know how to give and receive a mature love.

Our tutoring in that knowledge comes very early in life; it is at a time that nurturing, benignly or malignantly, can temper or distort our genetic endowment. Indeed, the more our cognitive, as distinct from our emotional, development is explored by the clinicians, as it has been so subtly by the British psychoanalyst Money-Kyrle, the more one has to acknowledge that in the first few months of an infant's life, the innate preconceptions with which we are endowed from the very first when, as it were, the auto-pilot takes the newborn babe to the nipple, there exists a vulnerability on the part of the baby, unless richly succoured, to form misconceptions which unconsciously persist into his adult sexual life. The conceptual differentiations between nipple, breast and mouth, between penis and nipple, between vagina, mouth and penis, if not established early can cause confusions that persist – as the analysands on the couch sometimes reveal – which can cause havoc in adult physical relationships. The proliferation of atactic modes of sexual expression like fellatio tell us of the failures of early mothering. Good mothering, for which there is no adequate substitute, marvellously guards us against the distortions which can so afflict us that we are never able to find full congruences in our intimacies.

It is fear of the intensity of such intimacies, entailing as they do the renunciation of so much of our narcissism, that gave us the ultimate absurdities in the 1999 Reith lectures given by Blair's guru Professor Anthony Giddens when we were told 'marriage was never in the past based upon intimacy', that romantic love is a modern invention and that 'what most of its defenders call the traditional family was in fact a late transitional phase in the family development in the 1950s'. Ferdinand Mount's stigmatisation of Giddens' sociology as 'negligent to the point of irresponsibility' is fully justified, as is his reminder to Giddens that some five centuries before the 1960s there was laid down in the marriage service of the *Book of Common Prayer* a paean to romantic love and an unblushing declaration of intimacy – both sexually and spiritually – as has ever been since composed. Marriage, it declares, is for the couple's 'mutual society, help and comfort'; they promise to love, honour and cherish each other 'for better for worse, for richer for poorer, in sickness and in health... with my body I thee worship'. It is a corollary of Giddens' wilful misreading of the past that he posits, as a replacement for the traditional family, what he calls 'a democracy of the emotions' in which we open up to one another and which would 'draw no distinction of principle between heterosexual and same-sex relationships'. The arena of personal life today, he reassures the promiscuous, is one of 'coupling' and 'uncoupling' rather than marriage and the family. Doubtless it is a reflection of his own predilections when he condones, if not incites, temporary liaisons and devalues permanency. The narcissistic professor is evidently frightened out of his wits of true commitment and would, in our 'couplings' have us behave, as Mount puts it, like 'ferrets or railway carriages'.

Such a philandering lifestyle harmonises with the rejoicing of the feminist tricoteuses of the so-called sexual revolution, applauding as they do the reduction still further of the shrivelled married couple's tax allowance and giving full support to Blairite Government intentions to re-engineer the family away from the model of children brought up within marriage to the model of the lone mother out at work while her children are cared for by the State. It is ironic that not a few of the young crusading women who have brought themselves into Parliament holding out hopes that their presence would bring a new sensibility into politics, acquiesce in this Blairite devaluation of mothering and the dismantling of the Welfare State, a welfare structure which itself was fundamentally a creation of the mothering, stay-at-home, non-crusading wives of yesteryear's South Wales' valleys. For although those wives did not overtly enter in any way into the Trade Union and political life of the little townships, and simply overwhelmingly voted as did their fathers and husbands, their influence as 'mams' was singularly persuasive in every facet of the policies which menfolk espoused.

That influence was not exercised by direct instruction; communication was not made by mere words. Within a culture well accustomed to the denunciations and diatribes of the offeriads and lay preachers of the chapel, eloquence was not rare and therefore was not over-valued; these wives were familiar with the pulpit histrionics of preachers who, with voices nicely tuned to crack with grief and passion, harangued racked congregations. So the women left their menfolk to their high-flown talk and let them soar to the stars in the miners' lodges, while they at home kept their feet well on the ground. In crises and strikes, their loyalty was absolute and supportive, but Mam, to a considerable extent, treated her men as chattering little boys and did not always regard their talk with high seriousness. Sceptical they may have been of rodomontade, and perilously near to infantilising their menfolk, but nevertheless the maternal values they possessed became encapsulated in their sons. When the hour struck and the Welfare State was born, it was Jim Griffiths, former President of the South Wales Miners, who brought to the House of Commons the legislation that set up the whole of our national insurance and industrial injury schemes and it was the South Wales ex-miner Nye Bevan who, despite Tory opposition, put through the Act creating the National Health Service.

Their intervention sang with love and maternal concern. Even as they were presenting their radical proposals, their gestures, body language and voices told of their mothers' biddings. James Griffiths, hand on hip, with feminine stance, was at the despatch box insisting on the passing of his legislation to support those maimed and unemployed, and out of the huge bulk of Nye Bevan's frame came a falsetto woman's voice rising ever more passionately as he insisted upon the need of care for the sick.

From their back benches there came total support, for the traditional Labour Party was essentially mother-orientated, even as the Tory Party, before it fell into total disarray, was essentially father-orientated. The Conservatives, until recent days, have been sternly authoritarian in mood, believing in an élite, at ease in a structured fag system, and in the Commons ready to accept the Whips' rule that would have been intolerable to a party more democratic and more sceptical of leadership principles. Contrariwise, the Labour Party was maternally concerned – the provider, the bountiful, the welfare party. Indeed, if a leader did evoke the image of the tyrannical father, all hell was let loose, for the rebellious temperaments which brought so many of my generation of Labour members into politics were then at once provoked. The Party is more at ease when its leaders are, or give the appearance of being, neutral; of being chairmen rather than leaders. That was Attlee's strength, and Gaitskell's weakness, in relation to the party; Wilson's colourlessness may explain in part the absence of effective rebellion against him during his premiership.

But today the gender confusions that envelop our society have permeated the two political parties, and the distinctions between them, correspondingly, have become smudged. Hague struggles to democratise his Party and finds himself out of kilter with the nostalgic yearnings of Party members for strong leadership, and meantime Blair in his Party ruthlessly pursues his efforts to impose consensus by diktat ensuring estrangement between himself and the rebellious Party activists. And whereas doughty women fighters of the traditional Labour Party like Barbara Castle continue to battle to their last breath to maintain the maternal welfare state, many of 'Blair's Babes', lacking confidence in the lineaments of their own femininity, ambivalent about advocating policies which would unashamedly reflect what traditionally has been held to be a woman's especial virtues, simply acquiesce to the Blair agenda, for protest may be interpreted as breaching their ideological feminist convictions that differences between man and woman are mere cultural constructs and should have no place in the determination of social policies. Such women can have no love-in with their electorates; that, for such women, would be demeaning. We cannot look to them to give birth, as the miners' wives did, to social legislation informed with love.

In itself, of course, social legislation cannot guarantee to us an endowment of love, but it can certainly create an environment in which it is more likely to flourish. It can, too, as we well know in the post-Thatcherite era, so pollute the climate of opinion that our couplings can be misshapen, or stunted and anaemic, for love does not grow but withers in the narcissistic society we have created. To prescribe conditions for love to be love to be attained would indeed be a pretentious, didactic exercise, but some of the obstacles to its attainment can with certainty be clearly identified.

Only political pusillanimity causes the acceptance of the
inevitability that leprous social sores must be passively endured as
the price of economic growth; there are alternative nascent
political agendas that could be thought through, and another
ethos than that prevailing come into existence. I am ever mindful
that although it took me almost a decade of failed efforts and a
punishing work programme to precipitate my 1967 legislation
that ended the criminality of homosexuality, and that it took a
similar span of years for me to achieve a fundamental legislative
change in 1969 to our barbarous divorce laws, and an even longer
span of campaigning to bring about the profound legislative
changes which for the first time ended children being treated as
property and gave them rights, in the end almost seismic changes
in public opinion were occasioned. What was heinous and
stigmatised became acceptable or sometimes, indeed, benign. In
terms of my own lifespan, the years spent crusading were of long
duration; in historical terms they were but a blink.

Perhaps today a new catalogue of stigmas should be drawn up and
emblazoned abroad and, against the tide, opprobrium should be
attached to modes of behaviour, now accepted or condoned or even
regarded with sneaking admiration, which maim the capacity of our
children to grow up to be loving adults. High on that charge-sheet
would be the absentee fathers of Britain. Each recent study of the
time given by fathers to their children reveals that it continues to
diminish, and now the stressed-out high-flyer is, on an average day,
spending as little as 15 minutes with his children. A sociological
report from Edinburgh University tells us that the majority of British
men are still enslaved by an office culture that regards the plea of
wanting to spend more time with their children as professional
vulnerability. What hope is there for the little girls when they grow
up to enjoy love when as children their fathers gave them such
perfunctory attention? A daughter's relationship with her father is
critical to the opening up wider horizons of difference in order that
she later can manage her intimate relationships with men. As family
therapists Pincus and Dare have written:

> The little girl needs to know that her father is a bit in love with her
> (just as the adolescent girl whose father feels absolutely no erotic
> interest in her cannot believe that anyone else could love her); a

little girl needs also to believe that her mother takes her seriously, as a rival to her father's affections; only so can she take herself and her own life seriously too.

And, for a son, the father can provide a role model in not only how to manage male aggression and power in and outside the family, but also how to bestow concern and support and love on another. The child needs the other parent to mediate, to avoid the suffocating and potentially manipulative closeness of the dyadic relationship with one parent. I have little doubt that, although it obviously cannot be statistically proven, that exclusive practising male homosexuality has increased in my lifetime, and that a major contributory cause of that increase is that so many boys have been brought up in what is in fact or in practice a one-parent family with no male model with whom they can identify.

Every child has the right to acquire the potential to enjoy fulfilled heterosexual relationship, and those feminists who, by advocating androgynous marriages blurring gender differences, or treating any stress of the values of permanent relationships within marriage as if it were a prim moralistic attack upon the unmarried or separated mother, are perpetrators of child abuse. Their propaganda helps to create conditions in which children, as adults, find they may only be able to participate in fixated homosexual relationships, lacking the options of hetereosexuality; this, self-evidently, is to diminish a child's possibility of future happiness; and to so acknowledge this disadvantage is in no way patronising committed gays but is affirming, when life is not easily lived for anyone, that in addition to social and legislative discrimination that the homosexual suffers, the gay has, by the nature of his condition, less possibility of gaining the happiness fuelled by that enduring love which for most of us, though rarely experienced, is at least potentially available.

Apparently endemic to the homosexual condition is the great divide between affectivity and sexuality caused, Michael Pollak tells us, by 'the lack of social and material cement that tends to make hetereosexual relationships last'. Drawing on the American research of Bell and Weinberg, Pollak asserts:

Often based only on the sexual act, a pair relationship rarely stands up to the test of time. Seldom lasting more than two years, it is often bedevilled from the start by dramas, anguish and infidelity. Faced with the example of the hetereosexual norm and without any real life-pattern of its own, the pair relationship still remains the deep-felt ideal in spite of successive and almost inevitable setbacks. How can sexual impulses stimulated by the existence of a highly accessible and almost inexhaustible market be reconciled with the sentimental idea of the stable relationship? This is the commonest problem that homosexuals who contact sexual and psychological consultants hope to solve.

Pollak may be excessively pessimistic, for lasting and enriching relationships between homosexuals most certainly do exist, although it may well be that the ideal of physical fidelity which governs the permanent heterosexual relationship – albeit so often in practice unobserved – does not belong to the homosexual world. But those living within that world, even although so many bravely and productively overcome the accompanying difficulties, so often have a tough fate, one which even the most liberal of parents would not deliberately choose for their children. To advocate as a model for future family relations to replace the traditional nuclear family, a model which insists upon gender symmetry and not gender difference, is irresponsible for it is an invitation to increase the incidence of adult homosexuality. It means the infliction upon children of an upbringing which can condemn them as adults to burdens, not least of which may be that their yearnings for a partner will be forever anguished by an antithesis of the loving couple ideal and the turbulence of the social market.

Such considerations never enter into the gender-feminist propaganda. The nineties have been malevolently influenced by views such as those set out in a notorious pamphlet written by Harriet Harman who, for a mercifully short time, was Secretary of State for Social Security and Minister for Women, a woman whom in the Commons I found possessed a conceit matching her obtuseness, and Patricia Hewitt, who became Economic Secretary to the Treasury in the summer of 1999. The notion that the prime and essential role of a father was to provide his sons with a separate model of confident and caring masculinity, and to ensure that the little ones had a clear window to an outside world, is not entertained; they opine that 'it is essential for men to change their role in the household and do more of the unpaid work' so that there may be an end to the 'separate spheres model of family life'. Confidently they assert that 'it cannot be … assumed that men are bound to be an asset to family life, or that the presence of fathers in families is necessarily a means to social harmony and cohesion'.

Such an approach reveals a compulsive need for total autonomy; for these women inter-dependence means, as they explicitly declare, 'equivalent skills status and power' – and how meanly they measure the distribution to ensure they never give one iota more than they receive. Not for them the observance of Goethe's adage: 'Give up what thou hast for then thou shalt receive'. Their approach to male-female relationships is worthy of cheating hucksters in the marketplace, and what they are selling is, as Melanie Phillips has challengingly asserted, indeed 'a programme for equality on female terms alone'. And thus wrapped up in their ideology, they would seek to hide their fears, for they lack the courage to let go lest it leads to dependence upon another; trusting neither themselves nor the other, they are perforce illiterates in the land of love.

But where they wreak the most havoc is in their marginalisation of the man within the family, in their minimising of the especial role of the man as father and their insistence that he must be a surrogate mother. Paradoxically, their approach fully accommodates the curmudgeonly resistance of New Labour to the EU Directives on working hours, and nowhere is this more clearly seen than in their failure to protest against the refusal of Blair's government to agree to give paid paternity leave. They can hardly demur while they continue to depreciate the significance of man as father that, unlike the rest of Europe, here it is intended to be unpaid. Such a deterrent to leave no doubt accommodates the Institute of Directors who, sheltering behind the genuine difficulties of the small employers, have, in the interests of the large employers, described the proposed curmudgeonly granted right to paternity leave as 'highly disruptive'. For it offends the employer's basic premise, that work, the profit-creator, must govern our humanity. And so it comes about again that the muddled thinking of the gender-feminists and the preoccupations of a government making 'flexible labour' the prerequisite to its attainment of the holy grail of yet more economic growth create a climate within the family unit where children growing up are unlikely to be tutored in the art of being loving spouses and parents.

The sad acknowledgement made during a July 1999 survey by more than one-third of 2,000 senior managers that they 'felt stressed' if they were not constantly under pressure at work, since they feared a lightening of their workload meant that they were 'no longer needed', tells us of men who evidently feel dispensable at home and turn for solace to work – their compensation for lack of domestic love. Work, not a woman, becomes their addiction and employers, the report tells us, have to force them to go on holiday, surely a very doubtful therapy. These men, doubtless, are among the million whom another report, that in August 1999 of the Institute of Personnel, describes as working on average 60 hours a week and who acknowledge they are addicted to their jobs. Among the afflicted senior managers one is unlikely to find much sympathy for the Government launch in the autumn of 1999 of a campaign to persuade employers to facilitate the granting of more breaks and holidays for their employees so that they may see more of their families. The managers may, however, take some comfort from the fact that the Government, fascinated by the economic theorists that tell them that Britain's flexible hours is the key to a superior performance over our continental neighbours, is to fund a Task Force manned by representatives of big business which will be 'expected to convince employers that there is a strong business case to be made for flexible working and that it should not be aimed simply at making life easier for "mothers and their children"'. More, lest there should be any misunderstanding, Margaret Hodge, Minister for Employment and Equal Opportunities, explicitly affirmed that 'the aim of the campaign is not to make people work less' and, echoing her reassurance, the banker appointed by the Government to lead the Task Force told how his company 'had saved £2,000,000 a year by having practices that enabled more women to get back to work after having children'.

But those of us retaining the core values of our socialist youth loathe the meanness and unimaginativeness of a defeatist Government making to capitalism obeisances of this order, for, from the moment of its creation, the dynamic behind the international Labour movement was the ever-present demand for a shorter working week and the emancipation from the tyranny of work. Always there was a yearning for leisure and the millennarian belief that within that leisure love could flourish, not least in the form of the brotherhood of man. When the International Socialist Congress of 1889 met, they designated 1 May as 'International Labour Day' on which, in meetings and in marches, workers in all lands could demonstrate, demand that labour not be exploited, and insist upon a shorter working week. In Britain it was left to Michael Foot when Leader of the House to implement the century-old demand that May Day should be a statutory holiday but, evoking as it did the demand for fewer working hours, the Tories shifted the day so that it had no international chimes, and disconnected it from its original purpose – to make explicit a bonding of workers everywhere, united in an affirmation that work and capital must be subordinate to the needs of humanity. Now it has become just another trivial and meaningless Bank Holiday.

But across the Channel, the French have not forgotten the call of the early socialists who put life before work, and refused to accept the canons of dehumanising capitalism. There, as the *Guardian*'s European correspondent has recently reported, the French 'reject Tony Blair's "flexibility" (the very word makes them spit) for fear of cutting leisure hours by stealth'. The prime minister Lionel Jospin has been paying homage to my favourite Marxist, Karl Marx's coruscating wilful Cuban son-in-law, Paul Lafargue, the handsome bon viveur who shone out among his grey, serious comrades and so often exasperated them. In my teens, when I was working long hours in a factory where no paid holidays were formally granted, I revelled in my first encounter with his book *The Right to be Lazy*, where he presented his vision of a socialist society in which workers would man their machines for three hours a day leaving 'the rest of the day and night to do absolutely nothing and banquet copiously', fainéanter et bombancer. There was to be plenty of time available for love in Lafargue's Utopia.

And I recall my delight when, in France's first Socialist-led Government of 1936, the prime minister Léon Blum, himself a notable author of a book on love, took up Lafargue's gospel and introduced a 40-hour week and a fortnight's paid leave. Nostalgically and with pride, Mitterand's administration in 1981, inspired by Lafargue and Blum, defied the French capitalists and raised the holiday quota to five weeks, lowered retirement age to 60 and introduced the 39-hour week. Now Jospin is to add to the range of France's unique public breaks, like Armistice Day and VE Day, the bounty of a 35-hour working week from the year 2000.

Work, it must be acknowledged, can, although less than yesteryear, provide us, as Freud has put it, 'with a secure place in a portion of reality in the human community', but a balance needs to be struck between work and leisure. The current imbalance, which the French appear to be attempting to redress, is leaving us emotionally distraught, as contemporary capitalism increasingly creates a culture that incites us to measure ourselves entirely in terms of work achievement, and this at a time when, for most, work is becoming dead and mechanical and leaving us lonely in workplace or office.

To enjoy working as do so many in the embellishment, with the aid of B&Q, of our homes, is an experience which we lack in our daily employment; but the adjustment necessary to mitigate the pains of our working lives subvert the foundations upon which modern capitalism, and containers of its values, like New Labour, rest. That is why in Britain the French challenge is being met with spurious and dire prophecies coming from within government, the City and major employers – that Jospin's 35-hour week will wreck competitiveness in the world's fifth richest nation, taking along with it the Euro and the Western Continent's political ambitions. The reactionary forces, in and out of France, that brought down Blum's government and more recently, in March 1999, succeeded in the removal of the German Finance Minister Oskar Lafontaine who shared Jospin's aspirations, are once more on the move, but this time their sabotaging efforts will not necessarily succeed. Despite the leisure already enjoyed by French employees, and despite the handicap of an uncomfortable unemployment rate, France has achieved high productivity, a healthy balance of trade, non-existent inflation, scientific innovation and a splurge of inward foreign investment.

With the ruthless leisure industry and shoddy television services lying in wait to exploit our free time, there is certainly no guarantee that increased leisure in itself can give love the chance that it is presently denied, that it can give elbow-room, free us from the constrictive embrace which squeezes the life out of us, leaving us so drained that we lack the libido to give and receive from another. And the assertion of the overwhelming need for unhurried leisure to which work must take second place means that we could abandon the destructive notion that our worth as human beings depends upon our capacity to stay on a treadmill; perchance government may begin to acknowledge that its role is to strive to create the conditions in which citizens may enjoy not the bitter-sweet fruits of economic growth but, rather, the wondrous produce of emotional growth.

At present Britain has the longest working hours in Europe, an average of 44 hours a week compared with 38.8 in Italy and 40.5 in the EU as a whole. The Rowntree Foundation report of August 1999 tells us, yet again, how miserable we are in our work. The report concluded:

> In the short term this drive to reduce costs and/or increase profits has intensified work and may well have increased 'efficiency' but in the long term the forces that are driving Britain's industry have worrying implications for...the health of Britain's social environment...We need to change the rules by which dominant stake-holders (in the private and public sectors) are controlling employment if we take seriously the quality of our working and family lives.

As a schoolboy I attended a run-down, fund-starved secondary school; in its vain struggle to match the status of the nearby fee-paying school, although drawing back from insisting we wore a school blazer which was well beyond the means of most of the impoverished parents, it required that we always wore the school cap. Upon the cap was woven the austere school motto 'Labor omnia vincit'. I hated then wearing a cap which taught that work conquered everything; it peddled a lie. Would that I then wore a cap which all little boys should now be wearing – it would carry the motto 'Amor omnia vincit'.

What is Love?

We should not concede that love has irrevocably slipped away, that triumphant modern capitalism dooms us without hope to a loveless sex, where the ejaculation or orgasm of the copulating couple only corroborates, not mitigates, their essential aloneness. There have been other times when there have been massive changes in the ethos of society, sometimes caused by shifts in governance, in religious beliefs, and often by painters and poets, which have resulted in social norms encouraging the pursuit of the holistic platonic ideal, that have opened the door to 'the force which calls back the halves of our original nature; it tries to make one out of two and heal the wound of human nature'. That force, Freud, following Plato, called Eros.

One such shift came with the emergence of 'courtly love' which Sheila Sullivan includes in her recent illuminating survey of Western literary movements which challenged their society's stereotypes of love and both altered and reflected contemporary attitudes to love and sex. From the twelfth-century troubadours in a flowering of lyric verse, came the cult of 'Fin'amors' and its 'code' of adultery which celebrated love by turning a new rapt attention inward, to individual experience, and helped re-humanise the former crudity of dominance and sex. By encouraging sensitivity, it took men nearer to the holistic ideal, giving as it did some release to man's feminine aspects. It may not contradict Sullivan's proposition if one stresses that the release of

148

which she writes was of unsatisfied homoeroticism demanding to be satisfied. The explanation of 'chivalry', with its exaggerated and often visibly affected adoration of women, surely lies in the phenomenon described as 'compulsive heterosexuality', the man's affective displacement of a man's attraction to a man to a woman. In order to free themselves from their attraction to men, chilvaric knights became the slaves of women.

The love songs that troubadours sang were hearkened to by Dante, Petrarch and, a little later, Chaucer, who began the long task of liberating love from the oppression of property and hence to help bring about the existence of the then new notion that marriage could take place for love, not money. As illustration, Sullivan cites the lovers' charter, Pope Alexander's 1215 decree, that marriage was 'valid through the free consent of the spouses' no longer requiring parental consent. Lovers were permitted to love and not necessarily to submit to their relationships being governed or outlawed by dynastic and property considerations.

We can too take courage and comfort from other historical precedents, periods when emotional life evaded the prevailing stern and stifling societal injunctions. One such time was the late seventeenth to eighteenth century, where the social historian Lawrence Stone places his 'affective individualism', the first acceptance of the 'close, affectionate nuclear family based on free choice and the domestication of love'. It was the period during which powerful advocates emerged of the cult of 'sensibility'. A softer attitude, a new respect for gentleness, a new emphasis, as Sullivan puts it, on the 'coeur sensible', and on the value of the emotions, expressed in words, deeds and fears. These were moods reflected in the work of writers like Richardson and Sterne. It was an influential cult that encouraged men to exhibit some of the 'feminine' qualities rejected by the patriarchal gender role.

And there was the time, much nearer to us, of the Romantic Movement – the time when Keats would affirm 'I am certain of nothing but the holiness of the heart's affection...' The high priest of the Romantic Movement, Shelley, albeit no exemplar of the high ideals he preached, elevated sexual love into a creative experience of better physical sanctity: 'sex-love was to be the redeemer of humanity, transforming sexuality, and leading to transcendence and intimations of eternity.' And with Byron forever seeking, although unsuccessfully, to negotiate on behalf of Eros against Thanatos's melancholy lures of incest and death, we saw the apogee of a movement that defied the shibboleths of traditional values gutting man's emotional life.

No doubt, in our current materialistic and cynical mood, we can mock these movements as unrealistic, treat them as the vapourings of delayed adolescence, subversive posturings or defiances of adult order; or we can patronise their claims as elaborate rationalisations and justifications, wrestling performances grappling with guilt induced by original sin. But we need to hesitate before concluding that they have manically overloaded sexual union with individual and social significances which it cannot possibly bear. Such assessments may only be advertisements of our own failures of imagination, our timidity, our fear of the consequences if we trigger off the full potential available to us lest the resulting explosion brings to an end the mean configuration within which we and our politics dwell.

There are works, from the East as well as the West, which woo us away from our acceptances that rutting and fumbling into tumescence are equivalences to sexual union. *The Kama Sutra*, no sex manual, is perhaps the supreme example of such persuasiveness, teaching us how niggardly one-dimensional sex is, and telling us that even Karma – 'the enjoyment by the five senses assisted by the mind together with the soul' – is by itself no route to happiness. That requires the additional practices of sanctification, Dharma, obedience to the command of the Holy Writ, and of Artha, the acquisition of arts and friends as well as of property. The ideal is the practice of all three which results in happiness both in this world and the next; but if this is too demanding for practitioners, nevertheless the warning is that 'an action which is conducive to the practice of one of them at the expense of the remaining two should not be performed'. That prohibition is nowadays blatantly ignored as economic growth, money and property are so singlemindedly assumed; in the resulting balance there is no place for Karma. Bliss is denied us, here and hereafter, and happiness postponed for ever.

When we limp, cursed by our lopsidedness, each step taking us further away from, not towards, happiness, we desperately need guides distilling this Eastern wisdom in Western idiom, able to redirect us. None can excel that bequeathed by Stendhal. His nineteenth century novels are still avidly read, but the book which he always considered his principal work, his two-volume *De L'Amour*, in which with such extraordinary subtlety he explores what he describes as the science of happiness, remains almost as neglected today as it was when first published, and probably for similar reasons. For this work on love – given to me some 30 years ago by that great romantic, Michael Foot – is prefaced by counselling that it should be left unread by those so chronically addicted to pelf and place that they are beyond understanding the sentiment it expresses:

> The active, hardworking, eminently respectable and positive life of a Privy Councillor, a textile manufacturer, or a clever banker reaps its reward in wealth but not in tender sensations. Little by little the hearts of these gentlemen ossify; things positive and useful posses them utterly, and they lose the capacity for that sentiment which, above all, requires leisure...

And mocking those whose unhappiness was sordid, he said because they did not know the unhappiness that love could bring, they would never know enriching happiness:

> If you have never experienced an unhappiness beyond worry over a lawsuit, failure to be elected a Deputy at the last election, or not being witty enough when you were taking the waters at Aix last season, then...this book will rouse your anger against its author, for it will make you suspect that there is a certain kind of happiness you do not know...

And the triumph of Stendhal is that, even in his whole searching study of the various stages in love that have to be endured or overcome to reach happiness, he never allows the analysis to be coldly calculating; always it is suffused with affect, with the unspoken personal dilemmas which had precipitated and sustained this work written over decades. This is why he lays it down that no-one who could not answer 'yes' to the question 'Have six months of your life ever been made miserable by love?' qualifies as a fit reader of his work.

It was only amour-passion, intense, romantic, often unrequited and perhaps impossible to requite, that was worthy of the name of love. Stendhal did not despise sex, amour-physique, of which in his lifetime he had his fill, but in this work he puts it firmly in its place:

> Although physical pleasure, being natural, is known to all, it is only of secondary importance to sensitive passionate people. If such people are divided in drawing-rooms or made unhappy by the intrigues of the worldly, they possess in compensation a knowledge of pleasures utterly inaccessible to those moved only by vanity or money.

The love of which Stendhal spoke was:

> ...like the heavenly phenomenon known as the Milky Way, a shining mass made of millions of little stars, many of them nebulae. Four or five hundred of the small successive feelings – so difficult to recognise – that go to make up love have been noted in books, but only the most obvious ones are there.

The cluster of emotions, with all their refinements and nuances, to which Stendhal draws our attention, was certainly not one of the 'obvious' ones; he was proclaiming 'the raptures of passionate love which practically efface the memories of bodily delights'. The enemy of this amour-passion was the vanity-love of the French bourgeoisie of his day, whose obsession with status and money was stifling true love. In vanity-love, the 'hierarchical principles' ruled. The higher the social status of the captured lover or mistress, the most the 'insipid relationship' could yield was:

> ...physical pleasure going with habit. A semblance of love; there is the pricking at your pride and the sadness and satisfaction; the atmosphere of romantic fiction clutches you by the throat, and you believe yourself lovesick and melancholy, for vanity will always pretend to be grand passion.

For Stendhal the power of love, if its potential was not choked by the vanities of the prevailing social mores, was boundless. Even death could not conquer love; on the contrary, love was not terrorised by its threat:

True love makes the thought of death frequent, easy, without terrors; it becomes merely a standard of comparison, the price one would pay for many things.

And from the disconcerting hotchpotch of this book's analyses and anecdotes, argument, apothegms and poetry, there emerges a piercing criticism of the affectations of the bourgeois society, where no duchess exceeded the age of 30, where there was no danger in leaving a girl alone with a handsome stranger for she would be thinking of nothing but the income of her future husband; and envy, in the world Stendhal hated, stirred by a corrosive competitiveness leading to all constantly matching themselves against the other, tainted all emotions and behaviour.

Many people, although inquisitive, are shocked at hearing news for they fear to feel inferior to the person informing them.

All the stripping by Stendhal of the artificiality and artifices of the meretricious bourgeois world is part of his overriding quest to find happiness which, like unhappiness – as Stendhal the master of understanding of ambivalence put it – could be found in true love. As Jean Stewart writes in an introduction to *Love*:

Happiness is a key word with Stendhal. He sought it unremittingly, not mere pleasure or the satisfaction of desires, but a rapture accessible only to natures of rare quality... the light that comes from intense feeling, lucid awareness, passion and energy; the happiness of reverie, of response to beauty, of the free imagination – and such happiness he found in loving, even without return.

The resonances today which Stendhal occasions come because we have fallen into the same trap as that set by the society of his day. We too, seduced by gee-gaws of modern capitalism and rushing frenetically through our lives, have no time for

the pleasure of indulging the soul as one lies languidly upon a divan, a pleasure inconceivable to those who rush about all day on horseback.

Or, indeed, in planes and Jaguars.

These people would die of boredom upon a divan. There is nothing in their souls for them to reflect upon.

For such people, their lot is jet-lag and being jerked off; there is no time for genuine love-making.

But there is a further reason why Stendhal speaks to us today, spurring us to raise our sights from the trough, and to love. He senses that although he may be striving to exorcise the 'madness' of love, he know he cannot kill it by dissection, that his telling is no arid didactic exercise, no resiling from a romantic belief in its magic capacities to take us in and out of despondency and yet keep us on course for happiness. In short, he gives us hope and, because above the hum of his whirling cerebrations we hear the beatings of his heart, we believe that, realistically, his ideal of love is attainable:

> I am trying extremely hard to be dry. My heart thinks it has so much to say, but I try to keep it quiet. I am continually beset by the fear that I may have expressed only a sigh where I thought I was stating a truth.

Stendhal's productive and essentially hermeneutic meditation contains a warning: if we are to create in today's conditions the political ecology within which authentic love can flourish, we need mentors and leadership that have more resource than the computer. Cerebrally, we shall never even discover the nature of the healing love which our fractured society so desperately needs. The required balm is to be found neither in counterfeit love-making, in promiscuous fellatio, in the acting out of the pornographic fantasies enveloping our video and television screen, nor, as now seems fashionable, in more subtle retreats from genital sex by way of dissecting intellectual dissertations like that of the philosopher Wilham Dilman who, in his 1998 work *Love*, would seek to persuade us that Freud is mistaken – that love can have an identity totally independent of sexuality.

These over-intellectualised dissertations are heirs to the pontifications on the nature of love made by Leonardo da Vinci, who provided us with a key to his own nature but not to the nature of love when he averred:

nessuna cosa si può amare nè odiare, se prima non si ha cognition di quella (one has no right to love or hate anything if one has not acquired a thorough knowledge of its nature)... For in truth great love springs from great knowledge of the beloved object, and if you know it but little you'll be able to love it only a little or not at all...

Leonardo's assertion is obviously false. As Freud has commented:

It is not true that human beings delay loving or hating until they have studied and become familiar with the nature of the object to which these affects apply. On the contrary they love impulsively, for emotional motives which have nothing to do with knowledge, and whose operation is at most weakened by reflection and consideration. Leonardo, then, could only have meant that the love practised by human beings was not of the proper and unobjectionable kind; one should love in such a way as to hold back the affect, subject it to the process of reflection and only let it take its course when it has stood up to the test of fault... And in his case it really seems to have been so. His affects were controlled and subjected to the instinct for research; he did not love and hate, but asked himself about the origin and significance of what he was to love or hate... In reality Leonardo was not void of passion; he did not lack the divine spark which is indirectly the driving force – il primo motore – behind all human activity; he had merely converted his passion into a thirst for knowledge; he then applied himself to investigation with the persistence, constancy and penetration which is derived from passion...

He was, consequently, left for all the latter portion of his life sexless. Cerebral knowledge alone will certainly not tell us of the potential love of which human beings may be capable and which particular societal conditions may quench or, alternatively, tease out. It may be more rewarding to take a more hermeneutic approach, taking account of the irrational and acknowledging how various true love can be, whether it be that of a young man and woman, or the Darby and Joan love of an old couple who have shared so many tribulations, children and joys, or indeed the love across generations which is now being described as the May-December love, one which may not necessarily be as mercenary as the cynical would have us believe. Robert Burton, in his *Anatomy of Melancholy* spoke truly when he told us, 'Love's limits are ample and great, and a spacious walk it hath...'

No incorrigible agitator, as I have been all my life, always possessed by the conceit that many of the world's ails can be soothed and much of society's unhappiness alleviated, can offer a political prescription accommodating a rare genius like Leonardo, or, indeed, a prescription sufficiently capacious to embrace the very small minority who can and do turn away from fully sensual love to aim-inhibited love – to those, as Freud has it, fond of:

> ...making themselves independent of the object's acquiescence by displacing what they mainly value from being loved on to loving; they protect themselves against the love of the object by directing their love not to single objects but to all men alike; and they avoid the uncertainties and disappointments of genital love by turning away from its sexual aims and transforming the instinct into an impulse with an inhibited aim. What they bring about in themselves in this way is a state of evenly suspended steadfast affection, affectionate feeling which has little external resemblance any more to the strong agitations of genital love from which it is nevertheless devised.

That may be achievable by the St Francises of this world. However, renunciation of genital sex is unappealing to me, as I am sure it would have been to those on the electoral roll of my constituency. My electors were possessed of the same human frailties as I am, and for them, as for me, happiness was possible only if sensual love was their central value.

Now that we are in the millennium year, I am told that I may claim to having sponsored in the twentieth century more Private Member Bills than any other MP. All those Acts impinged upon human relationships, and all were largely put in place because of my belief that politics is the art of the impossible, not the possible; but there is a difference between the delusionary goal, and the impossible one. To accord to passionate love the seemingly impossible potential with which Stendhal endows it can be inspirational; it can move us to fulfilment. Few can find that in renunciation; and none of us can find it in the ugly discourtesies that our society is now heaping upon sensual love.

Legislating for Happiness

Any Government which becomes destructive of man's inalienable right to the pursuit of happiness should be abolished. This was stated, without equivocation or qualification, by Jefferson in his blunt credo subscribed to by the 13 former colonies which were to become the United States of America. For the signatories to the 1776 Declaration of Independence, the right was sacramental, and its breach by any Government blasphemous

> ...We hold these truths to be self-evident, that all men are created equal, that they are endowed by their Creator with certain unalienable Rights, that among these are Life, Liberty and the pursuit of Happiness...That whenever any Form of Government becomes destructive of these ends, it is the Right of the People to alter or to abolish it, and to institute new Government, laying its foundation on such principles and organizing its powers in such form, as to them shall seem most likely to effect their Safety and Happiness.

Was there ever a more arrogant political assertion than that the prime duty of the State was to safeguard the rights of its citizens to pursue happiness? It pre-supposes that Governments have the capacity to define happiness and to know the route by which it may be reached; how otherwise could Government protect what it declares to be so fundamental a right? The Declaration of Independence is the most unashamed and eloquent advocacy of the duty of Government to protectively intervene into the most delicate of human relations.

It is, of course, scandalous, unnerving to all those public schoolboy political leaders who, carrying forward into adulthood the ambivalence they have to their own nannies – carers not known to most of us – have persuaded us that 'interventionism' is a scabrous word and a 'Nanny State' an abomination.

The paradox of the Declaration of Independence is that it declares freedom from the mother country but, like most adolescent responses, when worked through, leads to the assumption in adulthood of the very parental role which had been violently rejected. Since perhaps the signatories to the manifesto had been as ill-served as infants as they were by the king-father, their sustained private and public protests may have been congruent. Their assertion that happiness was the required gift that governments must seek to bestow was a pledge that they would do better than their parents: would give the love, which probably privately had been denied to them, and which had certainly been denied to them publicly by George III: they had divined that without love happiness is a quarry that can only be fruitlessly pursued.

Today no political party would have the courage or imagination to advertise in their declarations of intent a promise to create or maintain the conditions which could spur us on to pursue happiness. We are incited to pursue more 'realistic' goals – to work hard, to make money, to be rewarded with ever-growing economic wealth – and yet another penny off the income tax, to enable us to gorge ourselves further with consumer goods and let the children of a huge under-class go to hell and sink schools.

No-one should instruct or lead the electorate; that would be unpardonable, élitist behaviour, and government must be by referendum and focus groups. The legislators must be reduced to a seismograph registering the passive caprices and prejudices of the majority. Social engineering is to be regarded not merely as a politically incorrect peccadillo, but as Satan's work, invariably performed by bureaucrats, arrogantly interfering with our chosen modes of living.

And so we applaud leaders who, shirking the responsibility of decision-making, leave the difficult choice of entering the ERM to my good feather-brained barber and the sweet girl at the check-out desk of my local supermarket, shed the burdens of overseeing our utilities, give back the Bank of England to the Bank, and distance themselves even from their own departments by the creation of 'special advisers'. The gospel of privatisation, with all its accompanying pseudo-epigrapha, pervades our political scene and ensures that no busybody pointing the way to happiness is available; and, unsurprisingly and consequently, we have lost our way.

Yet now, in the late autumn of my life, when I muse upon the legislative changes for which I must take a large measure of personal responsibility, the one that was the most outrageous, the one that intervened into the very heart of family life, was the one that I can most confidently assert added to the capacity of hundreds of thousands to enjoy a happier life.

It was a reform, when its legislative implementation was imminent, that caused Jim Callaghan, a complex man too often regarded as simply another cynical opportunist politician, to write to me, over-generously and spontaneously: 'This is another reform that your own activity and zeal has been largely responsible for. You will have a wonderful collection of worthwhile scalps under your belt before you finish. And you do much more good in terms of human happiness than 90 per cent of the work done in Parliament on what are called "political issues".' And it was this reforming Act that in 1999 attracted this verdict from an All Souls' former Law Commissioner, lawyer and legal historian: 'The Act is a landmark in twentieth-century child law...the Act has stood the test of time.'

To proffer such testament to the Children Act of 1975 may be interpreted as a distasteful boast but I hope that acknowledgement of other motivations will be granted and so mitigate a condemnatory judgement. For the Act stands as a paradigm for all – few though they may be these days – who, when auditing legislation, first ask, is it a mere response to a present abuse or is it that most difficult of political arts, prevention of abuse, and who will then ask, does it add to or detract from the potentiality for happiness within our society?

I deprecate the usual political methods of exhortation and coercion, methods which assume the role of politics is to solve the conflicts when they have happened. Rarely do political demands which spring from such techniques produce permanent reduction in the tension level of society; the ideal of the politics of prevention is to obviate conflict by the reduction of tension levels and this means an insistence upon a continuing audit of the human consequences of social and political acts. That audit, if it is to be genuine, requires the unashamed use of a happiness scale. The problem of politics is less how to solve the conflicts than how to prevent them; less to serve as a safety valve for social protest than to apply social energy to the abolition of recurrent strains in society.

In these New Labour days, when ideology has become a filthy word and socialism a street curse, the threadbare thinking of those who so eagerly escape from such contaminations and who swagger in their 'pragmatic' suitings, leads them so often to deal only with symptoms, not causes. Then their ill-thought-out knee-jerk responses, like those of Home Secretary Jack Straw, ensure they scramble in unseemly disarray from one crisis to another. Quite often the 'solutions' that emerge are 'magical' ones; they are often semantic and incantatory ones, deliberately presented by the odious spin doctors as a manipulation designed to drive the controversy out of the public's mind. Too often all that consequently happens is that the community is distracted by another set of equally irrelevant symbols and catch phrases, and the politicians and the lackey spin doctors, to the delight of a hungry tabloid press seeking a new headline every day, deliberately create new controversies as a part of the technique of distraction. I saw too many pretentious statutes pass through the Commons, which in fact changed nothing in the permanent practices of our society, not to be keenly aware of the role of spurious 'magic' in politics.

The American political scientist Harold Laswell, who more than two generations ago attempted to assimilate the implications of psychoanalysis for the study of politics, affirmed: 'Our problem is to be ruled by the truth about the conditions of harmonious human relations.' But this is not the problem being faced by our present-day politicians, preoccupied as they are with the belief that politics is about holding office and about power, rather than about people. Our total aim should be the creation of a society which improves the quality of human relationships and we should not permit the maladoption of the professional politicians, panting for deference, and only capable of endowing vitality upon a political movement provided it is sufficiently loaded with the displacement of their private affects, to confuse us. Nor must we allow our impatience to mislead us. The politics of prevention are slow and laborious, but at least no shoddiness is attached to their aim.

The Children Act was no exception to the rule that in practice such politics of prevention meet strong resistance. Central to its purpose was the total overhaul of our adoption laws; fundamentally it was an assault upon the proposition that children are property with no rights of their own. Adoption is an ambitious technical method of resolving problems of sterility, illegitimacy and the nurture of the rejected or unattached child; it is also an imaginative and sensitive human enterprise where biology jostles passion, and where irresponsibility, inadequacy or wickedness is met by pity, concern and love. To presume to intervene by laws in this subtle and complex process is, inevitably, to invite condemnation as an intruder; reason and insight embedded within such laws, however mildly coercive, can be speedily resented.

Conscious of these hazards and of the need to proceed with political delicacy, when I started agitating in 1964 I moved more cautiously than is my wont. Yet the need for sweeping legal changes was overwhelming. Because of the lack of any comprehensive adoption service, giving support and guidance to the unmarried mother as well as would-be adoptors, available to all those needing it throughout the country, the choosing by society of parents for thousands of children each year was little more than a sinister game of roulette. Scores of voluntary adoption societies existed, unevenly distributed throughout the country, some purporting to serve a locality and others claiming to operate nationally. Many of them had standards of service which were abysmal; they lacked any professional skills or staff, dealing only on the basis of often bizarre criteria. The dilettante nature of the characteristics of too many of the adoption societies was encouraged by the perfunctory surveillance to which, by law, their operations were subject. Indeed, approval of their registration had become reduced to little more than a formality and was done by local authorities, more than half of whom shirked exercising their own existing powers to make their Social Services departments act as adoption agencies.

Outside the purview of these adoption societies of such varying quality, many adoptions were arranged privately by matrons, gynaecologists, health visitors and busybodies. Choosing parents for someone else's child was certainly too awful a responsibility to be left to any one person, but the muddlers and meddlers who for morbid or mercenary motives intervened to play God were given a dangerously free hand under our laws. One of the most hazardous direct adoptions were those arranged by a mother with colluding grandparents, aunts or elder sisters who wished to create legal relationships which differed from and distorted the natural relationship between not only child and adoptors, but also of the child to his own mother. Too often in such adoptions the real circumstances were hidden from the child and his later discovery that his 'parents' were really his grandparents and that his older 'sister' was really his mother was a final damaging blow to a child who had already been brought up in an inevitably guilty and anxiety-ridden home.

Yet despite the damage that could be caused to the child's life when his future was settled by concealment strategies in the family, or when the child was handed over to a stranger by some untutored third party or by bungling untrained adoption societies, the public reaction to such practices was extraordinarily mild. I realised that although we had reached the position that a woman was no longer regarded as the property of her husband, a child was still widely held to be the property of the parents. I became aware that we had a public still indifferent or blind to the consequence that the resonances coming from the continued mismatching of so many children would cause thousands of them to become adults who lacked the security to give love, or the courage to surrender to its demanding embrace.

Sándor Ferenczi, the most daring and elastic of Freud's early collaborators, 70 years ago told how the chances of adult happiness for a child who feels an unwelcome guest in the family could be blighted:

> [a] child has to be induced, by means of an immense expenditure of love, tenderness and care, to forgive his parents for having brought him into the world without any intention on his part; otherwise destructive drives begin to stir immediately. And this is not really

surprising, since the infant is still much closer to individual non-being, and not divided from it by so much bitter experience as the adult. Slipping back into this non-being might therefore come much more easily to children. The 'life-force' which wears itself against the difficulties of life has not therefore any great innate strength and it becomes established only when tactful treatment and upbringing gradually gives rise to progressive immunisation against physical and psychical injuries.

An adopted child, already rejected or by external circumstances compulsorily abandoned by the parents, has greater needs than most, if he is not to be afflicted by a diminished desire for life. Moral and philosophic pessimism, scepticism and mistrust, can become character traits which can especially burden the mismatched adopted child. According to Ferenczi, and to Georg Groddeck, the German physician who was the father of psycho-somatic medicine, such 'unwelcome guests' in adulthood have a vulnerability to illness, and to suicide, that exceeds the norm.

The issues that I was raising impinged upon a statistically significant section of the electorate: natural parents giving up their children, would-be adoptors, foster parents and adults who had been adopted. Yet, despite forming a group of MPs to support me in my representations to Government, I initially received only negative responses from the Home Office, and meagre media and public opinion encouragement. But then, after unrewarding years of attempting to coax and to alarm public opinion, there came a serendipitous intervention.

In 1967 Jim Callaghan became Home Secretary. He came to his new office shell-shocked. Devaluation and his subsequent resignation from Chancellorship of the Exchequer had left him stunned and depleted. He was poor in his boyhood and it led him to be over-fascinated by money. Mixing with bankers and economists had shored him up, leaving him with a profound sense of security that he had rarely been able to enjoy. The total collapse of his assumptions and of the pound was felt as more than a policy failure; he was a shaken man. Bewildered, he invited me, as doubtless he invited other backbenchers who had in the past fully involved themselves in political programmes that were part of the responsibility of the Home Office, to come and talk to him privately; he wanted instruction. I seized the moment, and told him he could be remembered as the man who had revolutionised Britain's child laws. The notion of being the 'Children's Protector' immediately appealed to him; as a very young boy, Callaghan lost his seaman father and the widow was left to fight a bitter struggle to maintain the family. The impress of those early years is irrevocably stamped upon the adult man; in this case, it acted to my advantage.

Callaghan agreed to my suggestions that an advisory committee be immediately set up to review the laws and make proposals for legislative changes, that it should be composed of those with expertise in fields of childcare and those familiar with the operations of the existing laws, and that I should sit upon it. The Home Office civil servants, as ever, stalled, claiming their Children's Department which was already over-stretched. Then, in a rearguard action, they sought to limit the terms of reference of the proposed committee. But my incitement of Callaghan to resist proved successful, and for three of my most arduous parliamentary years, I sat with the committee to produce, finally, an exhaustive and unanimous report whose recommendations could be legislatively implemented.

Soon after the report's presentation, David Owen drew a high place in the annual Private Members' Ballot which entitled him to time to bring in a Bill. He readily agreed to sponsor one implementing the committee's proposals. Together we steered the Bill through the Commons, and then, before it reached the statute book, an election was called and the Bill fell. On Parliament's return, however, the Labour Government took it over and, although it was still to be some years before it was fully implemented, it did become the Children's Act in 1975.

David Owen, writing of this period in his autobiography, paid a comforting tribute: 'I could always rely on Leo Abse, an influential Labour MP who had been the most important single influence behind the adoption reform movement, to put a little pressure on in the correct places. He was generous with his advice, having steered through more controversial legislation than any other MP.' Now, after twenty-five years the workings of the Act clearly need reviewing, not least because with more women working and with the coming of in vitro fertilisation, there is a paucity of suitable would-be adoptive mothers; the horrific Waterhouse Report on child abuse in children's homes has now precipitated such a review, one which I hope, like the preview to the 1975 Act, will be a painstaking enquiry, not an instant politics response.

But it remains the Act that, in retrospect, makes me feel all the slog and drudgery of my parliamentary life was well worthwhile. However, by recording some of the encomiums the original 1975 Act justifiably attracted, I risk being labelled a Mr Toad, but I do not do it for my own sake. A secondary justification, apart from the prime purpose of proffering the Act as a concrete illustration of the fulfilment of the Jefferson command that the legislature must always engage itself in the pursuit of happiness, is to reprove the sloth of many of our present backbenchers. By complaining, as some of them have, that their workload – despite their having cut down their working hours – is far too light, they both advertise their own indolence and their dismaying dependence upon executive initiative. Panting for advancement, diligently repeating the soundbites of their leader and so falsely claiming to be 'reformers', they forfeit independence and, fearing to be abrasive, fail to demand or to initiate legislative changes which may alleviate some of the sorrows of their constituents. With the collusion of cunning Whips – glad to be rid of them lest, as idle hands, they will turn to mischief – they retreat from the Commons to their constituencies where they play-act as social workers when they should be in the Commons implementing changes which may prevent many of the problems now burdening the authentic social worker.

Overpaid, endowed with a surfeit of non-taxable allowances, supported by researchers and communication technologies never available to previous generations of backbenchers, their present contribution is demonstrably disappointingly meagre. The back-bencher with the capacity to avoid the bars and possessed of stamina and single-mindedness, if prepared to forfeit immediate acknowledgement and lack of notice by press and public and engaged on painstaking obscure committee work, can, while tolerating present abuse and postponing accolades for a decade hence, achieve more than most ministers who, while awaiting the next reshuffle, absurdly only have a department for a couple of years at most. But the backbenchers whose one desire is to join in the game of musical chairs and scramble from the back bench to sit on the front bench are, by their restlessness, doomed to constant personal discontent, and their electorates will find them, as many of them presently are, a poor investment. A considerable number of them are in their place unlawfully, selected, as a blow to misogyny and a sop to feminism, by the imposition of women-only shortlists which are probably illegally discriminatory against men. To ask them to cultivate a political environment in which the pursuit of happiness has the highest place on the agenda is to invite a rebuff, for they themselves are part of the problem to be resolved if love, the prerequisite to happiness, is to flourish in our society.

The shifts in the structure of the economy and social division of labour, the growth of flexible low-paid part-time work replacing older manual jobs in a burgeoning service-based economy, all give full opportunity to the highly competitive woman to inflame the wounds displaced men have suffered, not least those endured by huge numbers of working-class boys who, while their sisters work, are left to languish in unemployment hell. Women MPs who created or colluded in a system which insisted candidates should be chosen not by merit but by gender are hardly likely to have the pacific sensibility required to engage in salutary legislative processing aimed to apply balm to gender-inflicted wounds.

It is unfortunate that too many women, eager to engage in public life, by their aggressive stances give credence to the inadequate construct of womanhood that early psychoanalysis provided. That construct was based on the clinical interpretations of the dilemmas of women who were patients; they came for help because they were at odds with their womanhood and with the permanent inequalities which seemed to doom them. What those women patients suffered was revealed on the couch in the privacy of the consulting room; nowadays these resentments are publicly acted out, and we have the spectacle of what one well-known but repentant feminist, Rosalind Coward, bemoans in a 1999 work as 'feminism', the philosophy that men are the problem and answerable for all the negative aspects of society, like criminality and war. She calls for the end of this 'male bashing' and for women to give support to the young men who she claims lie stricken by the onslaught feminism has made upon them.

The women, the erstwhile feminist chastens, have certainly increased in numbers, but ruefully now recalling how in Parliament such women, ever paranoiac about male motivation, obstructed for some years my divorce legislation, I do not regard them as a new phenomenon in public life. The most formidable of those at the time was Edith Summerskill, Minister for National Insurance & Industrial Injuries (1950-51) and Chairman of the Labour Party (1954-55), a veritable case history of the type of woman whose womanhood hinged on the so-called 'genital trauma'; that is, the little girl's sudden comprehension of the fact that she does not have, and never will have, a penis. Reverberating throughout Summerskill's spirited attacks on my divorce proposals, in which she insisted that women required constant attention from marauding aggressive philandering men, was envy of male sexuality. Certainly, her lurid accounts of the potency and promiscuity of the Casanova-type man which my legislation was about to release upon the community were the products of a rich fantasy life; she was the forerunner of those feminists who today seem to regard every man as a potential rapist.

Such women provide misleading evidence for the elaboration of the genital trauma hypothesis claiming to explain the nature of femininity. The assumed prevalence of envy in women; the assumption that the future baby is a substitute for the penis; the interpretation of the girl's turning from the mother to the father because she finds that the mother not only cheated her out of her penis but has been cheated herself; and the woman's disposition to abandon so-called 'male' activity and aggressivity for the sake of a passive-masochistic orientation; all of these depend upon the 'trauma' and all of them are built into elaborate explanations of femininity.

These assertions are surely psychic half-truths, drawn from a scrutiny of dysfunctional women, women who can be found on Commons benches as well as in yesteryear's Viennese culture and certainly, to attempt to create a blueprint for a society in which men and women can be happier, predicated on the assumption that half the human race is disabled, would indeed be folly. In the development of an infant girl to adulthood, it is unreasonable to believe that she would exclusively focus on what is not there. Far more likely, the female child will observe evidence in older girls, women and animals of the fact that there exists an inner-bodily space with productive as well as dangerous potential. Erik Erikson, the psychoanalyst whose divination often had the vision of a great artist rather than a scientist, indicated:

> Here one thinks not only of pregnancy and childbirth, but also of lactation, and of all the richly convex parts of the female anatomy which suggest fullness, warmth and generosity...Sensory reality and logical conclusion are given form by kinesthetic experience and by series of memories which 'make sense'; and in this total actuality the existence of a productive inner-bodily space safely set in the centre of female form and carriage has, I think, a reality superior to that of the missing organ.

Too many feminists, having achieved a relative emancipation reluctantly 'granted' by self-made man, tacitly accept and recommend to their sex his self-made image as a model to be equalled; their blunder is costing women dearly and causing a destructive turbulence which sweeps away love in man-woman relationships. Love is lost and all that is gained is limited access to career competition, standardised consumership and strenuous one-parent family home-making. Meantime, the frightened man, his dreams now haunted by reactivated infantile connotations of a vagina as a devouring mouth or eliminating structure, in his waking life unconsciously fearing emasculation or expulsion, fumbles, leaving the woman unfulfilled and himself unsatisfied.

A heavy price is being paid by an absurd denial or smudging of the biological differentiation between man and woman, the rock-bottom of which is the woman's productive inner space. The human foetus must be carried inside the womb for a given number of weeks, the infant must be suckled or at any rate raised within a maternal world; years of specialised woman-hours are to be devoted to the child. No wonder that the little girl, the bearer of ova and maternal powers, tends to survive her birth more surely and is a tougher creature, able as she grows up to be more resistant to not a few man-killing diseases and to enjoy a longer life expectancy. The survival of the species depends upon her physical strength, and upon her capacity to fulfil biological imperatives, to react as an adult more vividly, more personally and with great compassion to the differential needs of others – her reactions stemming from her primal responses to her child. For a woman to deny biology, to engage in an act of self-immolation, is a disastrous course; it impoverishes her own personal relationships and it deprives all of us of the new social inventions and institutions which we desperately need to guard and cultivate that which nurses and nourishes, cares for and tolerates, includes and preserves.

Repeatedly during my legislative efforts I was made aware of the importance of this 'inner space' in the feminine cycle. Before entering the Commons, as a solicitor with a substantial divorce practice, I had already been made acutely conscious of the profound despair and hurt a woman can suffer on the breakdown of a long-term marriage, pain that so often, in the case of the husband, was a wonder, arousing both his empathic horror and a refusal to understand. During the long campaign before my Divorce Act of 1969 reached the statute book, the anguishes that engulfed me, from the negative and positive responses coming from women throughout Britain, brought me an understanding that the woman's inner space was not only the very centre of fulfilment but was also the centre of despair, for to be left empty was to be drained of the blood of her body, the warmth of a heart, the sap of life. I do not believe Erikson was exaggerating when he wrote that such hurt can be re-experienced in each menstruation: 'It is crying to heaven in the morning over a child; and it becomes a permanent scar in the menopause.' It is an impertinence on the part of men to interpret that suffering by suggesting that women want, above all, what man has: an exterior equipment and traditional access to 'outer space', and it is foolishness on the part of militant feminists who, by their shrill demands for so-called equality, provide corroboration of simplistic penis-envy theorising. The 'void' that can arise within the inner space of a woman has a tragic profundity that cannot be explained away by male chauvinistic presentations, or by the denials of gender-feminists.

In the years following the Act of 1969, acutely aware of its blemishes and knowing that more could fill benignly at least some of this 'void', I worked hard to meet the painful grievances that avalanched upon me from women who felt that whatever gains had been made in my Act, there were serious post-divorce financial, property and custodial issues. After many difficulties in mobilising sufficient parliamentary support, I helped initiate the Divorce Bill in 1983 that, taken over by the Government, became the Matrimonial and Family Proceedings Act of 1985. Only then did the guilt that I might have added to, rather than lessened, the woes following upon a true Dolorosa – a woman full of sorrows – begin to evaporate.

But it is not only male legislators' insensitivity to woman's fated despairing potentiality that can add to her burdens; so can male antagonism to the creativity within her inner space. The male fear and envy of woman's inner creative space can permeate desire with ambivalences fatally despoiling love between partners; but there can arise in the public realm too those self-same ambivalences, and then, unless controlled, they can in extraordinary fashion invade the legislative process inhibiting changes likely to lighten the burdens destiny has decreed we must all carry. At no time in my parliamentary life did I see those syndromes more exotically displayed than during my involvement in the first direct intervention the State made in the field of family planning. To recall again the male moods which enveloped the issues is to illustrate not only the appalling reticences relating to contraception – so inimical to family happiness – that were in place over the greater part of our century, but also how irrational can be both the evaluations by men of the importance of the penis and their fear of the vagina.

However, I acknowledge that there were personal reasons why I found the challenge to introduce a family planning Act irresistible; it would be repayment of a debt that I owed to my mother, for her great heroine was the redoubtable Annie Besant. When I was a child the praises of Annie Besant were ever sung to me. Indeed, it was only when I was grown up, and knew that my mother's age precluded the possibility, that I really understood her regular recital of the details of the remarkable trial of Besant in 1876 for defying the law and publishing a pamphlet on contraception was not an eye-witness account. Marie Stopes and Annie Besant were women from whom I would undoubtedly have fled; but at least my mother's odd choice of mentors had helped to blow some of the cobwebs out of the mind of a callow provincial youth. Whatever the deeper motivation of those campaigning feminist birth-controllers, or indeed that of my own mother, I had been the beneficiary; the legacy needed acknowledgement. As a fortunate result of an adjournment debate that I initiated in 1966 I was able to discharge the obligation in full.

Over the years I had frequently probed in the House the inadequacies of family planning services in Britain and its dependencies. I had used a number of stratagems to focus public attention on existing needs, not least in a series of attacks on the abuses and prices of the monopolistic rubber contraceptive industry and ultimately, much later in 1972, I was to have the situation referred to the Monopolies Commission. My commentaries on the situation in some overseas countries had led to not a little turbulence. After a parliamentary visit I made to the Seychelles, the Earl of Oxford and Asquith, grandson of the former premier, dominated by his attractive opinionated Roman Catholic wife, had indeed threatened to resign governorship of the Seychelles when Nigel Fisher, the courageous Tory minister at the Colonial Office, was willingly yielding to my demands that the Governor should cease to obstruct the establishment of family planning clinics in the over-populated islands. All these, and other involvements of mine in the issue, had, I thought, clarified to me the nature of the resistances to State involvement in family planning services.

I had sensed, in almost all those hostile to my encouragement of contraceptive services, a keen personal resentment; I was taking away from them the enjoyment experienced by the pure and chaste which springs from their greater virtue. It was the same resistance that I had experienced in my attempts to remove legal disabilities from the illegitimate. The birth of children, and especially of illegitimate children, was seen as the rightful punishment for sexual indulgence, exposing the shame of the participants and imposing pain, responsibility and anxiety as the price of the illicit sensual pleasures that had been enjoyed. If the wicked could, with the aid of contraceptives, sin without fear, what reward was there for the chaste? The notion that punishment was the justifiable consequence of sin is deeply rooted; to outwit God's laws is the crime of humans and the wrath of the Lord was brought down upon humanity for behaving with such cunning. Such primitive apprehensions, albeit expressed in a more sophisticated and theological vocabulary, had ensured that political parties and individual MPs, conscious of the Catholic vote, firmly left the spread of family planning to voluntary agencies, often under-funded, and to barber shops. Our courageous crusading press was no less pusillanimous, almost all of them banning advertisements for contraceptives and, indeed, the Independent Television Authority was to ensure for years that our screens were similarly left unsullied.

Many politicians in the past had possessed the temperament which collaborated rather than challenged the consequences of this guilt-ridden theology; it would otherwise be difficult to understand how it took almost a century from the time of Besant's campaign to my precipitation of the first Family Planning Act in Britain. There is, of course, a curious ambivalence in man's attitude to his sexual impulses and organs, even as there is to the interior space of the woman. Man's organs are regarded, in traditional Christian morality, as the source of impurity and sin, treated with contempt and attempted to be sternly controlled; yet, they can also be a source of pride, intimately connected with self-esteem, dignity and power. And few are more concerned about prestige and power than the politician; potency and virility are, at least unconsciously, equated with that self-same power and indeed with ability in general. The virtue of this equation, not only the specific sexual capacity but the whole individuality, can be felt to suffer an affront, or an emasculation, by the idea of a curtailment of fertility. The preoccupation of Hitler, Mussolini and Pétain with the necessity of a high birth-rate reflected their feelings of personal insecurity at the prospect of any reduction in the rate of increase of population; men more confident of their potency would not have screamed for the reassurance of more and more births. There can indeed be sinister repercussions in the political field when some of the varieties of the castration complex produce distortions of this order. Although in Britain we were spared some of these excesses, in the post-war years Quintin Hogg, who was to become Lord Chancellor, was putting forward in an influential book, *The Case for Conservatism*, the argument that this country was going to be so short of manpower that there was an urgent need in the long run to increase the birth-rate.

With the intake, however, of a new House in 1966, I felt it likely that there were more balanced opinions available to be mobilised against the prissy traditional State attitudes. When the Ministry of Health wanted doctors employed within the service to have the right to charge patients for contraceptive prescriptions, I was able to seize my opportunity and initiate an adjournment debate criticising the decision. It was harsh that my criticism had to fall upon Kenneth Robinson, then the Health Minister, for, to his credit, he had issued earlier in that year a circular giving some encouragement to local authorities to give help to family planning services. That circular ended a period of 30 years which had passed without a single word of advice on family planning coming from any of the successive cowardly governments. The minister, however, acknowledged to me in the debate that it was a source of disappointment to him that he had discovered that there were statutory limitations on local authorities which compelled them to confine their activities severely to those who because of very strict medical requirements might be in need of contraceptive advice. The surprise Robinson felt in finding himself, by law, so hamstrung was not shared by me; my previous involvement had made it clear to me that my goal must be to remove those very restrictions.

The debate confirmed to me that there were now new responses abroad. A listening new member, the young geographer Edwin Brooks, who was then unknown to me, introduced himself after the debate. He had drawn a place in the Private Members' ballot and generously offered to co-operate with me in any Bill I might have in mind to increase family planning facilities. We put together a Bill which gave local authorities for the first time the right to set up or support family planning clinics where contraceptive advice and contraceptives could be given to all, married and unmarried, and for which some or no payment need be charged. The Bill also gave the local authorities power to undertake domiciliary visits which enabled the doctors and social workers to reach homes where advice was much needed. We carefully avoided making the duties mandatory, and by allowing the local authorities to choose to what extent they would, if at all, exercise these powers, we sought to avoid any provocations to Members of Parliament, particularly those with a Catholic electorate, where prejudice might be strong. The Bill in this form attained the willing approval and active help of Kenneth Robinson and his department.

Then came my astonishment. I had commenced on my familiar task of mobilising the lobbies that would be likely to assist, wooing the journalists, discussing issues with those active in the family planning field, sounding out influential members of all parties who would help us put the Bill through the House, and not forgetting to tackle those who I anticipated would oppose. I found, however, that we had no opposition whatsoever. Unknown to me, and apparently to anyone else, the rapid change of public opinion and private conduct had already totally undermined, by 1967, the walls of former prejudice. Bradlaugh's battle had been won years ago; and cowardly politicians and reformers had in fact been afraid of joining forces against an enemy who had long since fled. The religious opposition that in earlier years I had encountered had shamefacedly evaporated; the Pope's followers were no longer obeying him and in vain he was to insist that all but the rhythm method of contraception must cease. Old traditional attitudes were no longer meaningful and the caution and pussy-footing of those engaged in family planning propaganda came from an appraisal of what I found to be yesterday's opinion, not that of the 1960s.

Yet in many ways I found it more disturbing to be putting through a Bill without opposition than when I had hacked my way, inch by inch, towards a goal. In this area the enemies were in fact in the ranks of my allies, and I recoiled from the essential morbidity of their enthusiasm for my cause. I spoke of planning parenthood and personal choice; they spoke of birth control, with the emphasis on control. They described unplanned children as 'mistakes', with no appreciation of the unconscious need and demand of a woman for a child that often will mock at all contraceptives. They labelled the woman using no regular contraceptive technique as being 'at risk', as if pregnancy was a disease. I wanted to aid parents to have planned, well-spaced and happier families; they unconsciously begrudged the establishment of a family at all.

And, of course, these supporters were zealous population planners, as apocalyptic in their prophecies of the consequences of over-population in Britain, as in the 1930s and '40s the population fanatics had been of the consequences of under-population. It is perhaps a sociological phenomenon that earlier in the twentieth century the castration anxieties of many politicians were warded off by urging more and more conception; and yet, later in the century, using the well-worn psychological mechanism of projection preceded by denial, many politicians refused to acknowledge their own fear of the threat of castration and then dealt with their still acute anxieties by demanding the symbolic castration of all others through State population control policy.

However, one cannot in politics always choose one's allies; at the most one can strive to contain them. Edwin Brooks and myself did manage to distance them and simultaneously silence the last whimperings of opponents still expressing fears that knowledge of contraception would inevitably result in promiscuity. This indeed was to be the only piece of legislation with which I had been associated which reached the statute book without any vote being taken at any stage in the proceedings. It was to prove a more important measure than even I had anticipated, for the zealous use of its powers by many local authorities demonstrated its widespread need. When, in 1973, as part of the reorganisation of the health services in Britain, the Government decided to integrate local authority health services into the National Health Service, it found, in the Lords and Commons, an overwhelming demand that the services in use in some local authorities should now become nationally available. The Government yielded to our pressure and accepted that, as from 1974, within the NHS there should be provided a full family planning service with contraceptive advice freely given to all and with contraceptives available on payment of only the usual prescription charge.

I acknowledge that I do take some particular pride in having shaped the seminal Family Planning Act, one which was not debased by male Malthusian doctrines and yielded very little to sick puritanism. My mother gave birth to five children, one of whom she lost; her belated discovery of Marie Stopes ensured she did not follow the example of my grandmother who produced at least eleven children, of whom nine survived. My mother, unlike her mother, consequently did not find motherhood an intolerable restrictive burden, and, I am certain, the Act brought changes which meant my mother's relief from never-ending child-bearing would be shared by many women. Those who today regard any State intervention as necessarily the work of the devil, should think again; by bringing the State into the bed, the Family Planning Act helped many to make love without fear, an almost absolute prerequisite for so many people if they are to be a little happier. By passing the Act, the legislature performed what should always be its prime task: to direct the nation on to the path which, however long, does lead to happiness.

The Anal Society

Twenty-five years have passed since, stoically, as a parliamentary candidate, I endured participation in a campaign led by the man who famously recited the wonders that under his leadership technology would bestow upon us: the General Election of 1964 was fought and won on Harold Wilson's prognostications of the boons to be gained by the 'white heat of technological revolution'. In October 1999, repeating the same stale mantra, advertising, as ever, spurious claims to 'modernity', Blair explained the dynamic behind his policy: 'Behind it all, the urgency to modernise, because otherwise, in the face of technological revolution sweeping all before it, Britain will be left behind.' His Government, he said, was the 'enabler, equipping people to survive and prosper amid massive technological change'. Acting as an exemplar, he ostentatiously takes part in IT group lessons; in turn, his exemplar is the new technology billionaire and entrepreneur, Bill Gates. He declaims 'computers and the Net are empowering economic growth' and the overriding goal is the creation of a prosperous country.

Blair, like Wilson, is proffering us technology, the cornucopia which is to shower wealth upon us; but prosperity is no synonym for happiness, and when, at this time, as a nation, although wealth is cruelly unevenly distributed, we have never been more prosperous, it is only too clear that our discontents are profound. A child's wish for love is not met by stuffing him with sweets and toys; nor are our adult yearnings assuaged if desolately we live loveless in houses bulging with consumer goods. My self-made millionaire clients in their obsessional pursuit of ever more money I often regarded as mad; none were content and I cannot recall one who was happy. They were of the same ilk as those to whom Wilson in the past and Blair in the present sold peerages; these millionaires, confident New Labour will not curb their acquisitiveness, vainly hope a title, by its corroboration, will give them the sense of security, of identity, which they so lack. Politicians, baiting their electorates with promises of prosperity, seek to persuade us that these emotionally crippled men should be our mentors, and that by the enabling skills of our rulers, technology will make us all little millionaires.

These politicians cannot do their sums – money does not equal happiness. Their error has consequences; it incites us to attempt a grave maladaptation. There are two ways of adapting to reality: by means of adjusting reality to make it fit one's needs, or by means of changing oneself to fit in with reality. The psychoanalysts following Ferenczi have called these reactions 'allo-plastic' and 'auto-plastic' adjustments to reality. Politicians, lacking deference for the wisdom gained by the auto-plastically orientated civilisations of the East, and by the antiquity of our own Judaeo-Christian civilisation, choose to persuade us and themselves, despite so much evidence to the contrary, that the progress of technology can, by external changes, conquer everything. Worldwide environmental degradation and pollution are ignored, and the misgivings of those drawing lessons from BSE, or protesting against genetically modified food, draw Blair into chastening 'the tyranny of pressure groups' whom he dubs the 'anti-modernists'.

The psychoanalyst Robert Waelder, in his admonitory overview of the history of man, has spelled out how the post-Renaissance civilisation of Europe has been characterised by an ever-increasing and dangerous dream by such allo-plastic attitudes. Now accelerating technological leaps inflame the insolent politicians' hubris, and he contemptuously turns away from any intervention suggesting increased technological developments may increase unhappiness. Christian criticisms of the 'modern', as when Reinhold Niebur says that human history is not so much a chronicle of the progressive victory of cosmos over chaos, but story of an ever-increasing cosmos creating ever-increasing possibilities of chaos, are most unwelcome. And when, to his great credit, John Major came from the Queen to announce, as the new Prime Minister, that he wanted to create a nation at ease with itself, the sentiment, necessarily involving introspection, was speedily trampled upon by the 'bastards' in his Cabinet. They responded in the typical manner of the more extroverted politician who is expert in avoiding the painful insights that have to be faced through the calibration by introspective work into personal resource; they would sooner claim to be able to conquer the world than embark upon the arduous task of conquering themselves.

Essentially, what Thatcher-admiring Blair is inviting us to wallow in is an anal society. The allo-plastic notion, so compatible to the extroverted politician, that by control of technology prosperity will be delivered to us as never before, is an infantile anal fantasy. Many, I am aware, will respond to this interpretation with incredulity; it was ever so. More than half a century ago, Ernest Jones, Freud's colleague and biographer, wrote:

> Perhaps the most astonishing of Freud's findings – and certainly the one that has evoked the liveliest incredulity, repugnance, and opposition – was his discovery that certain traits of character may become profoundly modified as the result of sexual excitation experienced by the infant in the region of the anal canal.

And one of the main traits so modified is the attitude we strike to money. Certainly it is an offence to the grandiosity of the contemporary capitalist spirit now being urged upon us by Blairite exponents of 'enterprise' and 'modernity' to imply that the call they make with such great pride and self-importance to create more wealth, is a call on us to manufacture shit. Ferenczi wrote, more than 75 years ago:

> Whatever form may be assumed by money, the enjoyment at possessing it has its deepest and amplest source in coprophilia. Every sociologist and national economist who examines the facts without prejudice has to reckon with this irrational element. Social problems can be solved only by discovering the real psychology of human beings; speculations about economic conditions alone will never reach the goal.

The great economist Maynard Keynes, mocked during the insane monetarist Thatcherite years and now treated with renewed respect, well knew the validity of Ferenczi's assertion and, no less, knew the resistances such a view provoked. Even Keynes, who had immersed himself in Freud's works in 1925, was therefore circumspect in presenting his conclusion that the link between the infant's stools and money was clinically well established for, from one of Ernest Jones's papers, he was aware that of all the 'resistances' which arise when psychoanalytical interpretations are given, none produce greater storms of resistance than the interpretation of anal-sadistic traits. When publicly defending Freud's theory, Keynes took pains to mask himself behind a pen-name. But he well knew the score.

By the time Keynes published his *General Theory of Employment, Interest and Money*, he was adding to his view that the two motivations behind contemporary capitalism were love of money and a money-making 'instinct'. By emphasising a third motivation – a wish to control, a sadistic love of power – Keynes showed that he understood, as well as any psychoanalyst expounding the classical view, that we all, as infants, must pass through an anal-sadistic phase in which the anus and defecation are the major sources of sensual pleasure, forming the centre of infant self-awareness, and when mastery of the body, particularly of the sphincter and the socialisation of impulses are the infant's major preoccupations. Keynes wrote of the sickness of the search for money beyond any reasonable need. To him the love of money as a possession – as distinguished from the love of money as a means to the enjoyment of the realities of life – should be recognised for what it is: 'a somewhat disgusting morbidity, one of those semi-criminal, semi-pathological propensities which ones hands over with a shudder to a specialist in mental disease.'

But although in the extreme case the avid accumulation of money is indeed a symptom of mental disease, the central position occupied by the training of our excretory functions during our early years may, for all of us, be modified but can never be totally excluded from the rest of our lives. Our relationships with others, particularly those close to us, are influenced by our early experiences on the pot. The shit created by us, which in turn has created sensations for us, is a plastic source of fantasy and the very first object in which our relationship to others is concretised. To expel or hold back, to give or not to give, to submit or to disobey – the seemingly trivial contest of wills forges a link, a meaningful nexus between those involved. As Elvio Fachinelli, the Italian psychoanalyst, has emphasised:

> Within the nexus, a significant relationship of mutual tension and desire is gradually developed between the child and its mother. Moved by love for her, and by the fear of losing her, by the pleasure of gratifying its desire or the pleasure of being compensated for not doing so, the child slowly renounces total control over its new-found power and agrees to produce the golden eggs only when and where she demands. But in order to re-exert some authority over her in turn, to win her recognition and some revenge for all the wrongs inflicted on it, it learns at the same time to postpone, to disappoint her, to make her wait...

Yet, with sensitivity and love, a happy armistice can be achieved. The baby gives his great gift, the precursor to all gifts, and the mother's prohibitions are now felt as wondrous approvals.

But such peace treaties between mother and child are not always signed, and certainly will never be signed if the mother is, as at present, harassed by society's demand that she speedily return to employment and hustles the baby. Then the child, his anal delights unassuaged, does not wish to move on to genitality. In adulthood, nostalgia for those denied coprophilic pleasures expresses itself in marital money disputes, and in sadistic controlling – phenomena I so often found had wrecked the marriages of those attending on me in my divorce law practice. When one notes, as I have sought to do, the concatenation of events which link the parsimony of the grudging breast to today's widespread practice of fellatio, it is relevant to note too that the mother who is peremptory when the child wants satisfaction at the breast will be the same driven mother who denies herself and the child sufficient time to take pride in his first creations: the faeces.

With his sucking impulses left ungratified, when he moves from the oral phase to the next phase of his development, the anal-sadistic phase, desperately but in vain he seeks compensatory satisfactions. The resultant destructive traits which belong to the classical phenomenon of the anal character, and which are now so destructively playing havoc in relationships between men and women and which are catalogued in the depressing divorce statistics, are built on the ruins of an oral eroticism whose development has miscarried.

Curiously, one of the blessings that may be received by some homosexuals is, Freud once suggested, that they are less likely to be afflicted by the curse of the repugnant features that belong to the anal character – that of parsimony and compulsive money-making. Freud canvassed the view that:

> One may expect to find no very marked degree of 'anal character' in people who have retained the anal zone's erotogenic character in adult life, as happens, for instance, with certain homosexuals. Unless I am much mistaken, the evidence of experience tallies quite well on the whole with this inference.

It may well be that the ready availability of the 'pink pound', noticed these days by the advertisers of consumer goods, gives credence to Freud's surmise, but some may think homosexuality as a technique for by-passing the burdens of anal-character traits is a less than satisfactory option. Yet it may well be that Keynes' homosexuality played a not inconsiderable part in his bold economic theorising, castigating the folly of retentive monetarism and emphasising the benefits of a spending demand economy. His work has continued to infuriate over-cautious economists and politicians, loathing his expansionist theories; they wish, symbolically, to retain faeces in the form of significantly named 'nest-eggs'. Such indefinite postponement of future pleasures was not for Keynes, who never ceased to remind us that, 'In the long run, we are all dead.' However, whatever overdue acknow-ledgements are given to the homosexual for the societal benefits which flow from his lack of concern to gain immortality by crazily accumulating inheritance money for children, for most, the imperfect resolution of their infantile anal phase can only inject poison into their adult heterosexual lives.

Freud and his followers were, through their onto-genetic approach to human personality, the first to establish a nosology which classified anality, like Keynes saw it, as a potential mental disease, but they were certainly not the first to understand the modifications required if anality was not to bring about degradation in human personality and in society.

The Ancient Israelites, by their injunction that every 50th year there should come about a Jubilee, gave the most extraordinary recognition that greed and control over others must be curbed if man was not to be permanently enslaved by societal imbalances. The Jubilee Year was to be a year of perfect rest, where there was to be a cessation of money-making and no sowing or gathering of the natural products of the field and the vine, one which should be commenced with the liberation of all slaves and the restoration of all ancestral possessions. Liberation was to be proclaimed everywhere to everyone and the people were to return 'every man unto his possessions and unto his family' and all debts were to be remitted. In nineteenth-century Britain laws had to be passed modifying entailment of estates and, after one wealthy testator, Peter Thellusson, left his money to accumulate with interest so far into the future that the ultimate legatee would be the wealthiest man in the world, a Statute was passed to curb such posthumous accumulations. But such prohibitions were comparatively mild attempts to check the anal retentiveness which my ancestors saw could destroy man and society. The nomenclature they used to identify the iconoclastic force was different but its power was not underestimated, and in an endeavour to ensure that it be overcome, they evoked God to terrorise the accumulators and enforce their prohibitions. The fundamental principle was that the land was a sacred possession belonging to JAWEH and that therefore no-one could be permitted to alienate it permanently to themselves; God, not private property, was sacred.

The wisdom embedded in the concept of the Jubilee, the understanding that anality could, unless contained, destroy the whole social organism, was perpetuated within Christianity. No-one has more subtly spelled out the battles of the ecclesiastical authorities over the centuries to identify and prohibit the excesses of avarice than the economic historian R. H. Tawney in his classic work *Religion and the Rise of Capitalism*. The weight of his teachings, unsurprisingly, profoundly influenced the last wave of Labour Party reformers before Blair and his ilk affected to take over that role. He was the Christian Socialist guru at whose feet the anti-Bevanites sat and whose presentations completely captivated even as secular a man as Hugh Gaitskell and as wilful and raffish a man as Tony Crosland, who was to provide much of the intellectual weaponry for the reformers of his day. Tawney demonstrated how the Christian Church held a conception distinctively its own, committed to the formulation of a social theory – not as a philanthropic gloss upon the main body of its teaching, but one which was endemic and vital to its creed, and which insisted upon the superiority of moral principles over economic appetites. The Church thus knew, and passionately sought to ward off, the danger of that natural appetite which 'when flattered and pampered and over-fed brings ruin to the soul and confusion to society'.

Tawney's conclusion to his magnum opus was unequivocal:

> ...the quality in modern societies, which is most sharply opposed to the teaching ascribed to the Founder of the Christian Faith, lies deeper than the exceptional failures and abnormal follies against which criticism is most commonly directed. It consists in the assumption, accepted by most reformers with hardly less naïveté than by the defenders of the established order, that the attainment of material riches is the supreme object of human endeavour and the final criteria of human success. Such a philosophy, plausible, militant, and not indisposed, when hard pressed, to silence criticism by persecution, may triumph or may decline. What is certain is that it is the negation of any system of any thought or morals which can, except by a metaphor, be described as Christian. Compromise is as impossible between the Church of Christ and the idolatry of wealth, which is the practical religion of capitalist societies, as it was between the Church and the State idolatry of the Roman Empire.

Everyone knows, since he never ceases to tell us so, that Blair is the most Christian of Social Democrats, but in the moderate wing of yesterday's Labour Party, so influenced by Tawney, he would have been treated as a fraud. Funded and surrounded by his millionaires, his evangelistic preaching of the end of the class war, his constant accommodation to finance capital's vested interests and his incitements to follow him and become thriving earthworms, deny him any claim to be regarded as one of the heirs to Ruskin, Keir Hardie, Tawney and Cripps, whose Christian commitment considerably helped to shape the philosophy of the Labour Party.

Blair's claim to be a practising Christian does not, of course, draw upon Tawney's interpretation. Blair claims he was fascinated by the works of another academic, the Christian moral philosopher John Macmurray, which, Blair tells us, are central to his own thinking: 'If you really want to know what I am all about, you have to take a look at a guy called John Macmurray. It's all there.' His enthusiasm for this minor figure in academic theology was such that he trekked, as an undergraduate, to Scotland from Oxford in the vain hope of sitting at the feet of the then elderly guru. If he had met him, he would have received unpalatable advice, for on the philosophical peregrinations that this man trod, Blair would not have encountered any resting place where he could have found 'the coincidence between the philosophical theory of Christianity and the left of centre politics' to which Blair claims Macmurray led him.

When in my teens I first heard Macmurray lecture, he was over-praising the positive teachings of the Marxist philosophy of dialectical materialism and seeking, by way of subdued reservations, to accommodate Christianity to its tenets. Subsequently he abandoned these forays and, indeed, in a later book, the one specifically named by Blair as his 'guide book', Macmurray's earlier neo-Marxist essays are not listed among his previous publications. Macmurray ended his life as a pietist and a Quaker, and Blair most certainly could not have obtained any encouragement from him to seek any political answers to the woes of the human predicament. On the contrary, the late works which Blair, unconvincingly, claims to have read mock politics and politicians; community was to be found in religion and politics were to be eschewed. The warning Blair would have received from Macmurray was unambiguous:

> If we track the State to its lair, what shall we find? Merely a collection of over-worked and worried gentlemen, not at all unlike ourselves, doing their best to keep the machinery of government working as well as may be, and hard put to it to keep up appearances. They are, like ourselves, subject to the illusion of power. If we expect them to work miracles, we flatter them, and tempt them to think they are Supermen... Those of them who are wise enough to know their limitations, and to be immune to the

gross adulation of their fellows, will resign; and government will be carried on only by megalomaniacs.

The crusading Blair inciting Western Europe and the United States of America into battle, in Kosovo, drew nothing from the faith of the absolute pacifist Macmurray; nor does his outward display of Christianity, in his church-going and in his despatch of his children to a fee-paying Roman Catholic school, have as its source the self-abnegation which Macmurray urged upon his acolytes. We can no more expect that Christianity will inhibit this Prime Minister's eulogising of the materialism in this technologically advanced society than we can expect any brand of socialism to impress itself upon his New Labour policies.

There is no true parallel, as has sometimes been suggested, between the struggle in the 1950s and the 1960s of the revisionist Gaitskellites and the Labour Party Left, and Blair's present onslaught upon the values of the traditional Labour Party. The protagonists in the earlier Gaitskell-Bevan battle all had a common vocabulary; on economic issues, as distinct from the defence issue of unilateralism, they all spoke the same language. Gaitskell's favourite reading was Shakespeare's love sonnets and Tawney's *Equality*. The emphasis placed upon economic equality by the revisionists meant that they insisted that all private property was suspect and to be justified must be owned by only those who used it to perform a task of social value; today's fat cats would certainly have not been included in the revisionists' category of exemptions from the general rule that no-one should receive something for nothing. 'Socialism,' Gaitskell forever preached, 'was about equality.'

As the historian Brian Bravati, Gaitskell's biographer, has stressed, debate between the revisionists and the Left 'was an argument over the best means of organising society to promote equality and to intervene in order to change generation on generation the physical distribution of wealth'; both groups loathed the obscenity of mindless and endless accumulation of money. 'The focus of the debate was about the extent and nature of the increased role of the public sector; the extent to which the State could be enlarged...the Debate, though passionate at the time, appears with hindsight to have been about different formulations of the same basic approach.'

No such congruity exists between the Labour Party tradition-alists and Blair. No inhibition or constraints, such as a wish for equality or a distaste for the obsessive pursuit of wealth, must interfere with Blair's declared goal for the year 2000: the creation of a guarantee that Britain's future prosperity is assured by becoming a world leader in electronic information technology. And so, for the 2,000th parliamentary session, an E-commerce Bill takes central place.

Appropriately this Bill was heralded with Blair doctoring and adopting the slogan which his friend Clinton promoted in between practising irrumation, coition with the mouth; putting a hi-tech slant on a soundbite of Clinton's which is almost as well known as his taste for fellatio, Blair proclaimed: 'It's the e-economy, stupid.' E-mail, like fellation, so often results in quick communication between the parties, leaving them further apart; to link the two in the context of the promotion of a Bill aimed to excite a nation's lust for yet more money is apposite, not bizarre.

The biblical warnings, the admonitions of the Christian fathers and schoolmen, and the Christian ethics practised or borrowed by the Labour Party for almost a century have been swept aside by Blair as he advocates the return of an anal society for economic man. And in his enthusiasm to encourage the nation to wallow in filthy lucre, he sets an odious example: not for him, when he holidays, to be off like Harold Wilson to a Scilly Isles cottage or, like John Smith, on a walking holiday in Scotland. Millionaires of dubious provenance, wealthy Italian counts with ambiguous political affiliations and the taxpayers of Tuscany are all conscripted to provide him with ostentatious palatial villas so that he may live it up in the style to which, until his premiership, he was never accustomed.

Around him Blair gathers a clique of nouveau riche acolytes: slick Jack Cunningham, one-time enforcer of cabinet decisions, deservedly earning the title of 'Junket Jack' and seemingly blind to the follies of excessive covetousness despite the fate of a father gaoled for avarice; his Lord Chancellor play-acting as Cardinal Wolsey and insisting upon the notoriously lavish refurbishment of his private rooms which, although slightly shabby when I sometimes visited Gerald Gardner, the greatest of all Labour's Lord

Chancellors, certainly did not disadvantage that brilliant lawyer's reforming zeal; and, of course, the egregious Peter Mandelson, whose desire to acquire an up-market residence well beyond his bachelor needs led to scandal and ministerial resignations but only, unfortunately, to a brief hiatus in his contrived career.

It is not simply that one recoils from the vulgarity of these gaudy displays, and certainly it is not because one would wish to impose a joyless ascetic upon ministers; the objection is that they are holding out as exemplars to the nation a hollow and tawdry lifestyle, one where the capacity to flaunt a wealthy background is the desideratum for which, above all else, we are to strive. Within such a environment it follows logically that the only real issue which inspires political passions has the smell of ordure. The issue deciding and fracturing the parties is the future of the pound: should we or should we not exchange one symbol of faeces for another? Sterling or EMU? At the next election we shall witness the apogee of cloacal politics.

With politics thus demeaned, it is credible that the November 1999 government-sponsored report, 'Britain towards 2010: The Changing Business Environment', coming from the Economic & Social Research Council, will have its prophecies fulfilled: that disillusioned by politics, we shall, by the year 2010, be living in a more selfish and cynical era. Changing social structures, high divorce rates and a growing number of adults living alone will foster a 'me' attitude to which politicians and businesses will have to respond, and the interaction of social trends with economic and technological changes will give us an economically thriving but divided society.

If politicians continue to teach the nation to find love, not within human relationships but in money, then all these gloomy prognostications will doubtless prove correct, but there are no inevitabilities in human affairs, except dying and death. There are always alternatives and in this last half-century there have been dramatic switches, as often benign as destructive, in public and private attitudes; such changes can come again. But it means accepting that in this technological age, we need to battle, as perhaps never before, against the regressive expressions of anality in our private and public affairs.

Pilgrim's Way: The Journey

Since so many sages insist upon the transitory nature of happiness, is it folly to proclaim its pursuit as the ideal which should preoccupy our politics? And since, for most of us, happiness must rest upon sensual love, a state which Stendhal, the most subtle of explorers of the condition, affirms can only exist if capable of being defined in terms of the unhappiness it imports, what confusions do we bring, what Will-o'-the-wisps are we conjuring, in still insisting that the pursuit of so chimerical a phenomenon as happiness is the only enterprise capable of dignifying our politics?

Should we defy the wise men who counsel that we should cease our exactions and moderate our claims for happiness? Goethe tells us that man cannot tolerate sustained happiness:

> Alles in der Welt lässt sich ertragen,
> Nur icht eine Reihe von schönen
> Tagen

(Nothing is harder to bear than a succession of fair days)

And Freud, when scrutinising the condition, is at his most bleak:

> One feels inclined to say that the intention that man should be 'happy' is not included in the plan of 'Creation'. What we call happiness in the stricter sense comes from the preferably sudden satisfaction of needs which have been dammed up to a high degree,

189

and it is from its nature only possible as an episodic phenomenon. When any situation that is desired by the pleasure principle is prolonged, it only produces a feeling of mild contentment. We are so made that we can derive intense enjoyment only from a contrast and very little from a state of things. Thus our possibilities of happiness are already restricted by our constitution.

Thus discouraged, should we leave happiness to the dreams of poets or to the believers who promise it will be available in the next world, and, meantime, get on with the more mundane and prosaic, confining our politics to the obviously remediable, to the alleviation of some of the unpleasures which faults in today's laws and institutions may be causing? Should we, in short, abandon the Big Idea which today's politicians, unlearned in the compass of the human heart, rudderless on their non-ideological managerial pragmatic journey, so vainly seek in a quest to discover the elixir which will quicken their dead manifestos?

Or should we regard Freud's pessimism as suspect? The analogue which Freud had in mind when he warned us happiness is but a temporary and episodic phenomenon is clear: it is coition. Here it is Freud the biologist, not the psychologist, who speaks; indeed, even the 'mild contentment' which is at most, Freud concedes, possible, he regards as ever under threat, for biology decrees that discontent is endemic to the human condition, a necessity, since if man was sated, if there was no repetitive spur, if the itch subsided, the perpetuation of the human species would be at risk.

There are no such gloomy prognostications in Stendhal's thesis; for him, through love, happiness can be attained. Coition for him was not the template upon which happiness is shaped. Bodily delights may be part of the love route to happiness but is not utterly dependent upon them – indeed, the raptures of what he describes as 'passionate' love could efface their memory. How we respond to Freud's pessimism or Stendhal's optimism depends much upon our own life experiences and perhaps too upon our gender. But the politicians who believe they are powerless to contribute to human happiness – a condition whose existence they evidently doubt – and who fundamentally believe man's misery can, at best, be intermittently tempered by a judicious overview of the economic cycle are, while tinkering with their economic models, far more dangerous than the political idealist who, however delusionary the belief may be, believes men and women have the potentiality to live out their lives as happy, loving human beings.

In our politics it is far more important to know our destination than to arrive; our journey can be the reward, even if we are travelling to a mirage. En route to the heavenly city of happiness, which may always be the other side of the mountain, we may find love even though we certainly will encounter enemies; I am not seeking to enjoin that we love our enemies. We lose our capacity to give genuine love if in consensus politics we spread it so thin that we foolishly claim our ability to proffer it to hostile strangers. We are more likely to have a society whose political ecology fertilises love if we remember the assertion homo hominus lupus – man can be a wolf to man. It was the great ironist and idealist Heinrich Heine who drew the route to happiness when he confessed:

> Mine is the most peaceable disposition. My wishes are: a humble cottage with a thatched roof, but a good bed, good food, the freshest milk and butter, flowers before my window and a few fine trees before my door; and if God wants to make my happiness complete, He will grant me the joy of seeing some six or seven of my enemies hanging from those trees. Before their death I shall, moved in my heart, forgive them all the wrong they did me in their lifetime. One must, it is true, forgive one's enemies – but not before they have been hanged.

Bevan, Brown & Blair

In my lifetime it was Nye Bevan who, above all the politicians, explicitly presented the authentic 'vision thing' which eludes our present crop of grubby and unimaginative politicians. From the time of my teens when, as a young socialist, I proudly chaired some of his meetings in South Wales, to the time in 1955 when he came to Cardiff to support me as a candidate in a Tory stronghold, down to his last days, I heard him make speeches insisting that the ultimate goal of the true socialist was 'the serene society'. He was using an adjective unknown to today's political practitioners; he was externalising his conflict-ridden private life and reflecting his own interior battles, when he asserted that the serenity for which he yearned, and which could be the greatest blessing for society, could be reached only by unremitting political struggle. For Bevan, the private predicaments and society's dilemmas were all one. In singular form he was acting out, for all our benefits, the biological imperative that some psychoanalysts have suggested governs us: the law of psychic homeostasis. That decree instructs us that we have, inbuilt, a psychological system which seeks to attain a steady mental state, a condition of dynamic balance.

That harmony was to be denied to the man Bevan, and the more cynical will doubt, too, whether it can ever be achieved by society. But Bevan was no impractical dreamer and his perhaps impossible vision of a happy serene society gave him the courage to tackle even the greatest destroyer of man's equilibrium: death. Our own bodies are doomed to decay and dissolution and increasingly during our lifetimes there come the warning signals of anxiety and pain foretelling our extinction. Bevan's creation of the National Health Service in face of the opposition from the Tories and the leaders of the medical establishment was part of his defiance of all the intimations which death brings. Even the last enemy was to be denied the fruits of his victory, and the sufferings and sickness of the poorest man and woman in the land was to be alleviated.

How mean are the aspirations of our present politicians when contrasted with Bevan's views. Now we are invited to join the 'enterprise society' and put our snouts in the big trough that technology has created; success will come from our money-making, so we shall reach the top as a nation and as individuals. These are hopes that lack all generosity; their fulfilment is predicated upon the disappointment and failure of others. The top would not be worth reaching if there were room enough for everyone. Sometimes the disguise of this pseudo hope slips and it is then explicitly revealed as it was in Thatcher's aspiration: 'Let our children grow tall, but some taller than others.' To be envied is the quiddity of this form of pseudo hope.

And side by side with the call to enrich oneself in the shareholding society is untempered anger directed towards those who will not join in the scramble. No-one condones benefit fraud, but there is an over-determined emotionally toned antagonism towards those stigmatised as 'spongers' and suspected of living on disability and other benefit payments; it reveals a horror of dependency. It is the sin which Thatcher, the woman who can only be understood by her hostility towards her mother, whom she has always blotted out rather than acknowledge she was ever dependent upon her, regards as cardinal, an opinion shared by our bachelor Chancellor. I doubt his vigorous campaigns against those whom he regards as shirkers, not workers for gain, is to be wholly attributed to his Calvinism; his notoriously long engagement suggests an inability to take the step to unconditional commitment, to the authentic love life which, by its nature, requires mutual dependency. For some, the need for independence can be a neurotic compulsion, an incapacity to mortify narcissism in the service of another, and it can find expression in political testaments as well as private life.

It is not mutual dependence that defines Gordon Brown's policy; it is competitiveness which, he insists, must be the spur to bring us to the ultimate achievement – that of becoming a nation of entrepreneurs. In his 1999 autumn pre-budget statement, one meant to be about State finances, he cited competitiveness ten times – its virtues and the need to enforce it, have much more of it and promote yet more entrants to its world. For him, competitiveness is the doctrinal absolute of the enterprise society. But such competitiveness has a shadow side; an ethos inciting competition in the external world can invade the private domain. The inflamed rivalries in the commercial field and within the office and workplace can be brought home; and, with each protagonist fearing subjugation by the other, the battle of the sexes can be fiercely waged in the domestic arena. Interdependence is felt as a threat bringing, as it does, a genuine union of partners, and that is clearly terrifying for some. Gordon Brown is not the only man who has kept his fiancée waiting at the church. Increasingly men and women are cohabiting and, although divorce has never been easier to obtain, they are nevertheless frightened out of their wits to marry. Even as they dismiss the institution as of little importance, still marriage is felt to be a significant symbol bringing a union which is unconsciously interpreted to be a merger, with consequent loss of individuation.

This fear of merger is a phobic response so familiar to practised clinicians; to those so afflicted the bliss of intimacy is denied. And since it is a frightening condition to which in our earliest days we are all exposed, it becomes society to beware of the creation of a *Weltanschauung* which hinders our emancipation from the strangulation of an affect that otherwise may befall us in our adult life. Our initial intense need as babes for the mother creates a wish to merge with her, but that wish carries the implicit concomitant of the loss of a separate existence as an individual – annihilation. To avoid such a fate there is an intensive aggressive reaction aimed at self-preservation and the destruction of the mother; but such a destruction would lead to the loss of the mother, to total abandonment, so the babe's woes are compounded as the anxiety felt that he would be annihilated by a merger is now supplemented by the anxiety that he would be abandoned. The force of the aggression which he feels because he is thus entrapped in an impossible dilemma is not to be minimised, but although the babe cannot extricate himself from the predicament, fortunately the mother can come to the rescue. It is her ministering to our needs that helps us on our way. Gradually, if her mothering endows us with the confident self and diminishes our fear of individuation, the wish to merge becomes less insistent. Gradually the confidence grows that the mother's temporary absence does not mean abandonment; and so, the babe's aggression can be increasingly tempered and the consequent anxiety lessened.

But such a happy ending is not the lot of everyone, and when, for example, the mother has a markedly narcissistic character and she relates to a child in narcissistic terms, then her narcissistic over-attentiveness in treating him as part of herself reinforces his annihilatory anxieties and intensifies his aggression towards her. Her emotional self-absorption, her excessive commitment outside the home and her preoccupation with returning to work outside the home can all be factors resulting in an insufficient sensitivity to the child's needs which will both frustrate him, arouse abandonment anxieties and, again, intensify his aggression towards her. When the baby is bequeathed such a legacy, one lacking the constant reassurances which could lead him to acquire confidence in his own separateness from the mother, then we can expect that in adult life his capacity to merge with another can be impaired and fraught; acknowledgement of inter-dependence can only be grudgingly granted, for merger may unconsciously be equated with annihilation; with such annihilatory anxieties always lurking within his relationships with women, visible reminders of a woman's procreative capacity can be interpreted as threats. Our own Chancellor of the Exchequer, usually so ready to boast of his tax cuts, more out of fear than squeamishness could not even bring himself, when reducing the tampon tax in the March 2000 Budget, to announce that he was making tax savings for 11,000,000 women of £45,000,000 a year.

There may be a number of contributory reasons why marriage-shirking cohabitation has become widespread – the fiscal advantages attached to the single as against the married state may be one of them. But fundamentally the phenomenon is not to be explained in terms of rational couples making mathematical calculations; rather, it is the belief that freedom will be forfeited if they become bound, that their choices will not remain untrammelled if they change their status and formally acknowledge interdependence. They know not the golden chains of marriage, and they do not understand that far from being possessed of freedom, they remain entrapped, still caged within their apprehensions of their earliest months, still fearing that an overdose of love is fatal, that it is a dangerous potion that must be carefully measured. We have at least the right to be quizzical when we see a Chancellor who, on at least two occasions, sets up with the *News of the World* photo opportunities to draw national attention to his relationship with his girlfriend but ensures that there will be a long wait before a photograph will be shown of them together at the altar. Repeatedly since 1995 columnists have run the tale that soon the wedding bells will ring, but they toll not. In March 2000 his former spin doctor Charles Whelan, in teasing or mickey-taking mood, announcing the creation of his new web site devoted to Westminster gossip, claimed he would, as a 'scoop', be the first to announce the engagement of his former boss. Doubtless in the end the 50-year-old bachelor will be driven by the press to declare his intentions, but there will then surely have rarely been such a reluctant bridegroom.

But, it may be protested, whose business is it other than the parties concerned if two people decided to cohabit but not to marry? Certainly I do not intrude upon the Chancellor's private life because of some outmoded moralistic reservations. Indeed, long before it became socially acceptable, half a century ago I lived with my wife before we married and for me it was a valuable rite of passage on the way to an enduring marriage – and doubtless that has been the experience for many. But prolonged cohabitation may be no developmental stage – it can be an arrested emotional stage. Although such a judgemental view, if advertised, would likely be resented as an impertinence by thousands of cohabitees, there are good reasons to affirm that there are genuine public interest reasons, not manufactured prurience, to note our Chancellor's mode, for a diffidence to consummate a relationship within marriage is but one of the cluster of symptoms displayed in adult life by those who suffered a particularly uneasy and unresolved relationship with their mother in their earlier years. Another is intensive envious traits and these are characteristics which not only permeate our Chancellor's economic nostrums but also his relationships with political colleagues, notably and notoriously his relationship with Blair.

There will be those who will regard as preposterous an exploratory submission – even when acknowledged to be, of necessity, founded on inference – which directly relates Brown's policies and political behaviour to unhealed abrasions experienced as a babe. But those who noisily proclaim their 'independence', whether in the form of prolonged bachelorhood or less well-advertised displays, and who mock suggestions that, to an extraordinary extent, their adult lives may be in bondage to their earliest years, are suspect. However maniacally we assert our 'independence', we cannot step out of this world and all of us are born of woman. Our biology demands that, of all the species on this earth, none remains utterly dependent for survival on parental nurturing longer than homo sapiens, and that nurturing, good or bad, is etched upon our psyche and remains with us until we are dust beneath a few feet of soil.

And since it is the insufficiently empathetic mother who etches on her child's psyche a fear that if his independence is tempered dissolution will follow, we can expect too from such a nurturing that an exceptional envious disposition is likely to play a destructive role in that babe's adult life, for his envy may have a fatal precedent. It will have occurred soon after birth, as it does with all of us, when the infant becomes aware of the breast as a source of life and good experience. The clinical work of Kleinian child analysts has led to a view that the infant feels the breast, or other succouring object, is the source of all comforts, physical and mental, an inexhaustible reservoir of food and warmth, love, understanding and wisdom, and the blissful experience of satisfaction which this wonderful object gives will increase his love and desire to possess, preserve and protect it. But the same experience also stirs in him the wish to be the source of such satisfaction; he experiences painful feelings of envy which carry with them the desire to spoil the qualities of an object which gives him such painful feelings.

How, as adults, we cope with these infantile envious feelings largely depends on the quality of our very early environmental experiences. The fortunate may be so blessed that gratitude overcomes, or at least modifies, envy. If the child's fantasy of the incorporation of the good breast, or its symbolic substitute, repeatedly takes place, accompanied by feelings of love, gratitude and gratification, then it becomes integrated within his ego which is itself increasingly replenished with goodness. Envy lessens as gratification increases and then, in a benevolent circle, the diminution of envy allows more gratification and this, in turns, lessens the envy.

Such a benign personal history is not everyone's lot. The breakdown of the family and the competitive claims of work, career and the home mean that the strains of motherhood are felt and the goodness of the breast is experienced as too meagre to overcome the deep-seated envy. With envy untamed, it can be released in most destructive forms: the young delinquent can lash out, acting out the spoilation which in fantasy he had imagined against the grudging breast. Then we are left bewildered – not acknowledging the source – by the apparently senseless vandalism we witness. But sly politicians can disguise their envy in more subtle but not less destructive modes, and Brown's envy finds its expression in hypocritical sanctification. For him, envy becomes hallowed within theology where competition, the doing-down of the other, is holy writ; the deity to be worshipped is the green-eyed god.

Brown's envy is to be distinguished from the politics of envy sometimes preached by exponents of the hard left ideology of class struggle, and it lacks the refinements of Gaitskell and his heirs who, not satisfied with the Marxist doctrine 'from each according to his ability, to each according to his needs', always stressed that socialism was above all else about equality. This doctrine is not always conspicuous in their lifestyles and is far removed from the realities I had encountered in my teenage years on the factory floor when the battle was always for a fair wage and just differentials, not equality. An odour of envy pervaded many of the writings and speeches of the Gaitskell theoreticians and one suspects that in their early battles with their siblings for the love of their parents, they feel they lost out; a guarantee of equality means no-one else can be the favourite son. Sibling rivalry too is a feature of Brown's envious political dispositions;

indeed I doubt if the irrationality of his ill-considered and faultily-founded attack in May 2000 on the Oxford University entrance procedures can be fully understood without taking into account that, unlike Brown, Blair the surrogate brother is an Oxford graduate: envy can cunningly subvert judgement. Yet the fierceness of Brown's envious outburst suggests such rivalry is fuelled, rather than triggered, by competition with his talented brother. The source is more primal; more desperate.

And it is one that is destabilising the whole Party hierarchy, dividing it into Blairites and Brownies. The distinguished veteran journalist Ian Aitken, one not given to psychologising, ventilated the frustration and bewilderment of so many Party activists when in November 1999 he wrote of:

> ...the infantile feud between Brownites and the Blairites. What in God's name is this long-running vendetta actually about? If there are policy issues at stake, we should be told what they are, so that an informed and sensible debate can take place around them. But, on the contrary, the entire guerrilla war has been conducted in almost exclusively personal terms.

It is conducted in those terms because it is personal. Aitken is right to describe the feud as 'infantile', perhaps more than he appreciates. The origin of this feud is to be found in the cradle, not in any political issue.

The intense sibling rivalry, charged with the fierce envy coming from an untamed primal infantile source, can, as Edward Glover, doyen of the last generation of British psychoanalysts, always emphasised, lead to a positive homosexual attachment to brother substitutes. Early childhood impulses of jealousy derived from competition against rivals, usually with a brother for a mother's love, lead to hostile and aggressive attitudes towards those brothers which, in the unconscious, can reach to a pitch of actual death-wish; but these very dangerous impulses cannot maintain themselves. Under the influence of a decorous upbringing within a manse household, such as Gordon Brown had, there would be severe restraints on any untoward outward expressions of hostility. Still, in adulthood, we see Brown wrestling with that suppressed aggression as, fearful of releasing it, he masochistically turns it inward, eats himself up, forever gnawing at his fingernails. As a little boy, too, he turned inward, and with increasing awareness of his continuous powerlessness, the little boy in Brown's case became a withdrawn child, leaving the field to the displays of his extrovert older brother. Then the boy's impulses, as clinically would be expected, yield to repression and undergo a transformation, so that the rivalry of the earlier period becomes the first homosexual love object. The process, as Freud has explained, is:

> ... a complete contrast to the development of persecutory paranoia, in which the person who had before been loved becomes the hated persecutor, whereas here the hated rivals are transformed into love objects.

It is understandable that when quarrels occur between politicians who have long and deep friendships, and who share a common ideology, the cause of the break is attributed to 'ambition'; that is too simplistic a diagnosis. All of us, men and women, have homosexual components within our make-up, but how we deal with them, whether as in homophobia we fearfully and vainly endeavour to repudiate their presence, whether we sublimate them in a bonding to advance a political or religious cause, whether we deploy them within a heterosexual relationship to enrich our identification and empathy with our partner, whether they find expression in overt sexual conduct, what is irrevocable is their continuing presence; they cannot be cancelled out. And Edward Glover, who incited me to end the criminality of adult homosexual conduct, always reminded us that Freud had emphasised that hate constitutes one of the aetiological factors in homosexuality. As Glover expressed it:

> Earlier jealousy and rivalry can be resolved or countered or kept in successful repression by what we might call a reaction formation of homosexual attachment.

With jealousies and rivalries forever simmering beneath these homosexual elements, there are those who, because they find those elements to be too compulsive and untamed to be dealt with by any other means, turn to a 'reaction formation of homosexual attachment' which may or may not take an overt form. It is, however, a reaction formation which is fraught with hazards, for even if slightly punctured the jealousies and rivalries beneath burst, often with terrifying force. The disputatious Senior Common Rooms of Oxbridge colleges, as I have noted when invited to High Table, are littered with the intellectual debris of exploded homosexual attachments. The syndrome, notoriously displayed in those quarrelsome academic circles, is no less on show in Blair's inner circle and is witnessed, in its most exotic form, in prevailing bitterness between Blair and Brown, the pair once described as 'twins' and 'blood brothers' who entered Parliament on the same day and, during the years while I was in the House, shared an office in the Commons, living in each other's pockets. Even now, in March 2000, the *Observer*'s Andrew Rawnsley noted, 'Blair's favoured way of describing the closeness of his relationship with Gordon Brown is as a "marriage".' I doubt if, since 1994, Brown would so describe it.

That was when the explosion between Blair and Brown took place at Granita, a restaurant in Islington, at the height of the Labour leadership contest in 1994. The event and consequence have been accurately recorded by the *Express* correspondent Peter Oborne:

> Gordon Brown reluctantly agreed to stand down but insisted on conditions which Blair, guilt-stricken at the turn events had taken, was weak enough to concede. Brown demanded complete control over the economy and sweeping powers over other areas of policy as well. He demanded the ability to place his own people in key posts. In effect, he demanded, and got, something approaching a dual premiership.

And exercising that role, with his power base in the Treasury, it is Brown who is overwhelmingly determining New Labour's policies.

The feud between Blair and Brown yielded, in January 1998, the highly publicised taunt, never unequivocally denied as coming from Blair's aide Alistair Campbell, that Gordon Brown possessed 'psychological flaws', a taunt given by one who saw the mote in another's eye but not in his own. The taunt was intended as a smear with no purpose except to ensure that Blair's Downing Street camp maintained its ascendancy, for between Blair and Brown there is not even the pretence, a fig leaf, of ideological differences. Brown's envy is raw and unforgiving, and if this was directed only against Blair, one could leave it to two essentially immature men to get on with their unseemly quarrelling. But the psychological faults of Brown – not the ones, I am sure, that the malice of Downing Street was intending to pinpoint – overspill into almost every aspect of current public policy. Indeed, in some they are the sick dynamic that enables them to maintain their momentum.

Nowhere was this more clearly illustrated than in the 1999 budget. A close reading of its contents reveals a strategy to push women to take on the breadwinner role in a family structure – which is now to be redefined in economic policy as the mother and child alone. The bachelor Chancellor of the Exchequer, reflecting his lack of enthusiasm for marriage, is creating, as Melanie Phillips put it in her 1999 publication *The Sex Change Society*,

> ...tax and welfare policies amounting to a significant piece of social engineering which prefers lone mothers over married couples and working mothers over women who choose to look after their children at home... The changes to the tax system clearly signal a movement away from helping to buttress marriage and towards supporting all families regardless of whether the parents are married or not.

The insouciance Brown displays towards the personal commitments which can be so significantly, if not uniquely, sealed within marriage leads, with the acclamation of the gender-feminists, to the Government promoting a matriarchy at the lower end of the income scale. His is not a fiscal policy designed to buttress marriage and bless children with parents married to each other. On the contrary, as the economics correspondent Martin Wolf of *The Financial Times* has commented:

> In contemporary theory and practice, a family is a unit of mother and children. Men are seen as optional extras. Family benefits effectively 'belong' to the mother, since it is she who determines the family shape. By making more generous a benefit system that helps poorer families with children, particularly with the cost of childcare, the Government is providing a substantial boost to the resources available to mothers and improving their ability to dispense with both men and full-time motherhood.

Martin Woolf cannot be gainsaid when he concludes that the Government is creating a new subsidised industry of childcare, an industry indeed which is now, by the March 2000 Budget, bolstered by new Welfare-to-Work benefits for the single parent. And in that same Budget Brown, turning his back on any fiscal benefits accruing to marriage, announced his decision to replace the Married Couple's Tax Allowance with a new Children's Tax Credit, one that will mean tax-breaks for families will be 'attached' to the children and will therefore no longer depend on what kind of family they live in; cohabitation, not marriage, suffices in Brown's book.

When he introduces such changes, he is not blind to the impact that fiscal policy has on behaviour. On introducing his 1997 Budget, he did not hesitate to affirm 'the tax system sends critical signals about activities a society wishes to promote or deter'. His Budgets most certainly do not promote marriage; nor are they, as he claimed in his 1999 Budget to be, 'a Budget for women'; that Budget reality was more a budget for militant feminists. One needs to be on guard against Brown's sound bites; there is no languor in their delivery, no excruciatingly embarrassing histrionics in the Blair manner; they emerge out of a veritable torrent; his words pour out with extraordinary rapidity and, breathlessly, in highly-charged style, he tells us of the good tidings he brings. But there is a mismatch between the sanguine content and the lugubrious demeanour and, in the end, the delivery reveals rather than conceals the intense personal tensions of the inner man. His sound bites, like so many of this government's, should be treated for what they are: mere epiphenomena. We should not be duped into treating the political notions presented by this government as the offspring of pure reason; that would be assigning to them a parentage as mythical as that of Pallas Athene. The cliché-ridden librettos, however insistently and, in Blair's case 'passionately', delivered, should not deafen us to the underlying emotions, the discordant music to which the scripts are mere accompaniments. And that cacophony, in Brown's case, so often leaves his audience, in or out of the Commons, disorientated and perplexed rather than inspired.

Brown is now to take on the role of chief strategist for the General Election and responsibility for drafting the next Labour manifesto. It will contain no love lyric. Temperament bars him from giving us Labour's traditional promise of a co-operative commonwealth; that requires commitment, commitment to societal bonding from which, reflecting personal inhibitions, he shrinks. His fluency ends, and his stammerings commence, when support for institutions demanding intimacy like marriage is required; and since the tenderness of dependency is learned by a father or step-father through protectiveness for his little ones, the blank of bachelorhood in Brown's personal biography is ofttimes expressed in an insensitivity towards those weaklings who seek Social Security benefits; impatiently sweeping aside the inadequates in our society, who are and will always be with us, he rages against fraud, and proffers the populist working man alternative – work or starve. Thus his own loaded rivalrous disposition and his marked envious traits are disguised and subsumed under the rubric of 'competitiveness' and 'enterprise'; and if we join him, we are promised that at the terminus, at journey's end, there will stand a golden shopping mall under whose roof we all, except the undeserving indigent poor, will wallow in wealth and prosperity.

Conclusion

Is there then no hope? Are we bound to respond to the grim dirge of the joint premiers, the one smiling far too much, the other far too little, and accompany them through an arid political wasteland to reach so tawdry a destination? And en route must we uncomplainingly suffer the cacophonous hooligan noises from the front carriage where, in a struggle for priority, three second sons – Blair, Brown and Mandelson, fated by their place within the family constellation – now as adults brazenly act out the unassuaged rivalries of their childhoods? Is ideology so dead and religion so ineffectual that we must accept that we can no longer have available to us in any political party or the religious establishment the constituent and binding affects that can turn society into community?

Within the very questions there is an implicit defeatism; the temptation is to retreat to the stoicism of the distinguished French literary critic Romain Rolland, who, in dark days, when the world was out of joint and malevolence triumphing, affirmed: 'Even although I have no hope, still I remain committed.' More negative and inadequate are the responses of those many present-day disenchanted abstentionist voters who turn their backs on all our sordid and mean politics, wishing to invest all their expectations within a fenced-in private domain.

American sociologists like Talcott Parsons were, in mid-century, already emphasising the hazards of such excessive withdrawal of

binding libidinal urges away from the larger collectivity and
loading them upon the dyadic couple. Man's libido is essentially
finite; the libidinal diffusion, the social cement binding the wider
community together, needs constant replenishment. If it is
drained, if it is starved of sustenance, it suffers energic impoverish-
ment and then those larger co-ordinated aggregates, the
maintenance of which gives us the possibility of a civilised society,
can collapse.

The withdrawal of all societal allegiances in favour of
committal only to the personal is no answer to our predicament;
such an option has never been more seductively presented than in
Matthew Arnold's threnody *Dover Beach* where, faced with a
world 'swept with confused alarms of struggle and flight where
ignorant armies clash by night', we might almost believe it is an
attainable choice. But though at times 'the world, which seems to
lie before us like a land of dreams so various, so beautiful so new
hath really neither joy, nor love nor light, nor certitude, nor peace,
nor help for pain', Arnold's proffered course that we quit this
'darkling plain' and find our compensation in the strictly personal
– 'Ah love let us be true to one another' – is defective. For private
relations may provide the escapist honeymoon but its endurance
depends upon disloyalty. Without social oxygen the relationship
will wilt; if it is confined, lacking space, it cannot grow.

The balance between intimate family and supra-familial
collectivities has now been seriously disturbed; the glue that
bound us together has become unstuck. We have fitful surges of
patriotism but they soon subside – the passionate love of country
which in unison we shared has become anaemic. The Union Jack
is now only waved ironically at the Promenade concert. And the
fellowship found in the chapel and church has petered out; the
pews are empty. The glow of comradeship has vanished from the
Labour Party. All must be addressed as colleagues, not comrades,
and even trade unionists now flinch from calling their mates
brothers. The great political parties which drew together so many
to make common cause have now become the playground of
multi-millionaires and their Party conferences, once calling
thousands of the faithful to love-fests, complete with quarrels and
sweet reconciliations, are now media circuses. When they end,
'Auld Lang Syne' is sung tunelessly and although, out of habit,

hands are then linked, they are limp not firm. The Conservative Party has become a sick joke, the New Labour Party a shabby façade. The institutions which were the containers of sublimated libidinal urges are disintegrating and the disciplines of behaviour which governed us as group members, the checks upon our narcissism as we were invigilated and evaluated by others and by ourselves, have gone. Our present self-destructive promiscuity cannot be scrutinised in isolation; bereft, as we are becoming, of the former societal inhibitions, we regress and polymorphous perverse sexual antics can become the norm, not the deviant.

Yet all is not lost. When Yeats, reflecting upon the human predicament, wrote

Things fall apart; the centre cannot hold

he placed those often-quoted lines within a verse telling us:

Surely some revelation is at hand;
Surely the Second Coming is at hand.

And out of that present arid landscape he prophesied the sluggish emergence

... somewhere in sands of the desert
A shape with lion body and the head of a man,
... moving its slow thighs...

towards a blessed destination:

And what rough beast, its hour come round at last,
Slouches towards Bethlehem to be born?

We can dare share the hope contained in those final lines; the metaphor of that religious poem can be moved into secular world. It is true we are presently stranded. Once we were not alone, and shoulder to shoulder in unison we could sing 'God Save The Queen;' now, alas, we believe neither in God nor, thanks to the antics of a dysfunctional royal family, in the Queen. And like the Crown, once so unifying a symbol, no longer can Parliament, besmirched by its shabby political parties, gather us together, for party politics have become an enervating, not an ennobling, process. Yet, withal, Yeats's sighting was surely not a mirage. The 'rough beast' moves.

Despite the traditional institutions and political parties failing them, giving them no support or love and inspiring no common loyalty binding them to others, not all abandon hope. Slowly, protest is becoming institutionalised and within its organisation, men and women recover the mutuality that has been denied them by the depleted supra-familial collectivities. Many of the protesters know the specific enemy occasioning so much of the prevailing public and private dislocation, and do not scatter their fire, and the more discerning apologists for that enemy sense the danger. Viewing with dismay the swamping by thousands of protesters from all over the world of the Seattle meeting of the World Trade Organisation in December 1999, *The Financial Times* complained:

> The backlash against global capitalism is gaining force and power, and politicians so far have done little but sit back and watch it happen...The protests have real importance as a warning signal that public unease with capitalism and the forces of globalisation is reaching a worrying level.

In Seattle there was formed the most unlikely of coalitions: passionate environ-mentals, trade union members, church groups and that ultimate modern political oxymoron, organised anarchists, all took part in a demonstration telling the world how the American mainstream political system can no longer provide any outlet for opinions challenging the presumptions and values of global capitalism. At Seattle the protesters expressed their dissent with a verve that comes from conviction and commitment.

Now it is not only in Seattle that single-minded lobbies have revealed their élan. One of the most striking of political phenomena of recent years in Britain is the decline of party and the growth of single-issue protest lobbies. I can recall, when seeking to alter our divorce laws, finding that despite the oppression those laws were imposing upon so many, there was no extant organisation promoting their cause and, wanting outside support, I had to reactivate the one body formed decades earlier that had become almost totally dormant. Indeed, it was much later when leading, together with some Nobel Peace Prize-winning scientists and, less comfortably, with Arthur Scargill, Britain's first anti-civil nuclear march that I became conscious that the political parties were failing to capture the allegiances of large swathes of public opinion. The 10,000 young men and women, many with their families, that on that day I addressed from the plinths of Trafalgar Square, belonged to no party.

For me that day was the first real intimation that the established political parties – even though they were claiming to be parties of a 'broad church' – were disintegrating, and the binding forces in our society that they had hitherto provided were unlikely to endure. Nowadays lobbies proliferate. Some, it is true, are negative and self-interested but most, whether they protest against a bypass, a runway, a hospital closure, the rundown of the NHS, the state of our prisons, the poverty and disarray of our inner cities, the introduction of genetically manipulated foods, the desecration of the environment, the racialism and gender discriminations still prevailing, are providing an opportunity for men and women to be libidinally bound together, to be part of the civilising process. As Freud has put it:

> ... in the service of Eros whose purpose is to combine single human
> individuals and after that families, then races, peoples and nations,
> into one great unity, the unity of mankind.

This purpose, the wished-for unity, Thanatos, the eternal adversary of Eros, has, with terrifyingly destructive success in the twentieth century, endeavoured to thwart.

To posit such organisations in Britain with their various interests as the counterweight to all the formidable minions at the disposal of global capitalism could seem extravagantly sanguine, but it is not necessarily a triumph of hope over experience. No Party could have had a more untidy and fractious start than the Labour Party which, despite or because of the brevity of its periods in Government in the twentieth century, has, until its theft by Blair, so tempered private greed and indifference to the disadvantaged, been the single most civilising influence enveloping Britain in the twentieth century.

Yet, so ragged was its initial formation, that ambiguity still prevails as to when the Party can specifically be said to have come into existence; it is generally accepted that its birthday was exactly 100 years ago, in February 1900, when under the chairmanship of a trade union Liberal MP, 129 delegates of an extraordinary mixed tranche of interests assembled. Among them were 'Lib-Lab Possiblers', members of the Marxist Social Democratic Federation, representatives of gas workers and railway servants, radicals, and Keir Hardie of the Independent Labour Party; this somewhat motley crowd gathered together to form an alliance of mutual interests and interdependence. With bloated Imperialism abroad and the Boer War raging it was in some respects an inauspicious time but this coming together was to prove the most fruitful of miscegenations; at the time it was little remarked upon but it was to breed the most significant political party in Britain's history, a love-in not seen before or since. A huge family of socialists and trade unionists was to come into existence with the now much mocked brothers, sisters and comrades bound together, ever quarrelling like most families still do, yet ever preserving a fundamental unity.

But now that family is breaking down; increasingly the estrangement between Party activists and the manipulators of New Labour becomes irrevocable. With the Tories written off, the activists find the enemy is within and the mood has grown even among the most schismatic of Left groups to find common ground. The trend is clear: a new opposition is in the process of a long gestation; and the pangs of the London mayoralty elections are an intonation that painfully the process has begun. At some time, however long postponed, a coalescence will take place bringing together Party dissidents, the protesting lobbies, and those coming from the Scottish and Welsh devolved bodies – each of which is so likely to become a forum of discontent. And in that scenario a place will undoubtedly be found too for erstwhile Tories, possessed of probity, who turn away with disgust from the corruptions of their Party.

Such an alliance will undoubtedly be infiltrated by Thanatos's destructive legion, but within such a concordance it will be marginalised; for friendship, comradeship and bonding within large collectivities are, as Freud never ceased emphasising, expressions of aim-inhibited love, drawing their strength from the most powerful of man's urges, sex, and so always possessing a singular capacity to challenge the manifestations of the death instinct. That capacity holds out a promise to all who in their several ways may contribute to the creation of a new political configuration.

When it will arrive will depend not only on the dynamic of historical forces, it will depend too upon the living human will and, above all, upon hope – a special type of hope, not a political zealot's psuedo-millennarian hope, but one that takes hold of the present and is also not a mean private hope. For hope needs a present as well as a future and since hope is the emotional relationship between present and future, it can only become meaningful when it is perceived as part of a web of social relations rather than the lonely inexpressive end of individualism. When hope is privatised, when a man does not link his future destiny to others but becomes an isolated stranger – even to those with whom he sleeps – he is doomed to suffer, as so many are suffering today, the emptiness of which Pascal wrote:

> We never take hold of the present. We anticipate the future as though it were too slow in coming and we want to hasten its arrival ...the present never is our goal; the past and the present are our means; only the future is our end. Thus, we never live, we only hope to live; and in awaiting and preparing ourselves for happiness we inevitably never are happy.

Hope leached away from the present, as Pascal warns, indeed brings no real fulfilment; nor does hope wholly directed to personal achievement and personal fame. Hope privatised cancels itself out, leaving the bearer stricken.

Creative hope, informed by love, is essentially an activity affect needing personal commitment. This little essay therefore is intended as an incitement and a temptation; it invites an involvement in the politics of tomorrow, not as a debased career choice, but as a dedication. It is certainly not necessarily confined to the present decaying political parties; they, like the New Labour Party, want only the subscriptions of passive paying members but are embarrassed by its true activists. Such parties bring us no hope, for they cannot, through quiescent individual members, be journeying purveyors of hope since hope cannot be bought or sold. Only from relatedness does hope spring.

And that authentic hope can be actualised within all those burgeoning organised societies and lobbies whose concerns and ofttimes ennobling goals enhance their member participants. Sex is a bountiful source, and from it can come the aim-inhibited love of the worthy common cause and the terroir which in such collectivities promotes the growth of personal relations; then men and women can make love, not rut and fellate.

At 83, my day is almost done and the future belongs to younger generations. But those lacking faith in presumptuous prognostications that a new, benign political ecology may come into existence capable of remedying the imbalance between the social and individual domains which now over-burdens the intimate zone, leaving it oppressed and joyless, should take comfort. The last century brought terrible disasters and only by a hair's breadth has mankind avoided exterminating itself. Yet, in the end, Eros overcame. In the twenty-first century too, in the end, with courage and community hope, despite all the manifest obstacles, love, as always in the past, will find a way.

Sources

Abse, D. W., *Hysteria and Related Mental Disorders*, Wright, 1987

Abse, D. W., *Sexual Disorder and Marriage*, University of North Carolina Press, 1964

Abse, L., Finance Bill Report, *Hansard*, 1.7.1968

Abse, L., *Private Member*, MacDonalds, 1973

Abse, L., *Wotan, My Enemy*, Robson Books, 1994

Abse, L., *Tony Blair: The Man Behind The Smile*, Robson Books, 1996

Abse, L., 'The Politics of In Vitro Fertilisation', in *In Vitro Fertilisation: Past Present and Future*, Fisher, S. and Symonds, EM, eds, 1986

Aitken, I., ? title? *Tribune*, 12.11.99

Alizade, A. M., *Feminine Sensuality*, Karnac Books, 1999

Bataille, G., *Eroticism: Death and Sexuality*, trans. Dalwood, M., San Francisco City Lights Books, 1986

Blair, A., title? *The Times*, 11.10.99

Brivati, B., *Hugh Gaitskell*, Richard Cohen Books, 1996

Carlyle, T. B., *Signs of the Times*, 1829

Ceridian Performance Partners & Management Today, 'The Price of Success', *The Times*, 26.7.99

Clarke, J. R., *Looking at Love-Making: Constructions of Sexuality in Roman Art*, University of California Press, 1998

Cohn, N., *The Pursuit of the Millennium*, Secker & Warburg, 1957

Cook, M., *A Slight and Delicate Creature*, Weidenfeld & Nicolson, 1999

Coopersmith, J., 'Pornography, Technology and Progress,' *Icon, Journal of the International Committee for the History of Technology*, Vol. IV, 1998

Cork, R., 'A Miracle of Healing', *The Times*, April 1998

Coward, R., *Sacred Cows: Is Feminism Relevant to the New Millennium?*, Harper Collins, 1999

Cox, T., *Hot Sex and How To Do It*, Bantam, 1998

Dilman, W., *Love: Its Forms, Dimensions and Paradoxes*, Macmillan, 1998

Drindle, D., 'Despite the Red Rose Jollity', *Guardian*, 13.3.99

Eiguer, A., 'Cynicism: its Function in the Perversions', *International Journal of Psychoanalysis*, August 1999, Vol. 80, Part 4

Erikson, E., 'Inner and Outer Space: Reflections on Womanhood', *Dadelus*, 1964, 93: 582-606

Fachinelli, E., *Anal Money-Time in the Psychology of Gambling*, eds Halliday, J., Fuller, P.; Alan Lane, 1974

Fenichel, O., *Psychoanalytic Theory of Neurosis*, Routledge & Keegan Paul, 1971

Ferenczi, S., 'The Unwelcome Child and his Death Drive', *Collected Writings*, Penguin, 1999

Foucault, M., 'The Care of the Self', *The History of Sexuality*, Vol. III, New York, 1986

Frean, A., title? *The Times*, 23.7.99

Freud, S., 'A Case of Hysteria', SE Vol. VII

—'Three Essays on the Theory of Sexuality', SE Vol. VII

—'Group Psychology and the Analysis of the Ego', SE Vol. XVIII

—'Leonardo da Vinci', SE Vol. XI

—'A Child is Being Beaten', SE Vol. XVII

—'The Ego and the Id, SE Vol. XIX

—'Economic Problem of Masochism', SE Vol. XIX

—'Civilisation and its Discontents', SE Vol. XXI

—'Resistances to Psychoanalysis', SE Vol. XIX

—'Character and Anal Eroticism', SE Vol. IX

—'On the Grounds for Detaching a Particular Syndrome from Neurasthenia Under the Description "anxiety Neuroses"', SE Vol. III

Glancey, J., 'Dome Rule', *Marxism Today*, November/December

1998

Glasser, M., 'On Violence', *International Journal of Psycho-Analysis*, Vol. 79, Part 5, October 1998

Glover, E., 'Notes on Oral Character Formation', *International Journal of Psycho-Analysis*, Vol. 6, 1925

Halberstadt-Freud, H., 'Electra Versus Oedipus', *International Journal of Psycho-Analysis*, Vol. 7, p. 41, 1998

Harman, H., Cootes, A., Hewitt, P., *The Family Way*, IPPR, 1995

Hone, W., *Every Day Book*, Thomas Tegg, London, 1827

Hutton, W., 'The State We Should Be In', *Marxism Today*, November/December 1998.

—*Observer*, 24.1.1999

Jaques, E., *The Changing Culture of a Factory*, Dryden Press, 1951

Kahr, Brett, 'The History of Sexuality From Ancient Polymorphous Perversity to Modern Genital Love', *Journal of Psycho-History*, XXVI, Spring 1999

Kaletsky, A, 'America's open house for cheap labour', *The Times*, 11.5.00

Kampfner, J., *Robin Cook*, Victor Gollancz, 1998

Keuls, Eva C., *The Reign of the Phallus: Sexual Politics in Ancient Athens*, University of California Press, 1985

Keynes, J. M., *Essays in Persuasion*, Macmillan, 1972

Klein, M., *Envy and Gratitude: A Study of Unconscious Sources*, Tavistock Publications, 1957

—*The Psychoanalysis of Children*, London Hogarth Press, 1975

Lafargue, P., *The Right to be Lazy*, Fifth Season Press, 1999

Laplanche, A., *New Foundations for Psychoanalysis*, trans. Macey, E., Oxford Blackwell, 1989

—'Seduction, Persecution, Revelation', *International Journal of Psycho-Analysis*, Vol. 76, 1995

Laswell, H. D., *Psychopathology and Politics*, Viking Press

Marcuse, R., *Eros and Civilisation*, Deacon Press, 1956

Marx, K., *Selected Writings in Sociology and Social Philosophy*, ed. Tom Bottomore, Penguin, 1970

Miller, A., 'The Political Consequences of Child Abuse', *Journal of Psycho-History*, Vol. XXVI, No. 2, 1998

Money-Kyrle, R., 'Cognitive Development', *Collective Papers of Roger Money-Kyrle*, Clunie Press, 1978

Mount, F., 'Talking Rubbish in the Name of Reith', *The Sunday*

Times, 9.5.1999

Nagel, T., 'The Shredding of Public Privacy', *Times Literary Supplement*, 14.8.1998

Oborne, P., *Alistair Campbell, New Labour and the Rise of the Media Class*, Aurum Press, 1999

Owen, E., *Time to Declare*, Penguin, 1992

Parsons, T., *Social Structure and Personality*, Collier-Macmillan, 1964

Pascal, B., *Pensées, Oeuvres Complets*, Librairie Gallimard, Paris, pp.131-132

Phillips, M., *The Sex-Change Society; Feminised Britain and the Neutered Male*, Social Market Foundation, November 1999

Phillips, M., *Times Literary Supplement*, 20.3.1998

—'Man's Job is to Win the Bread, a Woman's Job is to Spend It...', *Observer*, 22.3.1998

Pincus & Dare, *Secrets in the Family*, Faber & Faber, 1978

Plato, *Symposium*

Powell, E. *The Evolution of the Gospel*, Yale University Press, 1994

Reiche, Reimut, *Sexuality and the Class Struggle*, (NLB), 1970

Rignano, E., *The Nature of Life*, Keegan Paul, 1930

Roberts, A., *The Sunday Times*, 8.11.98

Rycroft, C., *A Critical Dictionary of Psycho-Analysis*, Nelson, 1968

—*Reich*, Fontana Collins, 1979

Schell, J., *The Gift of Time*, Granta, 1998

Smithers, L. C., & Burton, R., *Priapeia*, Wordsworth Classics, 1995

Solms, M., 'Controversies in Freud', trans. *Journal of Psycho-Analysis & History*, Vol. I, No. I, 1998

Stein, R., 'The Poignant, the Excessive and the Enigmatic in Sexuality', *International Journal of Psycho-Analysis*, Vol. 7, Part 2, April 1998

Steiner, G., *Observer*, 13.9.98

Stendhal, *Love*, Penguin Classics, 1975

Stone, L., *Family, Sex and Marriage in England 1500-1800*, Weidenfeld & Nicolson, 1997

Sullivan, S., *Falling in Love*, Macmillan, 1999

Tawney, R. H., *Religion and the Rise of Capitalism*, Penguin, 1964

United Nations Economic Commission for Europe, *World Robotics*, 1998

Vasari, G., *Lives of the Artists*, Penguin Classics, 1965

Vatsyayana, *The Kama Sutra*, trans. Burton, R., Wordsworth Classics, 1996

Veyne, P., 'Homosexuality in Ancient Rome', in *Western Sexuality, Practice & Precept in Past & Present Times*, eds Philippe Ariès & André Déjin, Blackwell, 1985

Waelder, R., *Progress and Revolution*, International University Press New York, 1967

Wallace-Hadrill, A., 'Under the Sign of the Goat', *Times Literary Supplement*, 12.6.1998

Webster, P., 'Idle Streak in the French Constitution', *Guardian*, 9.8.99

Wiseman, T., *The Money Motive*, Hutchinson, 1974

Wolf, M., the *Financial Times*, 31.3.98

Yeats, W. B., *Selected Poems*, Macmillan, 1955

Index